'The debates on populism may have reached a certain state of consolidation, but the search for a conceptual framework and the definition of its key elements is still going on. The book offers a wide variety of positions including the proposal to avoid the term altogether. It is an important contribution laying ground for further research. Populism is no longer seen as a transitional phenomenon, it is here to stay, and its meaning is inextricably linked to the meaning of democracy itself. Rich in theoretical and empirical information, the volume provides a comprehensive view of the state of the art and offers important considerations on how to deal with populist phenomena.'

Karin Priester, *Professor of Sociology and Political Theory, University of Münster*

'Populism and the Crisis of Democracy is a vital and sadly very necessary project for our troubled times after Brexit, the election of Trump, the rise of right wing authoritarian parties and regimes across Europe, as well as the success of the Five Star Movement and the Northern League in Italy. Questioning traditional concepts and theories of populism that too easily talk of a populism of the right and left, as if the middle-ground of liberal democracy has held firm, this important collection helps to shape new political imaginations. In the face of growing racism, anti-immigrant xenophobia and a politics of hate, the project helps to engage new globalised control technologies as we frame new forms of democratic resistance.'

Victor Seidler, *Emeritus Professor of Sociology, Goldsmiths University of London*

'This stimulating volume goes beyond theoretical self-absorption, sociological platitudes, the rounding up of the usual historical suspects, and journalistic exaggeration to provide conceptually sophisticated, context-sensitive, conjuncturally relevant, and profoundly nuanced analyses of the varieties and variegation of populism. Drawing on different theoretical paradigms and research methods, the contributors offer new and accessible insights into the complexities of populism, its recent resurgence, and its wider significance. In the face of populist disdain for intellectuals, this volume shows that serious scholarship can offer critical perspectives that clarify present discontents and future possibilities.'

Bob Jessop, *Distinguished Professor of Sociology, Lancaster University*

Populism and the Crisis of Democracy

There is no threat to Western democracies today comparable to the rise of right-wing populism. While it has played an increasing role at least since the 1990s, only the social consequences of the global financial crises in 2008 have given it its break that led to UK's 'Brexit' and the election of Donald Trump as US President in 2016, as well as promoting what has been called left populism in countries that were hit the hardest by both the banking crisis and consequential neo-liberal austerity politics in the EU, such as Greece and Portugal.

In 2017, the French Front National (FN) attracted many voters in the French Presidential elections; we have seen the radicalization of the Alternative für Deutschland (AfD) in Germany and the formation of centre-right government in Austria. Further, we have witnessed the consolidation of autocratic regimes, as in the EU member states Poland and Greece. All these manifestations of right-wing populism share a common feature: they attack or even compromise the core elements of democratic societies, such as the separation of powers, protection of minorities, or the rule of law.

Despite a broad debate on the re-emergence of 'populism' in the transition from the twentieth to the twenty-first century that has brought forth many interesting findings, a lack of sociological reasoning cannot be denied, as sociology itself withdrew from theorising populism decades ago and largely left the field to political sciences and history. In a sense, *Populism and the Crisis of Democracy* considers itself a contribution to begin filling this lacuna. Written in a direct and clear style, this set of volumes will be an invaluable reference for students and scholars in the field of political theory, political sociology and European Studies.

This volume, *Concepts and Theory*, offers new and fresh perspectives on the debate on populism. Starting from complaints about the problems of conceptualising populism that in recent years have begun to revolve around themselves, the chapters offer a fundamental critique of the term and concept of populism, theoretically inspired typologies and descriptions of currently dominant concepts, and ways to elaborate on them. With regard to theory, the volume offers approaches that exceed the disciplinary horizon of political science that so far has dominated the debate. As sociological theory so far has been more or less absent in the debate on populism, only few efforts have been made to discuss populism more intensely within different theoretical contexts in order to explain its dynamics and processes. Thus, this volume offers critical views on the debate on populism from the perspectives of political economy and the analysis of critical historical events, the links of analyses of populism with social movement mobilisation, the significance of 'superfluous populations' in the rise of populism, and an analysis of the exclusionary character of populism from the perspective of the theory of social closure.

Gregor Fitzi is Co-Director of the Centre for Citizenship, Social Pluralism and Religious Diversity at University of Potsdam, Germany. After his PhD in Sociology at the University of Bielefeld, he was Assistant Professor at the Institute of Sociology, University of Heidelberg, Germany, and held a temporary position as full professor at the University of Bielefeld. His most recent publication is *The Challenge of Modernity: Georg Simmel's Sociological Theory* (Routledge, 2018).

Jürgen Mackert is Professor of Sociology and Co-Director of the Centre for Citizenship, Social Pluralism and Religious Diversity at Potsdam University, Germany. His research interests are in sociology of citizenship, political economy, closure theory, collective violence. His most recent publication is *The Transformation of Citizenship* (Routledge, 2017), in three volumes, co-edited with Bryan S. Turner.

Bryan S. Turner is Professor of the Sociology of Religion at the Australian Catholic University, Honorary Professor at Potsdam University and Honorary Fellow in The Edward Cadbury Centre, Birmingham University. In 2015 he received the Max Planck Award from the Max-Planck Society and Alexander von Humboldt Foundation, Germany. He is editor of *Citizenship Studies*, the *Journal of Classical Sociology*, and the *Journal of Religious and Political Practice*. He is also Chief Editor of the Wiley-Blackwell *Encyclopedia of Social Theory* (2017).

Routledge Advances in Sociology

Indigenous Knowledge Production
Navigating Humanity within a Western World
Marcus Woolombi Waters

Time and Temporality in Transitional and Post-Conflict Societies
Edited by Natascha Mueller-Hirth, Sandra Rios Oyola

Practicing Art/Science
Experiments in an Emerging Field
Edited by Philippe Sormani, Guelfo Carbone & Priska Gisler

The Great Transformation
History for a Techno-Human Future
Judith Bessant

Occupying London
Post-Crash Resistance and the Limits of Possibility
Sam Burgum

Populism and the Crisis of Democracy
Volume 1: Concepts and Theory
Edited by Gregor Fitzi, Jürgen Mackert and Bryan S. Turner

Populism and the Crisis of Democracy
Volume 2: Politics, Social Movements and Extremism
Edited by Gregor Fitzi, Jürgen Mackert and Bryan S. Turner

Populism and the Crisis of Democracy
Volume 3: Migration, Gender and Religion
Edited by Gregor Fitzi, Jürgen Mackert and Bryan S. Turner

The Challenge of Modernity
Georg Simmel's Sociological Theory
Gregor Fitzi

The World Multiple
Everyday Politics of Knowing and Generating Entangled Worlds
Edited by Keiichi Omura, Grant Jun Otsuki, Shiho Satsuka, Atsuro Morita

For a full list of titles in this series, please visit www.routledge.com/Routledge-Advances-in-Sociology/book-series/SE0511

Populism and the Crisis of Democracy

Volume 1:
Concepts and Theory

Edited by
Gregor Fitzi, Jürgen Mackert
and Bryan S. Turner

LONDON AND NEW YORK

First published 2019
by Routledge
2 Park Square, Milton Park, Abingdon, Oxon OX14 4RN

and by Routledge
711 Third Avenue, New York, NY 10017

Routledge is an imprint of the Taylor & Francis Group, an informa business

© 2019 selection and editorial matter, Gregor Fitzi, Jürgen Mackert and Bryan S. Turner; individual chapters, the contributors

The right of Gregor Fitzi, Jürgen Mackert and Bryan S. Turner to be identified as the authors of the editorial material, and of the authors for their individual chapters, has been asserted in accordance with sections 77 and 78 of the Copyright, Designs and Patents Act 1988.

All rights reserved. No part of this book may be reprinted or reproduced or utilised in any form or by any electronic, mechanical, or other means, now known or hereafter invented, including photocopying and recording, or in any information storage or retrieval system, without permission in writing from the publishers.

Trademark notice: Product or corporate names may be trademarks or registered trademarks, and are used only for identification and explanation without intent to infringe.

British Library Cataloguing-in-Publication Data
A catalogue record for this book is available from the British Library

Library of Congress Cataloging-in-Publication Data
A catalog record has been requested for this book

ISBN: 978-1-138-09136-8 (hbk)
ISBN: 978-1-315-10807-0 (ebk)

Typeset in Times New Roman
by Florence Production Ltd, Stoodleigh, Devon, UK

Contents

List of figures and tables   xi
Notes on contributors   xiii
Foreword   xv

Introduction: Is there such a thing as populism?   1
JÜRGEN MACKERT

PART I
Conceptual debate   15

1   Populism as a conceptual problem   17
CATHÉRINE COLLIOT-THÉLÈNE

2   Why populism?   27
ROGERS BRUBAKER

3   Populism: An ideal-typical assessment   47
GREGOR FITZI

4   How to define populism? Reflections on a contested concept and its (mis)use in the social sciences   62
CRISTÓBAL ROVIRA KALTWASSER

5   Populism and 'unpolitics'   79
PAUL TAGGART

PART II
Theoretical approaches   89

6   'We the people': Liberal and organic populism, and the politics of social closure   91
JÜRGEN MACKERT

7 Past is prologue: Electoral events of spring 2012 and the
   old 'new' nationalism in post-security Europe   109
   MABEL BEREZIN

8 The coterminous rise of right-wing populism and superfluous
   populations   130
   DAVID A. SNOW AND COLIN BERNATZKY

9 Toward a strategy for integrating the study of social
   movement and populist party mobilisation   147
   JOHN D. McCARTHY

   Index   170

Figures and tables

Figures

6.1	The continuum of manifestations of the two versions of populism	103
6.2	The continuum of manifestations of liberal populism	103
6.3	The field of populist politics	104
7.1	Trajectory of right electoral salience 1970–2012; selected countries	114
9.1	Time-series of total and collective behaviour/social movement publications appeared in top four US sociology journals, 1960–2012	151
9.2	Estimation of income tax burden	161
9.3	Party identification and elector turnout in Western democracies	163

Tables

8.1	Selected word usage in Obama's and Trump's inaugural addresses	134
8.2	Usage of 'people' in Obama's and Trump's inaugural addresses	135

Notes on contributors

Mabel Berezin, Professor of Sociology at Cornell University, writes on challenges to democratic solidarity in Europe and the United States. Her works include *Illiberal Politics in Neoliberal Times: Culture, Security, and Populism in the New Europe* (Cambridge, 2009). Her current writing focuses on extreme nationalism in contemporary Europe.

Colin Bernatzky is a doctoral student in Sociology at the University of California, Irvine. His research interests include social movements, social psychology, culture and cognition, with a particular focus on the spread, persistence and revision of beliefs.

Rogers Brubaker is Professor of Sociology at the University of California, Los Angeles. He has written widely on social theory, immigration, citizenship, nationalism, ethnicity, and religion. His most recent books include *Grounds for Difference* (Harvard, 2015) and *Trans: Gender and Race in an Age of Unsettled Identities* (Princeton, 2016).

Cathérine Colliot-Thélène, Professor Emeritus at University Rennes 1 (France). Specialist in German and political philosophy. Her research focuses on the work of Max Weber and on democracy interpreted from the point of view of subjective rights *La démocratie sans 'demos'* (PUF, 2011); in English: *Democracy and Subjective Rights* (2018).

Gregor Fitzi is Co-Director of the Centre for Citizenship, Social Pluralism and Religious Diversity at University of Potsdam, Germany. After his PhD in Sociology at the University of Bielefeld, he was Assistant Professor at the Institute of Sociology, University of Heidelberg, Germany.

John D. McCarthy is Distinguished Professor in the Department of Sociology and Criminology at Pennsylvania State University. He served both as Graduate Director and Head of his Department. He has recently directed studies on public disorders, spiritual entrepreneurs, Tea Party mobilisation, and anti-Muslim events across the U.S.

Jürgen Mackert is Professor of Sociology and Co-Director of the Centre for Citizenship, Social Pluralism and Religious Diversity at Potsdam University,

Germany. Research interests: sociology of citizenship, political economy, closure theory, collective violence.

Cristóbal Rovira Kaltwasser, PhD, Humboldt University of Berlin, is an Associate Professor of Political Science at Diego Portales University in Santiago, Chile. He is one of the editors of the *Oxford Handbook of Populism* (Oxford, 2017) and, with Cas Mudde wrote *Populism: A Very Short Introduction* (Oxford, 2017).

David A. Snow is Distinguished Professor of Sociology at the University of California, Irvine. His extensive publications include *A Primer on Social Movements* (with S.A. Soule), the *Wiley-Blackwell Encyclopedia of Social and Political Movements* (with D. della Porta, B. Klandermans, and D. McAdam), and the new and expanded *Wiley-Blackwell Companion to Social Movements* (with S.A. Soule, H. Kriesi, and H.J. McCammon).

Paul Taggart is Professor of Politics and Director of the Sussex European Institute at the University of Sussex. He is author of *The New Politics and the New Populism* (1996); *Populism* (2000) as well as co-editor of *Opposing Europe? The Comparative Party Politics of Euroscepticsm* (2008) and *The Oxford Handbook of Populism* (2017).

Foreword

Western liberal-democratic societies have been confronted by the growth of populist movements and political parties since the 1990s. This development – at the time unexpected – has subsequently spread across much of Europe, but also included the unexpected electoral victory of Donald Trump. Yet another unexpected development was the outcome of the 2016 British referendum on membership of the European Union, which set 'Brexit' in motion. The British vote to leave encouraged strong movements, for example in the Netherlands, Germany and Austria, but in fact across almost all Europe from Scandinavia to Spain and Greece. Without any doubt, in recent years, liberal democracies, which for several reasons already traversed a profound crisis of political representation, have been severely challenged by the rise of populism. New right-wing and left-wing social movements have emerged, new populist political parties have been founded, and some of them have come to power and established autocratic regimes, as in Poland and Hungary. The core elements of democratic societies such as the separation of powers, protection of minorities, civility and the rule of law have become compromised. In the second decade of the twenty-first century nothing less than the survival of Europe's democratic political culture is at stake.

These volumes provide a critical assessment of the conceptual muddle surrounding the concept of populism and offer fresh theoretical approaches to the topic. They also provide a variety of empirical case studies of actual populist movements and parties.

Concepts and Theory discusses in depth ongoing problems of defining and conceptualising 'populism' as well as its theoretical reflection. *Politics, Social Movements and Extremism* contributes to the role populism plays in contemporary political contestations in the context of profound changes in economic, political and social conditions that have global consequences. *Migration, Gender and Religion* concentrates on the three most important aspects that play critical roles in populist discourse, politics and mobilisation.

The publication of these three volumes would not have been possible without the support of the Deutsche Forschungsgemeinschaft (DFG), the Alexander-von-Humboldt Stiftung and the Max-Planck-Gesellschaft. Finally, we would also like to thank Hannah Wolf for her indispensable work at the Centre for Citizenship, Social Pluralism and Religious Diversity at Potsdam University, and Sara Nothnagel for her assistance during the production of these volumes.

Introduction
Is there such a thing as populism?

Jürgen Mackert

There is no threat to Western democracies today comparable to the rise of right-wing populism. While in politics and society it has played an increasing role at least since the 1990s, the social consequences of the global financial crises in 2008 only added momentum to its growth, as manifest in the Brexit vote in the UK and the election of Donald Trump as US president in 2016. Moreover, the global economic crisis promoted what has been called left populism in countries that were hit the hardest by both the banking crisis and subsequent neo-liberal austerity politics in the EU, such as in Greece, Portugal, Spain, Ireland and Cyprus. In 2017, we have seen the Front National attracting many voters in the French presidential elections, the radicalization of the Alternative für Deutschland (AfD), and the formation of a centre-right government in Austria, with the Freiheitliche Partei Österreichs (FPÖ) as part of the coalition, propagating racism, anti-Muslim politics and a radical restriction of immigration. Further, we have witnessed the consolidation of autocratic regimes in Poland and Hungary, the establishment of authoritarianism in Turkey after the referendum in April 2017 and the elections in June 2018, and not least the formation of an extreme-right nationalist government in Italy in March of the same year. All these manifestations of right-wing populism share a common feature: they attack or even compromise the core elements of democratic societies, such as the separation of powers, protection of minorities, and the rule of law. The rise of populism has promoted a broad, vivid and flourishing debate in the social sciences that seems to have arisen even in the face of the ties between right-wing populism and the extreme right. Further, political debate has turned into a cacophony of aggressive, racist, misogynistic, and pluralism-adverse voices that has transformed democratic political culture and begun to dominate political debates. Various political parties in democratic systems in Europe, such as conservative parties in the UK, Germany, Austria, the Netherlands and so forth have reacted by adopting 'populist' discourse and positions surprisingly smoothly. Nothing has become more common in politics than politicians instinctively accusing each other of being populists while claiming democratic reason for their own position.

The social sciences are struggling with how properly to *conceptualise* and *theorise* populism as a social and political phenomenon. Consistently, social scientists express discomfort with competing concepts of populism in the debate. Yet, the recent debate on populism reveals that efforts to *conceptualise* populism have been a recurrent topic and problem in the literature (Crépon, 2006; Decker,

2004; Delwit, 2012; Mény & Surel, 2002; Mudde, 2004; Priester, 2011). However, far from being new problem, this complaint has been well-known in the debate at least since Wiles (1969), with obvious disappointment, stated that every scholar seems to have their own definition of populism, depending on his or her interest (Allcock, 1971). More recently, Moffitt and Tormey (2014) have argued that statements about difficulties in defining or conceptualising populism reveal that this debate has begun to revolve around itself, an impression that again has been supported by Aslanidis (2016, p. 89). Such statements simply resonate widespread discomfort with the notion of populism and its alleged 'chameleonic character' (Arter, 2011, p. 490).

Besides this ongoing search for *the* definition or conception of what populism may actually mean, the scope of *theoretical reasoning* on populism that could exceed the disciplinary horizon of political science has apparently been neglected so far. Only few efforts have been made to discuss populism more intensely within different *theoretical contexts* in order to *explain* its dynamics and processes. Approaches that would allow for discovering cause-effect relations, critical events and tipping points in the processes of mobilisation, or the link between populism and recent social phenomena, such as emerging superfluous populations, have been proposed only recently (see the chapters by Mabel Berezin; David A. Snow and Colin Bernatsky; and John D. McCarthy and Jürgen Mackert in this volume).

In this introduction, I would like to refer to some critical aspects of both conceptual and theoretical work that may help to overcome some of the current uncertainties, or perhaps misunderstandings, and which can be subsumed under four headings: *Contestation, Conceptual history, Context,* and *Capitalism*. In brief, the contestation surrounding populism as a concept is not at all a problem if it stimulates debate and leads to progress. Conceptual history reminds us of the changing dynamic nature of both the concepts – as for example populism – we develop in order to grasp reality, and the social conditions that shape these conceptualizations. Context matters, if not to say context is all. There will not be a convincing concept of populism that is not context-sensitive and thus specific rather than universal. Finally, the dynamics of neo-liberal capitalism being an unfettered system of free markets allow for explaining populism's dynamics and destructive effects on the fabric of liberal democracies.

Populism as essentially contested

In 1965, W.B. Gallie's famous article *Essentially Contested Concepts* engaged with problems of endless contestation in scientific work:

> Any particular use of any concept of common sense ... is liable to be contested for reasons better or worse; but whatever the strength of the reasons they usually carry with them an assumption of agreement, as to the kind of use that is appropriate to the concept in question, between its user and anyone who contests his particular use of it.
>
> (Gallie, 1956, p. 167)

Gallie's elaborations clarify that there will not be a final agreement on how to define and conceptualise populism, but also, much more important, they provide an explanation as to why populism is, and will remain, contested among scholars in the social sciences. A brief look at Gallie's 'framework' for contested concepts, listing seven criteria, helps to understand our recent problems with populism.

Appraisiveness. Essentially contested concepts are value-laden. However, rather than necessarily attributing a positive value to them, there is good reason also to include negatively valued social phenomena (Collier, Hidalgo & Maciuceanu, 2006, p. 216). Without doubt, populism today is a negatively as well as positively appraised concept, if we look at the US and Europe or at Latin America, respectively. By sticking to the context of established liberal democracies however, we clearly see the negative valuation of what is usually called right-wing populism.

Internal complexity. As this criterion refers to different usages of the concept in question that scholars may apply (Gallie, 1956, p. 167), populism fits perfectly: it is a highly complex concept that is optionally conceived as ideology, political strategy and tactic, socially disruptive and exclusionary politics, and so forth.

Diverse describability. Immediately linked to internal complexity, this criterion refers to the fact that any explanation of a concept's worth must 'include reference to the respective contributions of its various parts or features' (172). Different descriptions of populism may therefore show that 'there is nothing absurd or contradictory in any one of a number of possible rival descriptions of its total worth, one such description setting its component parts or features in one order of importance, a second setting them in a second order, and so on' (172).

Open character. 'The use of essentially contested concepts is radically context-dependent' (Boromisza-Habashi, 2010, p. 277). As Gallie convincingly argues, 'there is no "marking" or "points" system to decide who are the champions, so there are no official judges or strict rules of adjudication' (Gallie, 1956, p. 171). Thus, essentially contested concepts remain 'open in their meaning, i.e. subject to periodic revision in new situations' (Collier, Hidalgo & Maciuceanu, 2006, p. 218). The plurality of usages, applications and meanings of populism thus only shows how, in a vivid debate, we can observe a contest for coming to terms with a concept that remains in flux and that needs to be continually revised given rapidly changing social conditions.

Competition. This criterion sets the rules of the game of how to use essentially contested concepts in the rhetorical struggle. Each party in the contest has to recognise 'the fact that its own use of it is contested by those of other parties, and that each party must have at least some appreciation of the different criteria in the light of which the other parties claim to be applying the concept in question' (Gallie, 1956, p. 172). From this perspective, different conceptualisations of populism are an expression of competition. Rather than trying to find *the* definition or conceptualisation, debate in fact should promote ever better and more refined definitions and concepts of populism.

Exemplar. In order to understand the variety of usages of the concept in question, Gallie argues that this must be seen as a kind of 'derivation of any such a concept from an original exemplar whose authority is acknowledged by all the contestant users of the concept' (180). Yet, we have simply to concede that there is no such a thing as an exemplar from which we could easily derive new, maybe better meanings of what populism may denote.

Progressive competition. This last criterion refers to a critical plea with regard to scientific debate:

> Recognition of a given concept as essentially contested implies recognition of rival uses of it (such as oneself repudiates) as not only logically possible and humanly 'likely', but as of permanent critical value to one's own use or interpretation of the concept in question.... One very desirable consequence of the required recognition in any proper instance of essential contestedness might therefore be expected to be a marked raising of the level of quality of arguments in the disputes of the contestant parties.
>
> (Gallie, 1956, p. 193)

Instead of bemoaning conceptual competition and sometimes even confusion in the debate on populism we should appreciate this dispute with regard to its theoretical elaboration. Thus, ongoing efforts of conceptualisation should be of a kind to further advance 'the quality of argumentation using the concept' (Waldron, 2002, p. 151).

Gallie's framework points to necessarily existing difficulties to grasp a tricky, value-laden and normatively and politically contested concept of political sociology. At the same time, it suggests that we should not look for a single obligatory definition/conceptualisation of populism. In a similarly confusing debate as the one on populism, Charles Tilly simply remarked 'So what? No one owns the definitions of terror, terrorism, or terrorists' (Tilly, 2005, p. 18), and he referred to a justification for this somewhat sloppy remark by referring to his own methodological position:

> Although definitions as such cannot be true or false, in social science useful definitions should point to detectable phenomena that exhibit some degree of causal coherence – in principle all instances should display common properties that embody or result from similar cause-effect relations.
>
> (Tilly, 2004, p. 8)

Tilly reminds us that definitions and conceptualisations are important, as they are the indispensable working tools for both theoretical and empirical analysis. Yet, he goes one step further in pointing out that the social phenomena we try to understand have in some way been brought to the fore. Referring to cause-effect relations refers to the specific dynamics that underlie the (re-)emergence of what we call populism. To my mind, this historicity plays a critical role with regard to the still pending aspects of the debate.

Social change and non-simultaneity – a lesson from conceptual history

The contestation surrounding almost all critical terms, for example democracy (Collier & Levitsky, 1997), the rule of law (Waldron, 2012), human dignity (Rodriguez, 2015), or liberalism (Abbey, 2005; Gray, 1978) and its obvious inevitability show that as human beings we create concepts in order to make sense of the world we are living in. This basic insight from *conceptual history* may help to understand social scientists' problems with coming to terms with populism.

Without elaborating on this tradition in detail, I want to stress the important finding that denoting events in the real world with certain theoretical concepts has to take into account the temporality of both *factual history* and the very *concepts* with which we try to grasp certain events. This aspect of temporality explains how and why concepts and facts may diverge, why we wonder whether concepts may denote historical facts correctly and why there is competitive dispute. Nevertheless, and in spite of these serious obstacles, Reinhart Koselleck ([2003] 2010) has forcefully argued that human beings cannot avoid building concepts in order to gain experience and to make social and historical events part of our lives. Thus, in the very moment in that we turn from our basic human disposition to the content of concepts that capture real and concrete experience, a process of change begins.

With regard to the debate on populism, we may keep in mind that elements of conceptualisation may change. Democracy, being one of the core terms of definitions and conceptualisations of populism, has changed dramatically during recent decades. This necessarily leads to ongoing revisions with regard to conceptualising populism. Further, as possible transformations of meanings may change differently, the critical aspect of temporality makes it obvious that some things are changing rapidly while others are going on slowly; the meaning of certain words may change while this might not happen to others; meanings may change faster or slower. Koselleck shows how important it is to realise such different temporal structures in both factual history and conceptual work, as this makes the complex and difficult relation of a concept and the facts and circumstances it tries to capture comprehensible. This essentially temporal relation is the key to a *history of concepts*, because what can and has to be comprehended lies outside of concepts – the very reason why these two dimensions may and in fact do only temporarily correspond. There are four logical possibilities with regard to these dynamics:

> First, the meaning of a word and the issue covered remain the same, synchronically and diachronically. Second, the meaning of a word remains the same, while the covered issue changes, thereby evading the prior meaning. The changing reality has to be captured in a new way, i.e. it has to be understood in a new way. Third, the meaning of a word changes, yet, the previously captured reality remains the same. The changing semantics have to find new forms of expression to do justice to reality. Fourth, circumstances and the meaning of words can develop in completely different perspectives

in a way that a once existing assignment will be no longer comprehensible. How and which reality could once be comprehended by a specific term can only be revealed by methods of conceptual history

(Schultz, 1979, pp. 65–67, translation J.M.)

Incongruity or asynchrony of events in factual history and their being conceptualised is obviously critical with regard to the problems that arise with defining and conceptualising populism. Both the changing social conditions for populism to rise (again) since the late 1990s and possible shifts in the very meanings that are ascribed to the term today – in contrast to other historical periods or social, cultural, political or institutional contexts – need to be kept in mind.

Context is all

Both the debate on essentially contested concepts and this brief look at conceptual history remind us of the simple fact that context matters if we try to come to terms with defining and conceptualising populism. Much of the confusion of the recent debate seems to originate from too little context-sensitivity. I want to refer briefly only to some of the most obvious contextual obstacles that will bar the way to any one and only obligatory concept of populism.

First, a recurrent problem in the debate on populism are the different meanings it has in the US and Europe, and in Latin America, respectively. While the former are confronted with a reactionary variety of populist politics, scholars working in the Latin American context emphasise the progressive character of 'left' populism, illustrated by citizen activism against oligarchies and defending democratic rights.

Second, this debate not only shows disparities within the concept with regard to geographical and historical contexts, but no less with regard to institutional ones. Can we really assume that democracy in each of these areas means the same? To be sure, following Joseph A. Schumpeter's ([1942] 2008) minimal definition of democracy as nothing but a mechanism of regularly electing the ones to enact authority over the population, all democracies are democracies. Yet, does that help? Do we not have to take into consideration essential and incomparable features of democratic systems with regard to institutional differences, as well as the politico-economic foundations of the countries under investigation, with an idea of redistribution of wealth, the welfare state and social rights? Is it the same to talk about, say, Argentina, Russia, Israel, the Democratic Republic of Congo, the US, Poland, the UK and France – all democracies by definition? I doubt it, and I argue that institutional contexts matter whenever we denote certain political movements or parties within them as populist.

Third, Argentina as a case may shed light on problems and confusion arising out of context-insensitivity. Péronism has always been a populist movement that has dominated Argentina's politics for decades. Further, there is another strange complication as Péronism in itself is characterised by a left wing and a right wing. On the left side we have recently seen the Néstor Carlos Kirchner/Christina

Kirchner faction in power, while before them Carlos Ménem served as president, a Peronist neo-liberal right-winger. What do we do with this confusion, although it may be a national peculiarity?

Fourth, while the concept of left-wing populism may make sense in the Latin American context due to fundamentally different historical, political, economic, social and cultural trajectories compared with the US and Europe, one might wonder why we talk about left-wing populism under conditions of established democratic systems and formerly developed welfare states. To be sure, Podemos in Spain or Syriza in Greece use the term of 'the people' (albeit in very different senses). However, if one of the characteristics of populism is an aggressive exclusion in both the social and cultural sense, what do we do with the fact that the politics of these two parties are socially and culturally inclusive? Defending the political and social rights of citizens, the welfare state, and democratic accountability may be anti-neo-liberal strategies, but I would argue that denoting these movements or parties as left populist is simply a misnomer.

Fifth, quite regularly, from a historical perspective, authors refer to the nineteenth-century American populist movement, which was a kind of progressive rural movement for the rights of peasants. This may be the case but does this remark help us to come to terms with what populism might mean under profoundly transformed conditions in the twenty-first century? I would argue that it helps as little as generally referring to pre-Christian Roman tribunes of the plebeians, Tiberius und Gaius Gracchus, as prototypical populist leaders or Pied Pipers (Rebenich, 2007).

Finally, there are also some interesting contextual shifts in denoting political styles. In 1995 Gianfranco Fini in Italy founded the Alleanza Nationale, which came out of the neo-fascist party Movimento Sociale Italiano (MSI), while in France Marine Le Pen 'reformed' the Front National (FN) that Jean-Marie Le Pen had founded in 1972 as an extreme right, one might say neo-fascist, party after she became the party's leader in 2011. Still an extreme right party, the FN succeeded in being perceived as 'sovereignist', neither left nor right, and indeed populist, rather than being called extremist or neo-fascist, as the party still is. Morevoer: Why should we denote Germany's AfD and Austria's FPÖ as right-wing populist rather than (neo-)fascist? Too often it seems that 'populism' operates as a kind of euphemism for (neo-)fascism (Foster, 2017; Berman, 2016). This leads me to my last point.

Capitalism and the dynamics of populism

Economic history and the analysis of capitalist dynamics finally draw attention to explaining the rise and power of today's populism that I argue to be a mediate consequence of neo-liberalism's destruction of the social fabric, norms and values, and democratic institutions of Western societies. It seems obvious that all Western liberal democratic societies are struggling with these manifold effects of a now globalised free market. This perspective stresses the significance of political economy as the very context of the recent debate on populism.

To be sure, analyses of populism sometimes refer to neo-liberalism in mainly correlational analyses on populism. Yet, the debate so far has widely neglected neo-liberal capitalism's powerful and destructive dynamics as the major force that prepared the ground for today's populism to flourish (as exceptions see Berezin, 2009; Brown, 2015, 2016; Block & Somers, 2014; D'Eramo, 2013; Foster, 2017; Judis, 2016; Mair, 2013).

Not for the first time in history, Western liberal societies face the devastating consequences of globalised free markets. In his seminal study *The Great Transformation* Karl Polanyi ([1944] 2001) tried to come to terms with the dynamics that brought Europe to the abyss and finally into the catastrophe of two World Wars, authoritarianism and Fascism. Writing as an economic historian, he starts with referring to the fact of a remarkable One Hundred Year's peace preceding the outbreak of the First World War. Of course, there had been conflicts and wars overseas or smaller wars between European powers, such as the Crimean War or the Franco-Prussian War, but there was no greater or long-lasting war amongst the main European powers at that time. For Polanyi, nineteenth-century civilisation rested on four critical institutions. First, a system of power balance between the greatest European powers. However, more importantly for an explanation of today's rise of populism, were the interplay of three further institutions: the idea of a self-regulating market, the liberal state, and the international gold standard. In their illuminating analysis of this analysis, Fred Block and Margaret R. Somers show that Polanyi

> argues that the triad of the self-regulating market, the liberal state, and the gold standard were central to the growing prosperity of nineteenth-century Europe. He insists, however, that these arrangements represented a radical and dangerous break with previous institutional patterns and set off countertrends that would ultimately lead to crisis and war.
> (Block & Somers, 2014, p. 13)

Without going into detail here, Polanyi argues that the free market had destroyed the existing social fabric of European countries that tried to develop some protection against the ongoing catastrophic effects of the 'self-regulating' market. Yet, as he made clear, this *countermovement* does by no means have to be progressive: 'These counter movements are just as likely to be conservative, even populist and fascist, as market destabilizations will mobilize the right no less than the left' (10). Thus, in the 1930s, while the US reacted to the world economic crisis with the 'New Deal' and later with 'The Great Society', Europe was sunk in the fascism and militarization in the build up to Second World War that were both promoted and spread by German Nazism.

Why should we take a look at Polanyi's analysis? In a certain sense, economic history and world history may tell us that experiments with free markets, as we see today, are destructive for whole societies or continents. In contrast to classical liberalism that rested upon the allegedly 'peaceful' exchange on markets, neo-liberalism has implanted and finally established *competition* as the core value and maxim of all social relations. Today, from the PISA regime in schools to universities and the workplace, modern life is organised according to a single benchmark test; from the body and nutrition to sports and dating platforms, from the call to maximise one's own human capital in order to be able to make investments that outdo others in the marketplace (Michéa, 2009), all social practices have become competitive. None of them transcends individual egotism and utility maximisation that are constitutive in order to lead a life by the principle of competition, and neither activity is expected to be socially responsible in order to be capable to develop democratic participation, social responsibility or social integration.

The social consequences of enforcing neo-liberalism as the organising principle of modern life with regard to economic transactions, political decisions, social security, education, health, pensions and so forth have become obvious in all Western societies. They have reactivated old social cleavages and triggered new ones – citizens vs. migrants, old vs. young, urban vs. rural, wealthy vs. poor and so forth – and pushed liberal-democratic societies into a new 'war of all against all'.

After the banking crisis of 2008–2011, politicians and representatives of global financial capital were powerful enough to reconstitute the global neo-liberal regime through coordinated action (Crouch, 2011; Blyth, 2013; Mann, 2013; Mirowski, 2013) – a regime in which the state and the economy are ever more intertwined (Michéa, 2013; Vogl, 2017). In this process, politics has turned into a vicarious agent of the demands of a globalised neo-liberal economy, serving its new master instead of its democratic citizenry – its most distinguished task being the protection of the market against the protest of citizenries rather than protecting citizens against the intrusion of the market into their daily lives and private spheres.

Taking into consideration Polanyi's analysis may make us more cautious with regard to the dangers that Western democracies face. If there are parallels in today's politico-economic development with the dynamics Polanyi has presented in detail, we should be reminded of Hegel's remark 'that all great world-historic facts and personages appear, so to speak, twice'. Yet, in this case we would have to agree with Marx, who said in the *Eighteenth Brumaire of Louis Bonaparte*, that Hegel 'forgot to add: the first time as tragedy, the second time as farce' (Marx [1852] 2006). Given today's fierce and apparently reactionary movements against the socially disruptive effects of neo-liberal experiments within the free market that started with Thatcherism and Reagonmics in the late 1970s, we should at least be aware that right-wing populism may easily slip into fascism – if it is not just a matter of degree that distinguishes the former from the latter.

Methodological and theoretical considerations for future work on populism

To conclude this introduction, I would like to refer to three critical aspects with regard to the debate on populism that seem to be inevitable and to which the contributions of this volume intend to make a definitive contribution.

Conceptualisation. If we take populism seriously as a necessarily contested concept of analysis, we might on the one hand appreciate the many efforts that so far have been made to define and conceptualise populism and take it as a strength rather than a weakness of the debate. On the other hand, and there is good reason to argue that way, in her chapter Cathérine Colliot-Thélène argues in favour of completely abandoning the concept of populism, as it is neither clear-cut nor analytically convincing, thus obscuring what we are discussing rather than clarifying the whole affair. This argument should be taken seriously by everybody working in the field before continuing with everyday work. This is exactly what Rogers Brubaker does in his chapter, grounded in analytical distinctions and considering historical dynamics, leading to a 'populist moment' that opens the perspective for a forceful defence of populism as an analytical category. Beyond this opposition of determined standpoints of either abandoning or defending the concept of populism, one may also follow the currently dominant interpretation of populism as a 'thin' ideology. From this standpoint, Cristóbal Rovira Kaltwasser in his chapter goes ahead with one strategy within the contest by pointing out why he sees this conception to be more fruitful than competing ones. Contrary to that, the contribution of Paul Taggart takes a different direction. He agrees with the idealist perspective, but at the same time, he shows different strategies of how to enrich it and make it even more convincing. As another genuinely sociological perspective, Gregor Fitzi makes an emphatic plea to re-orient the discussion from its empirical bias, to step back and re-think matters of conceptualisation from a theoretical point of view. Following Max Weber's methodology, he argues in favour of developing ideal types of populism in order to gain a soberer examination of how, in a methodologically refined way, we can go on with the debate.

Contextsensitivity. There can be no doubt that with regard to necessary comparisons, future work should be more context-sensitive. Spatial as well as temporal comparisons demand a lot of attention in order to properly employ a certain concept of populism. In their methodological reasoning about the role contexts play in the analysis of political processes, Charles Tilly and Robert E. Goodin argue:

> Valid answers depend on the context in which the political processes occur. Valid answers depend on three considerations namely on context, with regard to understandings built into the questions, with regard to the evidence available for answering the questions, and with regard to the actual operation of the political processes. We take this position not as a counsel of despair, but as a beacon of hope. We pursue the hope that political processes depend on context in ways that are themselves susceptible to systematic exploration and elaboration.
>
> (Tilly & Goodin, 2006, p. 6)

Taking contexts seriously might at once help to avoid any 'overstretching' of concepts (Collier & Mahon, 1993; Sartori, 1970) such as populism. Jürgen Mackert in his chapter suggests a discussion of populism with regard to the field in which populism emerges. Liberal democracy is characterised by the precarious link of capitalism and political democracy. While the antipode to capitalism would be socialism, the antipode to political democracy would be fascism (see Foster, 2017). From this perspective, in liberal democratic societies, populism can only be right-wing populism that occupies a huge field as it is an intrinsic part of democratic politics but might develop into fascism. The task then is to further investigate the political styles, political semantics, degrees of exclusion and so forth, and clearly define the differences between democratic, populist and fascist politics. This emphasis on the significance of different contexts is also prominent in Mabel Berezin's chapter. She describes and explains the recent upsurge of scholarly interest in the social phenomenon of populism in Western societies as a consequence that emerged from three crises: austerity, security and refugees crises. Concentrating on the sovereign debt crisis, she shows that it is inevitable to take this context and the forces within it into consideration in order to understand the cracks in the European political infrastructure threatening and transforming its political culture.

Dynamics and explanation. Overcoming static analyses that are mostly based on variable sociology will definitely be important for the debate over populism to improve. As correlations cannot present proper explanations of how and why the social phenomenon of populism emerged, we need processual analyses that take contexts seriously while developing convincing explanations. To be sure, the necessity of forward dynamic and explanatory approaches that allow one to detect the social processes yielding specific social consequences is prominent in almost every chapter in this volume, most obviously in those of the aforementioned Berezin, Brubaker and Mackert. Such dynamics also become obvious in the chapter of David A. Snow and Colin Bernatzky, who link constructions of right-wing populism to the emergence of superfluous people. They point to the dynamics of right-wing populists frequently nurturing the construction of superfluous populations by engaging in their Manichean exclusionary identity work and politics, often by exploiting certain existing trends, such as the flow of uprooted peoples and immigrants. In an explanatory way, Snow and Bernatzky point to the different ways in which populists may strategically deal with superfluous populations of 'the negative other' variety, with both abeyance processes and fluctuations in the cultural span of sympathy also functioning as important intervening factors in this dynamic. John D. McCarthy takes a different approach to populism by bringing social movement mobilisation into the debate. This methodologically refined and theoretically elaborated chapter makes a plea to contextualise the research on populist party mobilisation within the wider research of insurgent collective action. This perspective allows for new research strategies that may enable us to examine the dynamics of insurgents' claim making populist movements.

References

Abbey, R. (2005) Is liberalism now an essentially contested concept?. *New Political Science*, *27*(4), 461–480.

Allcock, J. B. (1971). 'Populism': A brief biography. *Sociology*, *5*(3), 371–387.
Arter, D. (2011). *Inside the radical right: The development of anti-immigration parties in Western Europe*. Cambridge: Cambridge University Press.
Aslanidis, P. (2016). Is populism an ideology? A refutation and a new perspective. *Political Studies*, *64*(1), 88–104.
Berezin, M. (2009). *Illiberal politics in neoliberal times: Culture, security and populism in the New Europe*. Cambridge: Cambridge University Press.
Berezin, M. (2012). Events as templates of possibility: An analytic typology of political facts. In J. C. Alexander, R. Jacobs, & P. Smith. (Eds.), *The Oxford handbook of cultural sociology* (pp. 613–635). New York: Oxford University Press.
Berman, S. (2016). Populism is not Fascism, but it could be a harbinger. *Foreign Affairs*, *95*(November/December), 39–44.
Block, F., & Somers, M. R. (2014). *The power of market fundamentalism*. Harvard, MA: Harvard University Press.
Blyth, M. (2013). *Austerity: The history of a dangerous idea*. Oxford: Oxford University Press.
Boromisza-Habashi, D. (2010). How are political concepts 'essentially contested'? *Language & Communication*, *30*(4), 276–384.
Brown, W. (2003). Neo-liberalism and the end of liberal democracy. *Theory and Event*, *7*. Retrieved from https://muse.jhu.edu/article/48659.
Brown, W. (2015). *Undoing the demos: Neoliberalism's stealth revolution*. Cambridge and London: Zone Books.
Brown, W. (2016). Sacrificial citizenship: Neoliberalism, human capital, and austerity politics. *Constellations*, *23*(1), 3–14.
Collier, D., Hidalgo, F. D., & Maciuceanu, A. O. (2006). Essentially contested concepts: Debates and applications. *Journal of Political Ideologies*, *11*(3), 211–246.
Collier, D., & Levitsky, S. (1997). Democracy with adjectives: Conceptual innovation in comparative research. *World Politics*, *49*(3), 430–451.
Collier, D., & Mahon, J. E. (1993). Conceptual 'stretching' revisited: Adapting categories in comparative analysis. *American Political Science Review*, *87*(4), 845–855.
Crépon, S. (2006). *La nouvelle extrême droite. Enquête sur les jeunes militants du Front National*. Paris: L'Harmattan.
Crouch, C. (2011). *The strange non-death of neo-liberalism*. Cambridge: Polity Press.
Decker, F. (2004). *Der neue Rechtspopulismus* (2. Aufl.). Opladen: Leske und Budrich.
D'Eramo, M. (2013). Populism and the new oligarchy. *New Left Review*, *82*(July/August), 5–28.
Foster, J. B. (2017). This is not populism. *Monthly Review*, *69*(2). Retrieved from https://monthlyreview.org/2017/06/01/this-is-not-populism/.
Gallie, W. B. (1956). Essentially contested concepts. *Proceedings of the Aristotelian Society*, *56*, 167–198.
Gray, J. (1978). On liberty, liberalism and essential contestability. *British Journal of Political Science*, *8*(4), 385–402.
Judis, J. B. (2016). *The populist explosion: How the great recession transformed American and European politics*. New York: Cambridge Global Reports.
Koselleck, R. ([2003] 2010). Die Geschichte der Begriffe und Begriffe der Geschichte. In R. Koselleck, *Begrifssgeschichte* (pp. 56–76). Frankfurt am Main: Suhrkamp.
Macpherson, C. B. (1977). *The life and death of liberal democracy*. Oxford: Oxford University Press.
Mair, P. (2013). *Ruling the void: The hollowing of Western democracy*. London: Verso.

Mann, M. (2013). *The sources of social power. Volume 4: Globalizations, 1945–2011*. Cambridge: Cambridge University Press.
Marshall, T. H. (1950). Citizenship and social class. In T. H. Marshall (Ed.), *Citizenship and social class and other essays* (pp. 1–85). Cambridge: Cambridge University Press.
Marx, K. ([1852] 2006). *The eighteenth Brumaire of Louis Bonaparte*. Retrieved from www.marxists.org/archive/marx/works/1852/18th-brumaire/ch01.htm.
Meek, J. (2015). *Private island: Why Britain now belongs to someone else*. London: Verso.
Mény, Y., & Surel, Y. (Eds.) (2002). *Democracies and the populist challenge*. Basingstoke, UK: Palgrave Macmillan.
Michéa, J.-C. (2009). *The realm of lesser evil*. Cambridge: Polity Press.
Mirowski, P. (2013). *Never let a serious crisis go to waste: How neo-liberalism survived the financial meltdown*. New York: Verso/New Left Books.
Moffitt, B., & Tormey, S. (2014). Rethinking populism: Politics, mediatisation and political style. *Political Studies*, *62*(2), 381–397.
Mudde, C. (2004). The populist Zeitgeist. *Government and Opposition*, *39*(4), 542–563.
Polanyi, K. ([1944] 2001). *The great transformation: The political and economic origins of our time*. Boston: Beacon.
Priester, K. (2011). Definitionen und Typologien des Populismus. *Soziale Welt*, *62*(2), 185–198.
Rebenich, S. (2007). Populismus funktionierte schon in der Antike. *Neue Zürcher Zeitung*, 17 June. Retrieved from www.nzz.ch/feuilleton/populismus-und-demagogie-in-der-antike-volksverfuehrung-ist-keine-neue-erfindung-ld.1301297.
Rodriguez, P.-A. (2015) Human dignity as an essentially contested concept. *Cambridge Review of International Affairs*, *28*(4), 743–756.
Sartori, G. (1970). Concept misformation in comparative politics. *American Political Science Review*, *46*(4), 1033–1053.
Schultz, H. (1979). Begriffsgeschichte und Argumentationsgeschichte. In R. Koselleck (Ed.), *Historische Semantik und Begriffsgeschichte* (pp. 43–74). Stuttgart: Klett-Cotta.
Schumpeter, J. A. ([1942] 2008). *Capitalism, socialism and democracy*. New York: HarperCollins.
Shils, E. A. (1956). *The torment of secrecy: The background and consequences of American security policies*. New York: The Free Press.
Streeck, W. (2012). Citizens as customers. *New Left Review*, *76*(July/August), 27–47.
Tilly, C. (2004). Terror, terrorism, terrorists. *Sociological Theory*, *22*(1), 5–13.
Tilly, C. (2005). Terror as strategy and relational process. *International Journal of Comparative Sociology*, *46*(1–2), 11–32.
Tilly, C., & Goodin, R. E. (2006). It depends. In R.E. Goodin & C. Tilly (Eds.), *The Oxford handbook of contextual political analysis* (pp. 3–32). Oxford: Oxford University Press.
Vogl, J. (2017). *The ascendancy of finance*. Cambridge: Polity Press.
Waldron, J. (2002). Is the rule of law an essentially contested concept (in Florida)?. *Law and Philosophy*, *21*(2), 137–164.
Wiles, P. (1969). A syndrome not a doctrine: Some elementary theses on populism. In G. Ionescu & E. Gellner (Eds.), *Populism: Its meanings and national characteristics* (pp. 166–179). New York: Macmillan.
Wright Mills, C. (1956). *The power elite*. Oxford: Oxford University Press.

Part I
Conceptual debate

1 Populism as a conceptual problem

Cathérine Colliot-Thélène

Introduction

To say that the literature on populism today is inflationary is an understatement. The rate of publications on the subject has accelerated over the past two decades. The theme 'populism' has become critical in the studies on democracy; its importance is on the way to supplanting those on cosmopolitanism, which were dominant in the last two decades. However, the concept of populism is far from being clear. I will first summarise some reflections on this concept (see Colliot-Thélène, 2013, 2016). These analyses, however, need to be completed in view of the rapidly changing political situation in Europe and the United States. The second part of my chapter, centred on attempts to define left-wing populism, will be devoted to this supplement. Finally, I will come back to a few semantic remarks that concern our conception of democracy as well as the concept of populism.

A contested concept

Preparing the first article (Colliot-Thélène, 2013) I had consulted a large number of more or less recent works and articles on the subject, and found that all converged at least on one point, namely the difficulty in proposing an unambiguous definition of populism. Rather than attempting to elaborate such a definition myself, I was interested in the representation of the 'people' that was presumed by the overwhelming pejorative use of the term 'populism', at the time, in the language of the politics and the dominant media in France. The vagueness of the notion stems precisely from the fact that this term is above all deprecatory: it tends to disqualify any position or any political movement that diverges from the consensus by which political parties in recent decades have assumed, in turn, the responsibility of government in the countries of the European Union.

I therefore insisted above all in this article on the 'contempt of the people' (Rancière, 2005, p. 88) that underlies the most common uses of the term 'populism' today. That rulers mistrust the 'people' they are supposed to represent is nothing new. The theoreticians of representative democracy often justified this form of government with the argument of the irrationality of the 'masses'. However, this old topic, which can be found in different variants throughout the history of modern democratic regimes, is not sufficient to explain the current stigmatisation of 'populism'. In the today-dominant pejorative use of the term, the reference to the irrationality of the masses, or, at the very least, to their lack of competence, is certainly present. But it is not the principle of representative delegation that is at issue, at least not directly. The 'populist' movements do not usually contest the procedures of representative democracy: they play the game of electoral competitions by striving to win the majority of the voters. They certainly show a strong preference for the referendum, rather than for the votes of the elected assemblies, but the referendum is part of the panoply of instruments of modern democracies. And governments that are usually not suspected of being populist also resort to referenda, often with a plebiscitary intention. The dimension of the modern liberal democracies that some current 'populisms' openly put into question and others pay little attention to is not the principle of representation, but the institutional counter-powers (public freedoms and the independence of the judiciary, in particular). This is clear in the case of the 'populists' that have already acceded to governmental responsibilities, notably in Poland and Hungary.

From this first approach, I retain the idea that, in view of the inflationary uses of the terms 'populism' and 'populist' today, it is necessary to question first of all – even if this is not enough – the presuppositions of these uses in the ordinary language of the politics and the dominant media, rather than trying to circumscribe a phenomenon whose appearance of unity merely reflects these presuppositions. The impossibility of forging a concept that accounts for all the phenomena that are discredited as 'populist' stems from the fact that these presuppositions are generally implicit. In so far as the *populus* of populism must have some kind of relation with the *demos* of democracy, an analysis of populism always engages a determined conception of democracy. In order to achieve clarity in the problems posed by the current use of the term 'populism', one must begin by summoning its detractors and defenders to explain their conception of democracy.

I have developed this argument further (Colliot-Thélène, 2016) by inviting, in a provocative way, to renounce building up a concept of populism. Any attempt at a definition tends indeed to essentialise it, while forgetting that the consistency of the notion depends in each historical case of a determined conjuncture, that is to say of the dominant *doxa*, of which the populist movements challenge one aspect or another. This *doxa* consists of a fixed conception of political 'normality' (a *sensus communis*), which sets the limits between opinions that are acceptable to public expression and those that are proscribed or considered as suspicious. For instance, today's 'political normality' in Europe encompasses very heterogeneous elements: the necessity of specific institutional arrangements, adherence to certain values, such as the condemnation of racism and other categories of discrimination (against women, homosexuals and so forth), but also the support of a particular economic policy, the key words of which are freedom of markets, budgetary rigor and labour flexibility. The principles of political and cultural liberalism and a fixed conception of economic rationalism are linked together through a vague reference to 'openness', which embraces both adherence to humanist values and acceptance of neo-liberal globalisation. It is the heterogeneous nature of this conception of political normality that makes it possible to confuse, under the category of 'populism', xenophobic and non-xenophobic, 'souverainists' and neo-liberalist parties or movements that are favourable or hostile to budgetary rigor, and so forth.

We can distinguish two types of strategies implemented by analysts who try to elaborate a concept of populism. Some authors take it as a revealer of the difficulties and aporias of modern democracy in general (Rosanvallon, 2014), others build up an ideal type (Müller, 2013). The latter strategy is minimalist: it selects a few characteristic features to forge an ideal type of populism. The flaw in this process is that it excludes from the 'right' understanding of the concept some of the phenomena which are called 'populist' in the everyday language of politics and the media. Therefore, it cannot account for the ordinary use of the word. The flaws of the first strategy are on the opposite side. Rather than limiting the understanding of the concept, it elaborates a broad catalogue of characteristics, so that the presence of only some of these characteristics in practices, opinions and political movements suffices to justify the use of the terms 'populism' and 'populist'. The boundaries of this catalogue being inevitably imprecise, populism becomes a diffuse phenomenon that can be found everywhere, including in the most ordinary discourses and practices of traditional political parties.

I summarise the core of my argument: the term populism, rather than being a concept awaiting its clarification, constitutes an obstacle to an unprejudiced analysis of the causes of the phenomena to what it refers. Indeed, the term cumulates designative and explanatory functions: 'Populism', understood as the spontaneous dispositions of the popular strata, which spreads like a virus, is supposed to explain the development of 'populisms', that is to say of right-wing and extreme-left movements and parties that challenge the present 'political normality'. The pseudo-explanation inherent in the use of the term blocks any differentiated analysis of the phenomena concerned, and consequently also any in-depth reflection on their causes.

Some of these causes are general or valid at least as much for the United States as for Europe: *First* of all, the social consequences of neo-liberal economic policies, which no one can any longer ignore. After the Brexit referendum, the election of Donald Trump in the United States, the French elections (the regional ones of 2015 and the most recent presidential election) and the German national elections in September 2017, it has become impossible to explain the diffusion of populism only by the ignorance, the irrationality and the prejudices of the masses. Even the participants at the last Davos Forum (in January 2017) feel compelled to recognise that the deepening of social inequalities that result from the neo-liberal economic policies is a major cause of the diffusion of 'populism'. According to the French economic paper *Les Echos* these participants show themselves 'overwhelmingly convinced that the [populist] question is primarily economic' (Vittori, 2017).

The *second* general cause is directly related to the first. Because neo-liberalism is linked to the globalisation of the economy and the loss of control of national governments over their economic and social policies, protest against the impoverishment and degradation of social protections tend very naturally to be formulated in nationalist terms. 'Brexit' and Trump's 'America first' illustrate this dimension of contemporary populism. The defence of national sovereignty against 'globalism' was also one of the main lines of division in the recent presidential election in France.

To these two causes is added a *third*, also of general importance, namely migratory pressures. In the European and North American countries, the nationalist withdrawal is combined with a refusal of immigrants, who are accused of lowering wages or unduly benefiting from the protections guaranteed to nationals.

These three elements: the protest against the disintegration of the social state, the denunciation of globalisation and the refusal of immigrants are found in most of the right-wing populisms in Europe and North America today. The 'left-wing' populism (to which I return) rejects xenophobia, but in this case, too, social protest goes generally hand in hand with a refusal of globalism (in France, hostility towards the European Union, considered as the transmission belt of the global neo-liberal logics). However, these general causes, which give current populisms 'family resemblances' (Judis, 2016, p. 14), are overdetermined in each case by the particular configurations of the different countries. For example, in the Eastern countries of the European Union (Poland, Hungary), hostility to it has other reasons than in England, France or Greece, and xenophobia has a different story and other motivations than xenophobia in France (Krastev, 2017). To focus on the 'populism' understood as a global phenomenon to which all governments are confronted covers up these particular causes and diverts attention from political evolutions in certain countries that may be more dangerous for the future of our democracies than the alleged 'irrationality' of the masses, for instance the contempt for public liberties and the development of authoritarian forms of government ('illiberal democracy'). Current governmental practices (in particular security policies) bear a great part of the responsibility for the weakness of democratic culture in some Eastern countries or for the erosion of democratic culture in the West of Europe.

Populism of identity versus plebeian populism?

I extend my objections to a definition of 'populism' also to the attempts made by certain leftist theorists to build up and defend a positive concept of it. At first sight the distinction between right-wing and left-wing populisms may seem welcome by contrast with the confusion of the most common uses of the notion, which tend to disqualify in an undifferentiated way any questioning of the 'political normality'. To the extent that this disqualification goes hand in hand with a challenge to the intelligence and political capacities of the 'people', it is tempting to appropriate the notion by reversing its sign of value. It is also nothing outrageous to rely on 'popular sovereignty' to demand, in the name of democracy, that the people have a say in the decisions that concern them. This argument, however, may serve both the right-wing populism as well as the left-wing populism. Both use indeed the same language, invoking the popular will against the 'elites' and the 'system'.

Like the theorists who oppose populism and democracy, the defenders of leftist populism must therefore also distinguish between a 'good' and a 'bad' people, or between a good and a bad way of conceiving it.

To illustrate this point let me take the example of an article of a French sociologist, Federico Tarragoni (2013), dealing with the 'science of populism', that is, with the majority of the works devoted to this theme by political science or sociology. Tarragoni finds in this literature a 'learned' form of the contempt of the people that underlies the most common uses of the term today. The rehabilitation of the people that he calls for does not, however, cover all kinds of populism. He opposes an 'identitarian', that is a nationalist and xenophobic populism, which presupposes an 'already being' people, and a 'plebeian' populism, that of those excluded from politics or positions of power in general, which does not refer to a people already constituted, but to a people 'to be made', through the struggles against exploitation and oppression. Tarragoni finds the historical model of plebeian populism in the agrarian populism of the end of the nineteenth century in the United States and in the Narodniki at the same time in Russia. In these cases, we were dealing with movements whose social bases were quite clearly identifiable and the stakes could be thought in terms of interests of classes or specific social strata. That is why the term populism does not have always in the US, up to the present day, the negative connotation it has in Europe.

However, to project on these class movements – as Tarragoni does – the imaginary of the 'people to be made', which is characteristic of the 'democracy of the squares', from the Spanish *Indignados* or *Occupy Wall Street* to *Nuit debout* in France, appears to me as an anachronism. The demand for active participation in politics, as it is expressed today, is the result of a specific political experience that covers the last thirty years or so. The elective voting, which is supposed to be the major political activity of the citizen, has lost the significance it had during most of the twentieth century, when the great parties that disputed the suffrages of the electors seemed to represent different projects of society. It is true that, in general, every episode of popular protest is accompanied by an intensification of the politicisation of ordinary citizens and the formation of various associations, more or less formalised, more or less ephemeral or lasting. But what has been called the 'movement of squares' is not directly correlated with classes or social strata opposed to specific economic policies that threaten their living conditions, as was the case with the People's Party in America in the nineteenth century (Judis, 2016, pp. 21–28). The protest of the movement of squares is, first of all, more global and more directly political: it is a reaction against the technocratisation of governance that increasingly restricts all citizens to the role of consumers and 'managers of oneself', depriving them of all influence on the direction of public policy. Moreover, the social composition of these mobilisations is heterogeneous. Generally speaking, the popular strata (peasant or working class) are poorly represented. The majority of the participants are urban youths, most of them with a good level of education. This does not prevent them from being affected by unemployment and the precariousness of employment and status, which allows them to melt their protest into a general challenge to the social inequalities resulting from neo-liberal economic policies. However, the 'people to be made', through the invention and development of participatory and 'horizontal' forms of political activity, is very far from the true 'plebeian' people, which is always defined in contrast to an 'Other', be it the 'strangers', the 'elites' or other nations. On the other side the 'identitarian' populism cannot be attributed solely to the influence of xenophobic demagogues. Rather, we must understand the sociological causes of the success of their propaganda, which the abstract and exclusively political notion of the 'people to be made' does not permit. For this reason I persist in refusing to raise 'populism' to the rank of a concept, whether in the pejorative variant of the dominant discourse or in distinguishing between right-wing and left-wing populism. I do not mean that populism is a false problem. The term 'populism' – it is probably impossible at the present time to avoid it – refers to a field of problems facing democratic regimes today in Europe, the United States and elsewhere. But I maintain that the notion of 'populism', in itself, far from being able to enlighten and *a fortiori* to explain the phenomena in question, constitutes an obstacle to their analysis. If my previous analyses seem too short to me today, it is because, in view of the gravity of these problems, one cannot merely argue pedantically on the sole level of conceptual rigor. It is urgent, on the contrary, that critical thought should take these problems in charge, in the ways I have indicated above, that is in differentiated analyses which distinguish between the general causes and the particular causes of the different kinds of 'populisms'.

Questions of semantics

A few semantic remarks will allow me to address the most widely publicised notion today of 'left-wing populism', defended by Chantal Mouffe in the wake of Ernesto Laclau (Laclau, 2005; Mouffe & Errejon, 2017). The absence or disappearance of social classes in the vocabulary of populist movements, right-wing or left-wing, has often been noticed. Instead, the lines of the socio-political divisions go between the 'people' on the one hand, the 'elites' and the 'system' on the other, or between 'those from below' and 'those from above'. Chantal Mouffe and Ernesto Laclau have theorised this change in vocabulary, which reflected a paradigm shift in the analysis of political conflicts (Laclau & Mouffe, 2001). Mouffe inspired notably Jean-Luc Mélenchon, and she has close relations with the Spanish political party Podemos.

If Mouffe, whose positions I share in part, assumes and defends the denomination 'left-wing populism' to designate political movements which challenge both neo-liberal economic policies and technocratic governance (the two things are linked), it is not only for convenience. We all understand immediately what movements or parties are involved, if only because they are also designated by the same expression, taken in a pejorative sense, in the dominant discourse. Moreover, it is because she considers, following the analyses developed by Laclau in *On Populist Reason* (Laclau, 2005) that a radical democratic policy must appropriate the signifier 'people'. In a book that relates her discussion with Iñigo Erréjon (one of the founders, with Pablo Iglesias, of the Spanish political party Podemos) we find a very interesting passage relating to this point. The two partners generally agree. There are, however, divergences regarding the terminology that should be used to construct the decisive political boundary in contemporary democratic struggles. Erréjon expresses reservations about the expression 'left-wing populism'. On the other hand, Mouffe, who defends this appellation, is surprised, first, by the fact that Podemos avoids taking up the right/left opposition and, secondly, that this party prefers to speak of *gente* (as opposed to *casta*) rather than of *pueblo*. Concerning the expression 'left populism', Erréjon notes that the expression is too marked by its pejorative use so that a reversal of its value could be comprehensible by the broad public:

> [We] intervene . . . in politics and in doing so, we can not use a term that has been cursed by its use in the media. Anyone who claims to win one day cannot endorse a definition that, in the collective imagination, immediately means 'demagogy'. . . . [In] the language of the media in Spain, [populism] has become synonymous with lies and demagogy. Who would like to endorse such a label?
> (Mouffe & Erréjon, 2017, pp. 196–197 – translation C.C.-T.)

But there is another reason for his reluctance to speak of 'left-wing populism', which directly concerns the signifier 'people', namely that the sedimentations of its national linguistic variants are different. 'People' is not a sociological term, it does not designate an identifiable social stratum, even approximately. In the practice advocated by Mouffe and Laclau, it is an empty signifier that must be occupied in a political strategy aimed at the constitution of a new hegemony. But is it advisable, is it even possible in all languages? Erréjon notes that the term 'pueblo' 'is a bit archaic in Spanish political language, the *Francoists* having used it for a long time to designate a homogeneous will that does not need political parties to be represented' (Mouffe & Erréjon, 2017, pp. 213 – translation C.C.-T.). He also refers to a lecture at the University of Vienna, where he spoke of Podemos, in which the translator had difficulties in translating *pueblo* and *gente*, which had given rise to an interesting discussion of the problems posed by the use of the term *Volk* in German.

In support of these remarks, I will quote some passages from a recent book by the German historian Michael Wildt, who devoted part of his work to the history of National Socialism and anti-Semitism. This book, published in 2017, is titled *Volk, Gemeinschaft, AfD*. AfD – Alternative für Deutschland – is the name of the political party which was formed in 2013 in Germany, initially by an economist, Bernd Lucke, and on the basis of opposition to the single currency European, and which has evolved rapidly, notably by opposing the migration policy of Angela Merkel in the summer of 2015, towards positions very much at the right fringe, at the price of different splits. This party achieved great success in recent regional elections in 2016 (in Mecklenburg-Vorpommern in particular) and in the last national elections in September 2017. Wildt evokes the history of the notion of

Volk in Europe and Germany as well as the history of the expression *Volksgemeinschaft*, which also belongs to the AfD terminology. Regarding the AFD's claim to represent the 'true people' (*das wahre Volk*), he notes that it is too simple to oppose to the 'true' people of the populists the 'true' people, universal and inclusive, of liberal democracy, for the definition of what the people of democracy is has never been self-evident. Referring to the distinction between *demos* (political people) and *ethnos* (a people defined by ethnic characteristics, whatever they may be), frequently made by the theorists of liberal democracy, he recalled that the *demos* of modern democracies were also constituted on the basis of exclusions, internal ('passive' citizens, deprived of the right to vote, colonised, women), or external (other peoples). He again notes, referring to analyses of Michael Mann (2005), that the *demos* can easily be transformed into *ethnos*.

This last remark concerns the democratic-liberal criticism of populism, which is too simplistic in Wildt's opinion. It should not, however, be understood as a justification, even a relative one, of AfD's terminology and positions. On the contrary, Wildt stigmatised the attempt made by certain leaders of this party to revalorize expressions that belonged to the Nazi terminology: *Volksgemeinschaft*, in particular, but also *völkisch*. Commenting on the statement by a member of the Lower Saxony parliament in 2015 that neither the words *Volk* (people) and *Gemeinschaft* (community) nor the expression *Volksgemeinschaft* can be considered negative, Wildt argues that after the crimes of Nazism, 'there is no more "innocent" use of this concept' (Wildt, 2017, p. 116 – translation: C.C.-T.). More generally, he maintains that:

> the concept of the *Volk* (people), which was historically indispensable in the struggle against the ancient regime and during the formation of sovereign national states and which underpinned the demand for democratic self-determination, has become anachronistic.
>
> (Wildt, 2017, p. 116)

Shall we agree with this generalisation or does it require to be corrected by taking into account the difference between national histories? I leave the question open. My point here is only to show the difficulties, and perhaps the dangers to which the discursive strategy of construction of the people advocated by Laclau and Mouffe (2001) is exposed. We might approve of the criticism on the basis of which this conception was constituted (the criticism of the essentialist conception of social classes in Marxist dogma) and recognise the interest of the Gramscian conception of hegemony for the purpose of political strategy. It remains that a term such as that of 'people' is not only a floating or empty signifier that could be arbitrarily resemantised, but a term loaded with history, a history which differs according to the nations and their languages. The senses sedimented in the course of this history make the 'people' (*pueblo, peuple, Volk*) a definitively plurivocal notion, and it is illusory to believe that a theoretical construction, however elaborate, can neutralise them. Left-wing populists are concerned to disregard any ethnic connotations of their conception of the people – the rejection of xenophobia is the main point of their divergence from the right-wing populists – but they are less clear regarding the nationalistic interpretation of the term. The shift from popular sovereignty to national sovereignty is all the easier because neo-liberalism has monopolised the values of cosmopolitical openness, confused with economic globalisation. The 'people' of left-wing populist parties and movements is the 'bottom-up' people, but it may be also the nation from which it is expected that it will restore its sovereignty against supranational powers, whatever they may be. The 'France insoumise' of Mélenchon and the National Front of Marine Le Pen share a common hostility to 'Brussels': they are both 'sovereignists'. This is one of the reasons why a part of their voters can swing between one and the other.

As pertinent as the criticism of a mechanistic conception of the relations between social conditions and class consciousness may be, it does not justify abandoning the sociological determinations of political dispositions. By failing to compete with this, the defenders of radical democracy, under the pretext of rehabilitating populism in a left-wing version, foster ambiguities about the meaning of democratic sovereignty and its relation to nationalism. And these ambiguities make it difficult for them to fight against the right-wing versions of the 'hegemony of national identification' (patriotism) other than by a moral condemnation of xenophobia. This remark is an invitation to reflect on the possibility or the impossibility for the left to recover, namely – in the terms of Mouffe and Erréjon –, 'the strong idea of community... which conservative liberal fantasy has too quickly ruled out' (Mouffe & Erréjon, 2017, p. 106). Can this community, this collective identity, this 'we', still be national, or even regional (the European Union), without defining and defending borders that do not pass only between 'those from below' and 'those from above', but also between insiders and outsiders? The notion of populism does not allow the answering of this question, which is at the core of the modern concept of democracy.

Conclusion

The journalist John B. Judis recently published an excellent summary on populism, entitled *The Populist Explosion* (Judis, 2016). The title could suggest a continuity between the parties and movements studied, from the American People's Party at the end of the nineteenth century to the left-wing and right-wing populisms of today. However, this book shows the great heterogeneity of these movements and parties. Their only common point is to express a protest from some of the citizens of a country against a determined state of political normality. Populisms are heterodox forms of politicisation; their contents vary according to the orthodoxy they dispute. It is this orthodoxy that must be in each case questioned, rather than seeking to identify positions (anti-liberalism, xenophobia, nationalism and so forth) that would be characteristic of populism in general. The place 'populism' took in the studies on democracy in recent years has shifted attention away from more insidious phenomena, which gradually undermine the foundations of our democracies, such as the staggering growth of economic inequalities, the technocratisation of governance or the restrictions of individual and public liberties in the name of security. By stigmatising populism, the liberal elites avoid confronting the reasons for the protests channelled by populist parties, be they right of left. But the defenders of left-wing populism on their side, if they correctly identify some of these causes (the growth of social inequalities as a result of neo-liberal economic politics), avoid others, notably the question of migration, which is one of the main challenges facing democracies in the twenty-first century.

References

Colliot-Thélène, C. (2013). Quel est le peuple du populisme?. In C. Colliot-Thélène & F. Guénard (Eds.), *Peuples et populisme* (pp. 5–26). Paris: PUF.
Colliot-Thélène, C. (2016). Le populisme n'est pas un concept. *Les Cahiers de L'éducation permanente*, *49*, 105–117.
Judis, J. B. (2016). *The populist explosion*. New York: Columbia Global Reports.
Krastev, I. (2017). *Europadämmerung*. Berlin: Suhrkamp.
Laclau, E. (2005). *On populist reason*. London and New York: Verso.
Laclau, E., & Mouffe, C. (2001). *Hegemony and socialist strategy*. London and New York: Verso.
Mann, M. (2005). *The dark side of democracy: Explaining ethnic cleansing*. Cambridge: Cambridge University Press.
Mouffe, C., & Erréjon, I. (2017). *Construire un peuple. Pour une radicalisation de la démocratie*. Paris: Cerf.
Müller, J.-W. (2013). *What is populism?*. Philadelphia, PA: University of Pennsylvania Press.
Rancière, J. (2005). *La haine de la démocratie*. Paris: La Fabrique éditions.
Rosanvallon, P. (2014). Penser le populisme. In C. Colliot-Thélène & F. Guénard (Eds.), *Peuples et populisme* (pp. 27–42). Paris: PUF.
Tarragoni F. (2013). La science du populisme au crible de la critique sociologique: archéologie d'un mépris savant du people. *Actuel Marx*, *54*(2), 56–70.
Vittori, J.-M. (2017). Au Forum de Davos la grande peur du populisme. *LesEchos.* Retrieved from www.lesechos.fr/20/01/2017/LesEchos/22366-027-ECH_au-forum-de-davos--la-grande-peur-du-populisme.htm?texte=Davos%20forum.
Wildt, M. (2017). *Volk, Gemeinschaft, AfD*. Hamburg: Hamburger Edition.

2 Why populism?

Rogers Brubaker

Introduction

It is a commonplace to observe that we have been living through an extraordinary pan-European and trans-Atlantic populist moment.[1] From the Brexit and Trump shocks via the Austrian and Dutch elections to the French and German elections, populism has been in the headlines. Support for long-standing anti-immigrant populist parties has surged, while the Sweden Democrats and the Alternative für Deutschland achieved electoral breakthroughs in countries in which support for such parties had long been conspicuously weak. The regimes of Viktor Orbán in Hungary and the Law and Justice party in Poland have been tightening their increasingly authoritarian grip on power. At the same time, Podemos in Spain, Syriza in Greece, and the Mélenchon, Sanders, and Corbyn insurgencies – as well as the shape-shifting Five-Star Movement in Italy – have shown that resurgence of populism is far from being restricted to the right.

All of these have been called 'populist', as of course have many figures elsewhere, such as Prime Minister Modi of India, President Duterte of the Philippines, and President Erdogan of Turkey. But do they really belong together? Are we in fact living through a pan-European and trans-Atlantic populist moment? Or is the term 'populism' just a journalistic cliché or political epithet that serves more to stigmatize than to analyse?

Easy recourse to loose and loaded words such as 'populism' can certainly be a form of intellectual laziness that substitutes labelling for analysis. But I will argue that 'populism' remains a useful conceptual tool – and one that is indispensable for characterising the present moment. Yet this raises a second set of questions: What explains the clustering in time and space that constitutes the populist moment? Why populism? Why here? And why now?

The question in my title – Why populism? – is thus in fact two questions. The first is a question about populism as a term or concept, the second a question about populism as a phenomenon in the world. Or to put it somewhat differently, the first is a question about how to name and characterise the present conjuncture, the second a question about how to explain that conjuncture. I address both questions in this chapter, while limiting the scope of my explanatory argument to Europe and North America.

A contested concept

For half a century, the literature on populism has been haunted by doubts about the nature and even the existence of its object of analysis.[2] Students of populism have put forward three main reasons to be suspicious of populism as a category of analysis. The first is that the term lumps together disparate political projects: right and left, urban and rural, neo-liberal and protectionist, inclusionary and exclusionary, mobilising and demobilising. To be sure, all claim to speak in the name of 'the people' and against various 'elites'. But 'the people' is a deeply ambiguous notion, with at least three core meanings (Mény & Surel, 2000, pp. 185–214). It can refer to the common or ordinary people, to the people as plebs. It can refer to the sovereign people, to the people as demos. And it can refer to the bounded or culturally or ethnically distinct people, to the people as nation or ethnos. To speak in the name of the 'little people' against 'those on top' would seem to imply a politics of redistribution. To speak in the name of the sovereign people against ruling elites would seem to imply a politics of re-democratisation. And to speak in the name of the politically bounded and/or culturally or ethnically distinct people against threatening outside groups or forces would seem to imply a politics of economic protectionism or cultural or ethnic nationalism. What could be gained by subsuming these very different forms of politics under the label 'populism'?

Speaking in the name of the people, moreover, is a chronic and ubiquitous practice in modern democratic settings. This is a second reason for suspicion of populism as an analytic category. If populism is everywhere – as it appears to be in broad and inclusive accounts that focus on the claim to speak in the name of the people – then it is nowhere in particular, and it risks disappearing as a distinctive phenomenon.

The third problem is that 'populism' is a morally and politically charged term, a weapon of political struggle as much as a tool of scholarly analysis. As has long been noted in the literature (Taguieff, 1995), it is routinely used by journalists and politicians to stigmatize and delegitimize appeals to 'the people' against 'the elite', often by characterising such appeals as dangerous, manipulative, and demagogic. In this deeply pejorative usage, the term 'populism' serves to defend a thin, indeed anaemic conception of democracy – a conception of 'democracy without a demos' (Stavrakakis, 2014, p. 507). Some scholars, too, notably Jan-Werner Müller (2016) – build disapproval into the definition of populism; they define it as intrinsically anti-democratic. But others – in a mirror reversal – emphasise populism's intrinsically democratic nature. Canovan (2002) characterises it as 'the ideology of democracy', while Ernesto Laclau – no doubt the single most influential theorist of populism – goes so far as to identify populism (which entails 'question[ing] the institutional order by constructing an underdog as an historical agent') with politics as such, as distinct from administration (Laclau, 2005, p. 47). If 'populism' is such a deeply politicised term, and one that is used by scholars in such radically incompatible ways, can it serve as a useful category of analysis?

Populism as a discursive and stylistic repertoire

These objections are serious, but they need not be fatal. They can be addressed, I think, by treating populism as a discursive and stylistic repertoire.[3] Here I build on the well-established discursive and stylistic turn in the study of populism. This turn has allowed scholars –increasingly aware of the heterogeneous ideological commitments, programmatic goals, core constituencies, and organisational forms of populist movements and parties– to capture the discursive, rhetorical, and stylistic commonalities that cut across substantively quite different forms of politics.[4] Following Jansen (2016), I also build on the literature on repertoires of political contention (Tilly, 2006) and the broader literature on repertoires in the sociology of culture (Swidler, 1986).

The repertoire metaphor has three useful implications for the study of populism. First, it suggests a limited though historically variable set of relatively standardised elements that are well known to, and available to be drawn on by, political actors. Yet while the elements are more or less standardised, and in some ways even scripted, they leave room for improvisation and elaboration: they must be filled out with particular content and adapted to local circumstances. As general discursive templates, moreover, all of the elements can be elaborated in very different directions, specifically in ways that link up with projects and stances of the right or the left.[5] This helps to make sense of the deep political and ideological ambivalence of populism, and it helps to account both for the democratic energies populism may harness and for the antidemocratic dangers it may represent (Canovan, 1999; Mudde & Rovira Kaltwasser, 2012).

Second, the repertoire metaphor suggests that instances of populism are related by what Wittgenstein (1958, paras 66–67), writing about the difficulty of defining a game, famously called a 'family resemblance', rather than by strictly logical criteria.[6] Just as there may be no common feature shared by all games, but instead a 'complicated network of similarities overlapping and criss-crossing' (p. 66), so it may not be fruitful to seek to specify a necessary or sufficient set of elements for characterising a party, politician, or discourse as populist.[7] A further implication of the family resemblance idea is that elements of the repertoire, taken individually, are not uniquely populist, but may belong to other political repertoires as well, and that it is the combination of elements – rather than the use of individual elements from the repertoire – that is characteristic of populism. As I shall argue below, the repertoire is indeed built around a core element: the claim to speak and act in the name of 'the people'. But even this core element, though empirically predominant, is neither conceptually necessary nor empirically universal.[8] And it can be combined in differing ways with other elements from the populist repertoire, each of which can be given differing weights or inflections.

Third, the repertoire metaphor suggests a way of responding to the claim that populism is ubiquitous (and therefore cannot serve as a useful analytical category). For while the populist repertoire is chronically *available* in contemporary democratic contexts, it is not chronically *deployed*. The cultural resonance and political traction of the various elements of the repertoire – and therefore their attractiveness to political actors – vary systematically across political, economic, and cultural contexts. Moreover, the repertoire is drawn on unevenly *within* a given time, place, and context: some political actors shun the repertoire altogether; some draw on it only occasionally or minimally (and may do so even as they criticise others for their 'populism'); others draw more chronically and fully on a wider range of elements from the populist repertoire. Populism is thus a matter of degree, not a sharply bounded phenomenon that is either present or absent (Diehl, 2011a, pp. 277–278). But it is not *only* a matter of degree: populisms also differ qualitatively in the combinations of elements drawn on and in the directions in which the elements are elaborated and filled out.

In the name of the people: vertical and horizontal oppositions

The core element of the populist repertoire is the claim to speak and act in the name of 'the people'. That this is central to or even constitutive of populism has been universally recognised in the literature. But since this claim is central to democracy, not just to populism, some scholars add the specification that populism involves the claim to speak and act in the name of 'the people' and against 'the elite'. In the influential view of Cas Mudde (2004, p. 543), for example, populism is defined by a vision of society as divided between the 'pure people' and the 'corrupt elite'. Yet if the distinction between 'the people' and the 'elite' is indeed central for populism, 'the people' need not be represented as 'pure', not need corruption be the only or even the central failing ascribed to elites. More fundamentally, as I have argued elsewhere (Brubaker, 2017a), populism is based not only on the *vertical* opposition between 'the people' and 'the elite', but also on the *horizontal* opposition between inside and outside. The core element of the populist repertoire is thus better understood as a *two-dimensional* vision of social space, defined by the *intersection* of vertical and horizontal oppositions.[9]

In the vertical dimension, 'the people' are defined of course in opposition to economic, political, and cultural elites. 'The people' are represented as morally decent (though not necessarily as pure), and as economically struggling, hard-working, family-oriented, plain-spoken, and endowed with common sense, while 'the elite' – the rich, the powerful, the well-connected, the (over-) educated, and the institutionally empowered – are seen as living in different worlds, playing by different rules, insulated from economic hardships, and out of touch with the concerns and problems of ordinary people.

'The people', moreover, can be defined not only in relation to those on *top* but also – still in the vertical dimension – in relation to those on the *bottom* (Müller, 2016, p. 23). Those on the bottom may be represented as parasites or spongers, as addicts or deviants, as disorderly or dangerous, as undeserving of benefits and unworthy of respect, and thus as not belonging to the so-called decent, respectable, 'normal', hard-working 'people'.[10] The downward focus of populist anger and resentment has been much less widely discussed than the upward focus. But it should not be neglected, especially since the upward and downward orientations are often closely connected: those on top are often blamed for being overly solicitous of those on the bottom. Populism is keenly attuned to the distribution not only of *resources* and *opportunities* but of *honour, respect, and recognition*, which may be seen as unjustly withheld from 'ordinary' people and unjustly accorded to the unworthy and undeserving (Hochschild, 2016).

In the horizontal dimension, 'the people' are understood as a bounded collectivity, and the basic contrast is between inside and outside. Left-wing populism construes the bounded collectivity in economic or political terms and identifies the threatening 'outside' with unfettered trade, unregulated globalisation, the European Union (EU), or (especially in Latin America) American Imperialism. Right-wing populism construes the people as a culturally or ethnically bounded collectivity with a shared and distinctive way of life and sees that collectivity as threatened by outside groups or forces (including, of course, 'internal outsiders': those living on the inside who are seen as belonging to the outside).

What I want to emphasise here – since it is characteristic of the present European and North American populist conjuncture – is the tight discursive interweaving of the vertical opposition to those on top and the horizontal opposition to outside groups or forces. In both left and right variants of populism, economic, political, and cultural elites are represented as 'outside' as well as 'on top'. They are seen not only as comfortably insulated from the economic struggles of ordinary people, but also as differing in their culture, values, and way of life. They are seen as culturally as well as economically mobile – in effect, as rootless cosmopolitans, indifferent to the bounded solidarities of community and nation. Their affective and cultural as well as economic investments are seen as moving easily across national boundaries, while their moral self-understanding, cultural identity, and economic fate are seen as de-linked from those of the nationally bounded 'people'.

Left-wing variants of the intertwining of vertical and horizontal oppositions are more likely to emphasise the elite's economic outsiderhood, and their supra-national or global economic ties, horizons, and commitments. Right-wing variants are more likely to emphasise elites' cultural outsiderhood. They criticise elites for welcoming immigrants and financially supporting refugees while neglecting the hard-working 'native' population, and for favouring mixing and multi-culturalism while denouncing ordinary people as racist and Islamophobic, as Hilary Clinton infamously did when she characterised Trump supporters as 'a basket of deplorables'.

The intertwining of vertical and horizontal oppositions is also evident, of course, when those 'on the bottom' – for example, Roma in East Central Europe, certain groups of immigrant origin in Western Europe, and African Americans and certain other racialised minorities in the US – are simultaneously seen as 'outside', and when their putatively irreducible outsiderhood or 'difference' is seen as explaining or legitimising their lowly position. There is nothing specifically populist about this kind of culturalisation or even naturalisation of inequality. It only becomes populist when elites – domestic or international – are blamed for prioritising or privileging in some way those who are at once on the bottom *and* outside, while neglecting the problems and predicaments of 'ordinary people.'

Rounding out the repertoire

In addition to the core element just characterised, I want to briefly sketch five additional elements of the populist repertoire. These are best understood as elaborations or specifications of the vertical opposition between people and elite or the horizontal opposition between inside and outside. While my account of these elements is inflected by my concern with the euro-Atlantic populist conjuncture, none of the elements is restricted to this context.

The first of these is what I will call antagonistic re-politicisation: the claim to reassert democratic political control over domains of life that are seen, plausibly enough, as having been depoliticised and de-democratised, that is, removed from the realm of democratic decision-making. This has been emphasised by theorists and defenders of left populism in the Laclau tradition, notably Mouffe (2005), Katsambekis and Stavrakakis (2013), and Stavrakakis (2014). But it can be characteristic of right-wing populism as well (Probst, 2002). Antagonistic re-politicisation may involve opposition to the infamous claim that 'there is no alternative' to neo-liberal economic policies. It may involve opposition to the extension of administrative, technocratic, and juridical at the expense of political modes of decision-making. It may involve opposition to the stifling of debate about fundamental political questions that may result from grand coalitions or ideologically indistinguishable groupings of major parties. Or it may involve opposition to the abdication of key aspects of national sovereignty to the European Union, with its deep 'democratic deficit'.

In all these cases, contentious re-politicisation has an anti-elite thrust. Elites are represented – plausibly enough – as distrusting 'the people,' and thus as favouring modes of decision-making that are insulated from the pressures, passions, and putative irrationality of democratic politics. Contentious re-politicisation draws sharp and antagonistic boundaries between 'the people' and 'the elite'. Liberal anti-populists denounce this polarising language as 'Manichaean', but leftist intellectuals may defend this antagonistic language and the energies it can mobilise.

The second element is majoritarianism – the assertion of the interests, rights, and will of the majority against those of minorities. Majoritarian claims may be directed against those on top, those on the bottom, or those at the margins. They may challenge the privileged few in the name of the many. Yet they may also challenge the rights and benefits accorded to those on the bottom: means-tested welfare benefits, for example, or the procedural protections of criminal law, for which the 'decent, hard-working majority' must allegedly bear the cost.[11] Or they may challenge efforts to promote the interests, protect the rights, or recognise the dignity of marginal groups – defined by religion, race or ethnicity, immigration status, sexuality, or gender. They may reject discourses and practices of multi-culturalism, diversity, or minority rights, seeing these as disadvantaging or symbolically devaluing those in the mainstream. Majoritarianism thus again highlights the ideological indeterminacy and ambivalence of populism.

The third element is anti-institutionalism. This is of course a selective anti-institutionalism: populists in power may construct their own institutions and seek to dominate and work through existing ones (Müller, 2016, pp. 61–62). But as an ideology of immediacy (Innerarity, 2010, p. 41; Urbinati, 2015), populism distrusts the mediating functions of institutions, especially political parties, media, and the courts. Populists often deploy an anti-party rhetoric, even when they establish new parties in order to compete in elections, and the parties they establish are generally weakly institutionalised vehicles for personalistic leadership.[12] They often claim to promote direct rather than representative democracy. And even as populists seek to exploit or control the established media, they also seek to bypass it and to communicate directly with their supporters, as Trump and Wilders have done through Twitter and Beppe Grillo has done through an innovative blog. Populists also distrust the complexity and non-transparency of institutional mediation and the pluralism and autonomy of institutions. Thus Trump, for example, has ferociously attacked the legitimacy of the (mainstream) media and the legitimacy of the courts as well. And Hungary's Fidesz regime has pursued a comprehensive institutional 'Gleichschaltung' that has subordinated courts, media, the economy, and academic and cultural institutions to the party-state.

The fourth element is protectionism: the claim to protect 'the people' against threats from above, from below, and today especially from the outside. One can distinguish economic, securitarian, and cultural forms of protectionism; all three are central to the present conjuncture. Economic protectionism highlights the threat to domestic producers from cheap foreign goods, the threat to domestic workers from cheap foreign labour, and the threat to domestic debtors from foreign creditors. Securitarian protectionism highlights threats from terrorism and crime. Cultural protectionism highlights threats to the familiar life world from outsiders who differ in religion, language, food, dress, bodily behaviour, and modes of using public space.

The final element of the populist repertoire pertains not to the *what* of populist discourse but to the *how*: to matters of communicational, rhetorical, self-presentational, and body-behavioural style. In Ostiguy's (2009) terms, the populist style is a 'low' style: it performatively devalues complexity through rhetorical practices of simplicity, directness, and seeming self-evidence. This is often accompanied by an explicit anti-intellectualism or 'epistemological populism' (Saurette & Gunster, 2011) that valorises common sense and first-hand experience over abstract and experience-distant forms of knowledge. The 'low' style is enacted not only through ways of talking but also through embodied ways of doing and being involving gesture, tone, sexuality, dress, and food (Diehl, 2011b; Moffitt, 2016, pp. 63–68).

The populist style opposes common sense and plain speaking to the constraints and restraints of civility and political correctness. Populists not only criticise the rules governing acceptable speech, they relish violating those rules. Through an attention-seeking strategy of provocation, they celebrate their willingness to break taboos, refuse euphemisms, and disrupt the conventions of polite speech and civilised demeanour. As Coleman (2016) has noted, for example, Trump used conspicuous rudeness, crude sexual references, and a general 'bad boy' demeanour to project an image of authentic proximity to 'the people,' in contrast to Clinton's perceived scriptedness and inauthenticity.

Explaining the populist conjuncture

I turn now to the second question signalled in my title. What explains the clustering in time and space that constitutes the present pan-European and trans-Atlantic populist moment? Here too it is necessary to distinguish between different kinds of explanatory questions. Some of these pertain to specific events, especially the Brexit and Trump victories. Any explanation for why a close referendum or election result falls on one side or the other of the razor-thin line that separates victory from defeat must involve a great variety of time-and place-specific contingencies. Had some of these contingencies played out differently, Brexit and Trump might well have lost. On the other hand, had *other* contingencies played out differently, Norbert Hofer might be President of Austria and Marine Le Pen President of France. Analysts interested in explaining specific outcomes would then have faced radically *different* questions.

Yet for those more interested in broad tendencies than in particular events, as I am, the underlying question would have been precisely the same: namely, how did we reach the point at which Brexit, Trump, Hofer, and Le Pen – but also Sanders, Mélenchon, Syriza, and the 2015 Greek referendum rejecting the terms of further bailouts – *all* had a real chance of victory, and the Eurozone and Schengen system of free movement a real chance of collapsing, at around the same time?

Answering this question requires a layered explanatory strategy that integrates processes of different scale, scope, and temporal register (Sewell 2005, p. 109).[13] In the limited space available to me, I can do no more than gesture towards such an explanation. I will distinguish for convenience between structural and conjunctural temporal registers, though I would be the first to admit that the distinction is somewhat arbitrary.

Structural transformations

In the structural register, on a temporal scale measured in decades, two sets of structural trends have expanded opportunities for populism. The first involves what I call a crisis of institutional mediation. Everywhere we see a weakening of political parties and party systems (Mair, 2002, 2011; Kriesi, 2014). This is indicated by the sharp decline in party membership, trust, and party loyalty. It is also shown by the dramatic reconfigurations of many party systems, as parties that had long dominated the political landscape collapse, and new parties arise. The weakening of parties and party systems encourages politicians to appeal to the people as a whole, rather than to specific social constituencies represented by parties.

Changes in the relation between media and politics point in the same direction. The pervasive 'mediatization of politics' (Mazzoleni & Schulz, 1999), the commercialisation of the media, and of course the accelerated development of new communications technologies make politicians less dependent on parties and more inclined to appeal directly to 'the people. The mediatisation of politics and the commercialisation of the media also encourage both politicians and the media to adopt a populist style of communication. As media scholars have noted, this is a style characterised by simplification, dramatisation, confrontation, negativity, emotionalisation, personalisation, and visualisation (Mazzoleni & Schulz, 1999; Esser, 2013, pp. 171–172).

Transformations of party systems and of the relation between politics and media have fostered a kind of generic populism, a heightened tendency to address 'the people' directly. A second set of structural transformations – demographic, economic, and cultural – have encouraged more *specific* forms of protectionist populism.

The most strikingly visible of these is the large-scale immigration of the last half-century. This has obviously created and expanded opportunities for populist claims to protect the jobs, welfare benefits, cultural identity and way of life of 'the people' – meaning of course the 'native' or 'autochthonous people' – against migrants and increasingly, in the last fifteen years or so, against Muslims. And indeed, economically and culturally protectionist forms of anti-immigrant populism have become chronic since the 1990s throughout most of Western Europe.[14]

The opening of national economies to large-scale immigrant labour is part of a broader set of economic transformations that have fostered a partly overlapping yet distinct form of populism in Western Europe and the US. In relation to the rapid growth, relative stability, relative equality, and widely diffused prosperity of the immediate post-war decades, economic transformations of the last several decades have created opportunities for claims to speak in the name of the 'little people' or 'ordinary people' against 'those on top' as well as against outside groups and forces that are seen as threatening 'our' jobs, 'our' prosperity, 'our' economic security, or 'our' way of life. The litany is familiar: sharp increases in inequalities; the regionally concentrated collapse of manufacturing jobs; the dramatic opening of national economies; and the shifting of risks and responsibilities to individuals through neo-liberal modes of governance. It is worth emphasising that social-democratic parties did not seize the political opportunity created by these major economic shifts. The neo-liberal turn in recent decades left the field open to other parties, on the right as well as the left, to advance populist claims to protect domestic jobs and welfare benefits.

This description of economic transformations and the populist response to them applies to the US as much as to Europe. But the dynamics of Europeanisation (Berezin, 2009) and the institutional architecture of the European Union have provided a distinctive focus for both economic and cultural forms of protectionist populism, thanks to the EU's deep democratic deficit, its imposed policy straitjacket, its constitutionalisation of market freedoms (Grimm, 2015), its position as both 'on top' and 'outside' of national polities, and its foundational commitment to downgrading and in key domains dissolving national boundaries.

In the domain of the politics of culture, finally, new waves of emancipatory liberalism since the 1960s have created opportunities for populists to attack political correctness and to speak in the name of an aggrieved, symbolically neglected or devalued majority and against the alleged privileging of minorities.

These include religious, ethnic, and racial minorities, both immigrant and non-immigrant, on the one hand, and gender and sexual minorities on the other.[15]

Converging crises

The medium-term trends outlined above help explain the routinisation of a thin, generic, 'background' populism in recent decades. They help explain the tendency for political actors to address 'the people' directly and to adopt at least some elements of a populist style of communication. They help explain why anti-immigrant populist and (more recently) Eurosceptical parties have become a structural feature of the political landscape in most West European countries. And they help explain the periodic populist challenges to the American political establishment in recent decades, from George Wallace and Ross Perot to Pat Buchanan, the Tea Party, and Occupy Wall Street (Judis, 2016).

The problem with this account, though, is that it explains too much. If all of these trends favour populism, then we face the problem of explaining why populism is not ubiquitous. We could certainly define populism so broadly that it *is* ubiquitous under contemporary conditions. But then we would have to speak not of a populist *moment*, but of a populist *era*.

Thinking of populism as a discursive and stylistic repertoire offers a way around this difficulty. The trends sketched above have created incentives for almost all political actors to draw, in some contexts, on some elements of the populist repertoire. But 'thicker' forms of populism, drawing on the full range of elements from the repertoire, are *not* chronic or ubiquitous. The populist repertoire is indeed chronically available in contemporary democratic contexts, but it is not chronically or uniformly activated: it is drawn on unevenly, no doubt because the cultural resonance and political traction of the various elements of the populist repertoire vary systematically across political, economic, and cultural contexts.

What, then, explains the populist conjuncture of the last few years? Why now, rather than any other time in the last several decades? My argument – though again I can only gesture towards it here – is that several independent crises have converged in recent years to create a 'perfect storm' supremely conducive to populism, and especially to forms of right-wing populism that unite economic, cultural, and securitarian protectionism.

To be sure, crisis is not a neutral category of social analysis; it is a category of practice that is deliberately mobilised to do specific political work (Hay, 1995) – work that is particularly important for populists. As Moffitt (2016) has recently emphasised, crisis is not an external cause of populism but an intrinsic *part* of populist politics. With the help of the media, populists – and of course other political actors as well – contribute to *producing* the very crises to which they claim to respond. When I speak of a converging set of crises, therefore, I mean a cluster of situations that have been widely *construed and represented* as crises.

Let me begin with the economic crisis. The financial crash and Great Recession were compounded, in Europe, by the sovereign debt crisis and the deep institutional crisis of the Eurozone and the European Union itself (Offe, 2016, pp. 16–31).

The disastrous straitjacket imposed on debtor and trade-deficit countries by monetary union was aggravated by creditor countries' (especially Germany's) unwillingness to mutualise debt, and by the insistence on austerity as a condition for bailouts. This deepened and prolonged mass unemployment, especially in Spain and Greece, and it directly provoked the left populist reaction that brought the Eurozone to the brink of collapse in July 2015, when Greece voted to reject the terms of a further bailout.[16]

But the economic crisis cast a long shadow: its effects were felt well beyond the hardest-hit countries and well beyond moments of peak unemployment or maximum tension over debt. And the crisis energised the right as much as the left. Throughout Europe and North America, populists have used the crisis to dramatise economic insecurity and inequality, to tap into economic anxieties, and to highlight the disruptions of globalisation. And they have proposed a resonant counter-narrative emphasising the need to protect domestic jobs and markets. The counter-narrative informed the Brexit and Trump campaigns and the Mélenchon insurgency in France. But it also found expression in the striking shift in recent years to a protectionist and welfarist stance on the part of most of Europe's national-populist parties. These parties have increasingly targeted segments of the electorate – especially the so-called 'losers of globalisation' – that have been largely abandoned by European social democrats and by the Democratic Party in the US.

Outside of Spain and Greece, it was the European refugee crisis of 2015 that most immediately and visibly provoked a populist political reaction. The rhetoric of 'crisis' in connection with migration and asylum-seeking in Europe and North America is of course not new. And while the 2015 numbers were large, they were not objectively overwhelming. Yet the surge of mainly Muslim asylum-seekers afforded rich opportunities for dramatising – and televisualising – a sense of borders being out of control, an image of multitudes of strangers at the gates, indeed an apocalyptic narrative of Europe being under siege from a seemingly endless supply of desperate men, women, and children willing to face death at sea and violence and exploitation at the hands of smugglers in order to reach the promised land of Germany or Sweden. In a context in which European national-populist discourse had already come to focus on the threat of 'Islamisation', the fact that the large majority of asylum-seekers were Muslim gave additional traction to the trope of a Muslim 'invasion'.

The most direct political effects of the refugee crisis were felt in Germany, Sweden, and Hungary (even more than in Greece). In Germany, the crisis produced both a moment of extraordinary openness on the part of both government and civil society, and a strong reaction against that openness. The reaction was expressed – among other ways – in the transformation of the Alternative für Deutschland from a neo-liberal 'party of professors' to an anti-immigration, anti-Muslim party that achieved dramatic electoral breakthroughs the following year. In Sweden, which received even more refugees per capita than Germany, there was a surge in support for the far-right Sweden Democrats, bringing them neck and neck with the long-dominant Social Democrats. In Hungary, Prime Minister Viktor Orbán took the lead in constructing a razor-wire border fence, a step followed quickly by others. Orbán struck the posture of a lonely leader with the mission of saving Europe from itself, and notably from what he called Europe's 'suicidal liberalism'.

But the refugee crisis – like the economic crisis – cast a long shadow: its effects were felt throughout Europe and indeed beyond. Trump, for example, characterised Merkel's decision to welcome refugees as 'insane' and promised to 'send back' Syrian refugees arriving in the US, since they might be a 'Trojan horse' for ISIS. And fears of borders being out of control were central to the constellation of moods that made Brexit possible. A much-discussed UKIP poster during the campaign featured a 2015 photograph of refugees massed at the Croatian-Slovenian border with the slogan 'Breaking point: the EU has failed us all.'

The refugee crisis – again like the economic crisis – generated a broader crisis of European institutions (Offe, 2016, pp. 136–146). It overwhelmed the Dublin system that regulates applications for asylum, and it brought the Schengen system of internal free movement to the point of perhaps irreversible collapse. Free movement has been one of the most genuinely popular aspects of European integration, but its political viability depends on effective external border controls. By dramatising the porousness of external frontiers, the refugee crisis encouraged populists to stake out more radical forms of Euroscepticism.

The refugee crisis of the summer of 2015 was only the most visible and dramatic phase of a larger migration crisis. Like the United States and other rich countries, the European Union has resorted in recent decades to a system of extraterritorial 'remote control' – to use the late Aristide Zolberg's (1999) phrase – in order to keep unwanted migrants at bay. The fragile – and of course normatively problematic – March 2016 agreement with Prime Minister Erdoğan to cut off flows through Turkey is a well-known example. Less well known is the history of cooperation with Morocco, Tunisia, and Libya to prevent sea crossings to Spain and Italy. This cooperation has always been precarious, quite apart from the moral and political questions it raises. But a key link in the system broke down altogether with the collapse of state authority in Libya. Sea crossings to Sicily and the small Italian island of Lampedusa have surged since 2014, as has support for the radically anti-migrant Northern League. Deaths at sea have also surged, reaching a record level of more than 5,000 in 2016. Since the summer of 2017, however, crossings to Italy have dropped sharply, thanks to murky Italian initiatives to recreate a Libyan coast guard and to cooperate with Libyan militias.

The wave of terror attacks since 2015 also fed in to the 'perfect storm.' In historical and comparative perspective, of course, the number of casualties has been small. But the increased frequency and symbolic resonance of attacks in the heart of a series of European capitals have enabled the populist right throughout Europe and North America to cultivate and dramatise a sense of insecurity and vulnerability. The attacks have enabled them to combine the Schmittian political semantics of friend and enemy with the Huntingtonian thesis of a clash of civilisations between radical Islam – or sometimes Islam per se – and the West.

The perfect storm was created by the *coming together* – or rather the political *bringing-together* or *tying-together* – of the economic, refugee, and security crises. The populist right throughout Europe, for example, used the Würzburg,

Ansbach, and Berlin attacks – all committed by perpetrators who had applied for asylum in Germany – to link the refugee crisis and terrorism. And they (as well as Donald Trump) used the sexual aggressions in Köln, Hamburg, and elsewhere on New Year's Eve 2015 to dramatise the connection between the refugee crisis, ethnoreligious demography, cultural difference, and physical insecurity.

More generally, the Brexit, Trump, and Le Pen campaigns tied together economic, ethno-demographic, cultural, and crime- and terrorism-focused insecurities in a newly resonant narrative. This narrative defined the opposition between *open and closed* as more fundamental than that between *left and right*.[17] In this fundamentally protectionist narrative, the basic imperative is to protect 'the people' – economically, culturally, and physically – against the neo-liberal economy, open borders, and cosmopolitan culture said to be favoured by economic, political, and cultural elites at both national and European levels.

The Brexit, Trump, and Le Pen campaigns promised to defend and revive the bounded national economy in the face of 'savage globalisation' and the frictionless cross-border movement of goods, labour, and capital. They promised to defend national – as well as European and Christian – culture and identity from dilution or destruction through large-scale extra-European immigration. And they promised to protect public order and security against threats from both outside and inside – and against an elite portrayed as soft on crime and terrorism, in thrall to political correctness, deluded by the myth of multiculturalism, and insufficiently cognizant of the threat from radical Islam.

The final element of the perfect storm is the crisis of public knowledge that is suggested by talk of fake news, alternative facts, and a post-truth era (Brubaker, 2017b). This is not only a matter of fake news – of the proliferation of dis- and mis-information churned out for profit or propaganda (Persily, 2017, pp. 67–68). The crisis of public knowledge is also generated by seemingly positive developments, notably the superabundance and apparently democratic hyper-accessibility of 'information' in our hyper-connected digital ecosystem. Like other aspects of cultural democratisation, this has weakened the authority of the mediating institutions that produce and disseminate knowledge: universities, science, and the press. As a result, a cloud of suspicion shadows all claims to expert knowledge.

Anxieties about the convergence of media, commerce, and new communications technologies go back more than a century. But something fundamental has changed in recent years as smart phone and social media use has become nearly universal. Trump's spectacular use of Twitter to appeal directly to his huge and active following and to bypass and denounce the mainstream media – even as he skilfully exploited its dependence on him and used Twitter to make news the mainstream media felt it had to cover – would not have been possible even a few years earlier.

The crisis of public knowledge presents an opportunity for populists – and especially, in the current conjuncture, for the populist right. It is an opportunity to further undermine and discredit the press. And it is an opportunity to generate and propagate not just 'alternative facts', but an entire alternative world-view that is not only massively insulated from falsification but seemingly massively confirmed by a continuous supply of new 'information' (Calhoun, 2017). The hyperconnected digital media ecosystem enhances the performative power of populist discourse: the power to create or at least deepen the very crises to which populists claim to respond, and the power to sharpen and exacerbate the very divisions – between 'the people' and 'the elite', and especially between insiders and outsiders – that populists claim to diagnose and deplore.

Conclusion

I suggested above that my structural account of the medium-term trends conducive to populism explained too much. My conjunctural account of the 'perfect storm' explains both too little *and* too much. It explains too little in that this highly generalised sketch, which abstracts from the messy particularities and contingencies of time, place, and situated action, cannot account for the substantial variations across Europe and North America, in degrees and forms, of populist politics. It explains too much in that – like my account of medium-term trends – it would lead one to expect populism and nothing but populism.

Yet populism is of course not uniformly strong, even at this distinctively populist moment. I would like to speculate, by way of conclusion, about why we are not in fact trapped in an ever-escalating spiral of populism. I will briefly note three factors that can make populism a self-limiting (Taggart, 2004, pp. 276, 284) rather than a self-feeding phenomenon.

The first is what I will call poaching. As is often observed, there is no sharp boundary between populism and non-populism, or even anti-populism. Both substantive themes and stylistic devices from the populist repertoire are routinely appropriated by 'mainstream' political actors, sometimes precisely in an effort to combat populist challenges. A classic example was Dutch Prime Minister Mark Rutte's notorious open letter to 'all Dutch people,' published in all major newspapers seven weeks before the election. Rutte used simple, direct language to proclaim his identification with the discomfort felt by the hard-working 'silent majority' in the face of immigrants who 'misuse our freedom' to act in ways that are 'not normal'. And he called on immigrants to 'behave normally or leave' (Rutte, 2017). By selectively and strategically deploying populist tropes, as Rutte did, mainstream parties may be able to defeat populist challengers – in this case Geert Wilders, whose party had been leading in the polls in the run-up to the elections.

Secondly, while populism thrives on crisis, and while crisis often sells, it does not *always* sell. Just as populists perform crisis, other political actors – for example Angela Merkel or Emmanuel Macron – can be understood as performing *non*-crisis. This is one way of thinking about Merkel's famous 'Wir schaffen das' – 'We can do it' – during the height of the refugee influx. In the battle between representations of crisis and representations of non-crisis, crisis does not always win. And of course the materials for cultivating and deepening a sense of crisis are not always equally propitious. The absence – as of this writing – of major attacks in France after the spectacular horrors of the Charlie Hebdo (January 2015), Bataclan (November 2015), and Nice (July 2016) attacks allowed Macron to project optimism and perform non-crisis. And the sharp reduction in arrivals of asylum-seekers in Germany after 2015 allowed Merkel to do the same.

The third and perhaps most important limit on populism is what I will call the limits of enchantment. Populism depends on a kind of enchantment: on 'faith' in the possibility of representing and speaking for 'the people' (Canovan, 1999). It depends on an affective investment in politics and specifically in the idea of popular sovereignty. At the same time, of course, populism thrives on the *lack of faith* in the machinery and language of representation, on an affective *disinvestment* from politics as usual. So the resonance of populist rhetoric depends on a claim to *exceptionality*, a claim to be fundamentally different from politics as usual. But this claim can be discredited; it can ring hollow. The idea of popular sovereignty may be drained of its emotional potency, leaving only cynicism and distrust in its place. And that cynicism, that distrust, can extend to populists themselves. The affective constellation that *sustains* populist politics can thus shade over into a constellation that *undermines* populist politics as much as it does other forms of representative politics. This offers no reasons for complacency: cynicism and distrust are scarcely grounds for a democratic public life. It is important nonetheless not to exaggerate the strength of populism, just as it is important to take it seriously.

Notes

1 This is a condensed version of a paper originally published in *Theory and Society*, 46, 5, 357–385.
2 For early doubts, see Worsley (1969, p. 219) and, a decade later, Canovan (1981, pp. 3–7). For representative recent statements expressing or addressing these doubts, see Panizza (2005, p. 1) and Moffitt and Tormey (2014, p. 382). For a recent critical analysis of several generations of populism research, concluding with a cautionary note about the futility and empirical inadequacy of any global or strongly generalising account of populism, see Knöbl, 2016. On the history of the category 'populism', see Houwen, 2011 and Jäger, 2017.
3 This does not mean that populism should be understood as 'merely' discursive or stylistic. Any political practice, party, movement, figure, or regime that can be analysed as populist can (and must) also be analysed in terms of ideological commitments, substantive policies, organisational practices, bases of support, and so on. But what ties substantively different forms of populist politics together – what makes it possible to characterise them all as populist – is the discursive and stylistic repertoire on which they draw.
4 These commonalities have been construed in various ways: in formal terms as a discursive logic; more informally as a set of characteristic discursive tropes or interpretive frameworks; or in terms of communicational, rhetorical, self-presentational, aesthetic, or body-behavioural style. For the discursive logic approach, see Laclau, 1977, 1980 and Stavrakakis, 2004. For informal discursive, 'ideational', or ideological approaches, see Taguieff, 1995; Canovan, 2002; Mudde, 2004; Mudde & Rovira Kaltwasser, 2017 and Stanley, 2008. For approaches emphasising communicational (including body-behavioural) style, see Ostiguy, 2009; Diehl, 2011b, 2017; Moffitt & Tormey, 2014; and – for the most sustained discussion of populism as a political style

- Moffitt, 2016. Moffitt and Tormey, 2014 and Moffitt, 2016 present definitions of populism as an ideology, a political logic, and a discourse as alternatives to their preferred definition of populism as a political style. But as their own discussion suggests, these four are not sharply distinct. I therefore prefer to speak of a single broad discursive and stylistic turn.
5 For a critique of the widespread identification of populism with right-wing (or extreme right) forms of xenophobic nationalism in the literature on European populism, see Stavrakakis et al., 2017.
6 The 'family resemblance' metaphor has been more widely used in the discussion of literary and musical genres (Fishelov, 1991) than in the discussion of repertoires per se. But genre and repertoire are themselves closely related terms.
7 A Wittgensteinian, 'family resemblance' approach to defining populism has been proposed by Roberts, 1995; for a critique, see Weyland, 2001. Collier and Mahon, 1993 note the similarities between family resemblance approaches and Weber's ideal types.
8 As Diehl (2011b, p. 31) notes, the claim to speak and act in the name of 'the people' is extremely attenuated, if present at all, in the case of Silvio Berlusconi. Yet Berlusconi's mode of political communication and embodied manner of representing himself (by virtue of his origins) as 'one of the people' are classically populist. Diehl concludes that while Berlusconi is not *only* a populist, in that he also exemplifies an anti-political stance and mood and practices a form of 'politainment', he is *also* populist.
9 This is richly suggested but not quite made explicit in Taguieff, 1995.
10 The most striking contemporary instance of this downward focus of populism is that of Duterte in the Philippines; see for example Curato, 2017.
11 On 'penal populism', see Pratt, 2007 and Roberts et al., 2003.
12 On anti-party parties, see Tormey (2015, pp. 113–119). On personalistic leadership as a key aspect of populism, see Weyland (2001, pp. 12–14).
13 I should emphasise that what I seek to explain is the pan-European and trans-Atlantic populist conjuncture of the last few years, *not* the emergence and consolidation of anti-immigrant (and, increasingly, anti-Muslim) populisms in Western and Northern Europe since the 1980s. My explanatory argument is thus narrower in temporal scope than most discussions of European populism. But I conceptualise my explanandum more broadly than most discussions: I include Eastern and Southern Europe (and the US) as well as Western and Northern Europe, and I include left-wing and hybrid or hard-to-classify populisms as well as the right-wing populisms on which the European literature has overwhelmingly focused – a focus sharply (and in my view correctly) criticised by Stavrakakis et al., 2017.
14 For broad accounts, see Betz, 1994 and Kitschelt & McGann, 1995. On the politics of 'home' and autochthony, see Duyvendak, 2011 and Mepschen, 2016. On nativism and populism, see Betz, 2017.
15 On cultural backlash, see Bornschier & Kriesi, 2013 and Inglehart & Norris, 2016. The importance of honour, recognition, and respect to Tea Party and Trump supporters has been stressed by Hochschild, 2016. For an account of contemporary populism (with reference to support for Trump and Brexit in particular) as a 'rent-restoration project', emerging in response to the liberal 'rent-destruction project' that sought to overcome the structural disadvantages based on race, gender, and nativity, see Jackson & Grusky, (under review).
16 On Podemos, see Kioupkiolis, 2016; on Syriza, see Katsambekis, 2016 and Stavrakais & Siomos, 2016. For the left populist reaction generally, see Stavrakakis, 2014.
17 On the emergence of a new dimension of political competition in Europe defined by differing experiences with and stances toward globalisation, see Kriesi et al., 2006 and Azmanova, 2011.

References

Bornschier, S., & Kriesi, H. (2013). The populist right, the working class, and the changing basis of class politics. In J. Rydgren (Ed.), *Class politics and the radical right* (pp. 10–30). London and New York: Routledge.

Brubaker, R. (2017a). Between nationalism and civilizationism: The European populist moment in comparative perspective. *Ethnic and Racial Studies*, *40*(8), 1191–1226.

Brubaker, R. (2017b). Forget fake news. Social media is making democracy less democratic. *Zócalo Public Square* (blog), November 29. Retrieved from www.zocalopublicsquare.org/2017/11/29/forget-fake-news-social-media-making-democracy-less-democratic/ideas/essay/.

Calhoun, C. (2017). The big picture: Trump's attack on knowledge. *Public Books* (blog), November 29. Retrieved from www.publicbooks.org/the-big-picture-trumps-attack-on-knowledge/.

Canovan, M. (1981). *Populism*. New York: Harcourt Brace Jovanovich.

Canovan, M. (1999). Trust the people! Populism and the two faces of democracy. *Political Studies*, *47*(1), 2–16.

Canovan, M. (2002). Taking politics to the people: Populism as the ideology of democracy. In Y. Mény & Y. Surel (Eds.), *Democracies and the populist challenge* (pp. 25–44). London: Palgrave Macmillan.

Coleman, G. (2016). On truth and lies in a pragmatic, performative sense (with my respects to Nietzsche) or why reality . . ., *Medium* (blog), November 20. Retrieved from https://medium.com/@BiellaColeman/on-truth-and-lies-in-a-pragmatic-performative-sense-with-my-respects-to-nietzsche-or-why-reality-5c8400bd9ac2.

Collier, D., & Mahon, J. E. (1993). Conceptual 'stretching' revisited: Adapting categories in comparative analysis. *American Political Science Review*, *87*(4), 845–855.

Curato, N. (2017). Politics of anxiety, politics of hope: Penal populism and Duterte's rise to power. *Journal of Current Southeast Asian Affairs*, *35*(3), 91–109.

Diehl, P. (2011a). Die Komplexität des Populismus: ein Plädoyer für ein mehrdimensionales und graduelles Konzept. *Totalitarismus und Demokratie*, *8*(2), 273–291.

Diehl, P. (2011b). Populismus, Antipolitik, Politainment. *Berliner Debatte Initial*, *22*(1), 27–39.

Diehl, P. (2017). The body in populism. In R. C. Heinisch, C. Holtz-Bacha, & O. Mazzoleni (Eds.), *Political populism: A handbook* (pp. 361–372). Baden-Baden: Nomos.

Duyvendak, J. W. (2011). *The politics of home*. London: Palgrave Macmillan.

Esser, F. (2013). Mediatization as a challenge: Media logic versus political logic. In H. Kriesi (Ed.), *Democracy in the age of globalization and mediatization* (pp. 155–176). London: Palgrave Macmillan.

Fishelov, D. (1991). Genre theory and family resemblance – Revisited. *Poetics*, *20*(2), 123–138.

Grimm, D. (2015). The democratic costs of constitutionalisation: The European case. *European Law Journal*, *21*(4), 460–473.

Hay, C. (1995). Rethinking crisis: Narratives of the new right and constructions of crisis. *Rethinking Marxism*, *8*(2), 60–76.

Hochschild, A. R. (2016). *Strangers in their own land: Anger and mourning on the American right*. New York and London: New Press.

Houwen, T. (2011). *The non-European roots of the concept of populism*. Working Paper No. 120, Sussex European Institute.

Inglehart, R., & Norris, P. (2016). *Trump, Brexit, and the rise of populism: Economic have-nots and cultural backlash*. SSRN Scholarly Paper ID 2818659, Rochester, NY: Social Science Research Network. Retrieved from https://papers.ssrn.com/abstract=2818659.

Innerarity, D. (2010). *The transformation of politics: Governing in the age of complex Societies*. Brussels: Peter Lang.

Jackson, M., & Grusky, D. B. (under review). A cultural theory of structural loss.

Jäger, A. (2017). The semantic drift: Images of populism in post-war American historiography and their relevance for (European) political science. *Constellations*, *24*(3), 310–323.

Jansen, R. S. (2016). Situated political innovation: Explaining the historical emergence of new modes of political practice. *Theory and Society*, *45*(4), 319–360.

Judis, J. B. (2016). *The populist explosion: How the great recession transformed American and European politics*. New York: Columbia Global Reports.

Katsambekis, G. (2016). Radical left populism in contemporary Greece: Syriza's trajectory from minoritarian opposition to power. *Constellations*, *23*(3), 391–403.

Katsambekis, G., & Stavrakakis, Y. (2013). Populism, anti-populism and European democracy: A view from the south. *OpenDemocracy* (blog), July 23. Retrieved from www.opendemocracy.net/can-europe-make-it/giorgos-katsambekis-yannis-stavrakakis/populism-anti-populism-and-european-democr.

Kioupkiolis, A. (2016). Podemos: The ambiguous promises of left-wing populism in contemporary Spain. *Journal of Political Ideologies*, *21*(2), 99–120.

Kitschelt, H., & McGann, A. J. (1995). *The radical right in Western Europe: A comparative analysis*. Ann Arbor, MI: University of Michigan Press.

Knöbl, W. (2016). Über alte und neue Gespenster: historisch-systematische Anmerkungen zum 'Populismus'. *Mittelweg*, *36*(6), 8–35.

Kriesi, H. (2014). The populist challenge. *West European Politics*, *37*(2), 361–378.

Kriesi, H., Grande, E., Lachat, R., Dolezal, M., Bornschier, S., & Frey, T. (2006). Globalization and the transformation of the national political space: Six European countries compared. *European Journal of Political Research*, *45*(6), 921–956.

Laclau, E. (1977). *Politics and ideology in Marxist theory: Capitalism, fascism, populism*. London: NLB.

Laclau, E. (1980). Populist rupture and discourse. *Screen Education*, *34*, 87–93.

Laclau, E. (2005). Populism: What's in a name?. In F. Panizza (Ed.), *Populism and the mirror of democracy* (pp. 32–49). London and New York: Verso.

Mair, P. (2002). Populist democracy vs party democracy. In Y. Mény & Y. Surel (Eds.), *Democracies and the populist challenge* (pp. 81–98). London: Palgrave Macmillan.

Mair, P. (2011). *Bini Smaghi vs. the parties: Representative government and institutional constraints*. Working Paper. Retrieved from http://cadmus.eui.eu//handle/1814/16354.

Mazzoleni, G., & Schulz, W. (1999). 'Mediatization' of politics: A challenge for democracy? *Political Communication*, *16*(3), 247–261.

Mény, Y., & Surel, Y. (2000). *Par le peuple, pour le peuple: le populisme et les démocraties*. Paris: Fayard.

Mepschen, P. (2016). *Everyday autochthony: Difference, discontent and the politics of home in Amsterdam*. University of Amsterdam. Retrieved from https://pure.uva.nl/ws/files/4482851/168894_01_Introduction.pdf,%20page%2023.

Moffitt, B. (2016). *The global rise of populism: Performance, political style, and representation*. Stanford, CA: Stanford University Press.

Moffitt, B., & Tormey, S. (2014). Rethinking populism: Politics, mediatisation and political style. *Political Studies*, *62*(2), 381–397.

Mouffe, C. (2005). The 'end of politics' and the challenge of right-wing populism. In F. Panizza (Ed.), *Populism and the mirror of democracy* (pp. 50–71). London and New York: Verso.

Mudde, C. (2004). The populist Zeitgeist. *Government and Opposition*, *39*(4), 542–563.

Mudde, C., & Rovira Kaltwasser, C. (2017). *Populism: A very short introduction*. Oxford: Oxford University Press.

Mudde, C., & Rovira Kaltwasser, C. (Eds.). (2012). *Populism in Europe and the Americas: Threat or corrective for democracy?*. Cambridge: Cambridge University Press.

Müller, J.-W. (2016). *What is populism?*. Philadelphia, PA: University of Pennsylvania Press.

Offe, C. (2016). *Europe entrapped*. Cambridge: Polity.

Ostiguy, P. (2009). *The high and the low in politics: A two-dimensional political space for comparative analysis and electoral studies*. Working Paper No. 360, Kellogg Institute. Retrieved from www3.nd.edu/~kellogg/publications/workingpapers/WPS/360.pdf.

Panizza, F. (Ed.). (2005). *Populism and the mirror of democracy*. London and New York: Verso.

Persily, N. (2017). Can democracy survive the internet?. *Journal of Democracy*, *28*(2), 63–76.

Pratt, J. (2007). *Penal populism*. London and New York: Routledge.

Probst, L. (2002). Die Erzeugung 'Vorwärtsgerichteter Unruhe'. Überlegungen Zum Charisma von Jörg Haider. *Vorgänge*, *41*(4), 39.

Roberts, J. V., Stalans, L. J., Indermaur, D., & Hough, M. (2003). *Penal populism and public opinion: Lessons from five countries*. Studies in Crime and Public Policy, Oxford and New York: Oxford University Press.

Roberts, K. M. (1995). Neoliberalism and the transformation of populism in Latin America: The Peruvian Case. *World Politics*, *48*(1), 82–116.

Rutte, M. (2017). *Lees hier de Brief*. Retrieved from www.vvd.nl/nieuws/lees-hier-de-brief-van-mark/.

Saurette, P., & Gunster, S. (2011). Ears wide shut: Epistemological populism, argutainment and Canadian conservative talk radio. *Canadian Journal of Political Science*, *44*(1), 195–218.

Sewell, W. H. (2005). *Logics of history: Social theory and social transformation*. Chicago, IL: University of Chicago Press.

Stanley, B. (2008). The thin ideology of populism. *Journal of Political Ideologies*, *13*(1), 95–110.

Stavrakakis, Y. (2004). Antinomies of formalism: Laclau's theory of populism and the lessons from religious populism in Greece. *Journal of Political Ideologies*, *9*(3), 253–267.

Stavrakakis, Y. (2014). The return of 'the people': Populism and anti-populism in the shadow of the European crisis. *Constellations*, *21*(4), 505–517.

Stavrakakis, Y., Katsambekis, G., Nikisianis, N., Kioupkiolis, A., & Siomos, T. (2017). Extreme right-wing populism in Europe: Revisiting a reified association. *Critical Discourse Studies*, *14*(4), 420–439.

Stavrakakis, Y., & Siomos, T. (2016). *Syriza's populism: Testing and extending an Essex school perspective*. Paper Presented at the ECPR General Conference, Charles University, Prague. Retrieve from https://ecpr.eu/Events/PaperDetails.aspx?PaperID=31315&EventID=95.

Swidler, A. (1986). Culture in action: Symbols and strategies. *American Sociological Review*, *51*(2), 273–286.

Taggart, P. (2004). Populism and representative politics in contemporary Europe. *Journal of Political Ideologies*, *9*(3), 269–288.
Taguieff, P. A. (1995). Political science confronts populism: From a conceptual mirage to a real problem. *Telos*, *103*(March), 9–43.
Tilly, C. (2006). *Regimes and repertories*. Chicago, IL: University of Chicago Press.
Tormey, S. (2015). *The end of representative politics*. Malden, MA: Polity Press.
Urbinati, N. (2015). A revolt against intermediary bodies. *Constellations*, *22*(4), 477–486.
Weyland, K. (2001). Clarifying a contested concept: Populism in the study of Latin American politics. *Comparative Politics*, *34*(1), 1–22.
Wittgenstein, L. (1958). *Philosophical investigations*. Oxford: Blackwell.
Worsley, P. (1969). The concept of populism. In G. Ionescu & E. Gellner (Eds.), *Populism: Its meanings and national characteristics* (pp. 212–221). London: Weidenfeld & Nicolson.
Zolberg, A. R. (1999). Matters of state: Theorizing immigration policy. In *The handbook of international migration: The American experience* (pp. 71–93). New York: Russell Sage Foundation.

3 Populism
An ideal-typical assessment

Gregor Fitzi

Introduction

Although we often refer to populism as a consistent research topic nowadays, there is still no consensus about a definition of the concept of populism. After decades of scientific research, we return to the conclusions of the eponymous conference at the London School of Economics held in 1967 (Ionescu & Gellner, 1969). At different points in time and in distinct geographical regions of the world, populism has appeared in so many diverse forms (Priester, 2007; Puhle, 1986) that, in an attempt to grasp this concept, sceptical common sense ultimately prevails among specialists. In recent years, remarkable efforts have been undertaken to define the politological category of populism (Moffit, 2016; Müller, 2016) as well as to circumscribe crucial aspects of the phenomenon. To this effect, one can recall the diverse studies on populism as a symptom of the crisis of democracy (Albertazzi & McDonnell, 2008; Mény & Surel, 2002; Panizza, 2005; Pasquino, 2005; Urbinati, 2014). These include the analysis of the populist longing for a lost heartland (Taggart, 2000); the inquiry into the predilection of right-wing populism for stoking fears (Wodak, 2015) as well as the typological examination of the differences between populism on the left and right (Priester, 2012).

Nevertheless, there is an ongoing difficulty of establishing consensus about the definition of the phenomenon. This seems to suggest that different approaches to empirical research on populism imply the emergence of divergent operative definitions of the concept. This factor, above all, has consequences for the kind of research that is developed on populism. It discourages the attempt to examine the societal background for the rise of populism and disconnects politological from sociological research on the topic. Accordingly, the mainstream literature seems to agree that every effort to build an analytical category for exploring the populist phenomenon shall abandon the aim of explaining the possible social and economic reasons for the rise of populism, and concentrate instead on a typological classification of its external manifestation. Although there are some remarkable exceptions (Kriesi & Pappas, 2015), after more than three decades, one has to admit that Canovan's plea for purely descriptive populism research in 1981 was highly successful (Canovan, 1981). Presupposition-less research ending in a typology, yet without any pretence of explaining the social backdrop of the phenomenon, became the leading approach of populism research (Aslanidis, 2016). Following the example of politological studies on nationalism (Freeden,

1996), researchers produce comparative typologies describing 'thin' and 'thick' ideologies of populism (Mudde, 2007; Mudde & Rovira Kaltwasser, 2012) or the rhetorical styles of populist movements and parties (Moffit, 2016). This research provides crucial contributions to gain a better understanding of the development of the populist phenomenon and its proximity to the radical right-wing movements that try to establish neo-fascist ideas within political culture. Yet, it leaves open the question about the societal reasons for the rise of populism, and its possible success beyond the limits of the traditional extreme right-wing electorate.

As has been remarked by different observers, it cannot be overlooked that there is a substantial amount of mainly politological research concerning the multifarious appearance of the populist movements and parties, but also a conspicuous lack of sociological studies on the possible societal causes and effects of populism (Gidron & Bonikowski, 2013). Above all, the questions remain unanswered of how and why societies produce various forms of populist political enterprises as well as what the impact of populism is on the grounding societal arrangement, as for instance, access to welfare services and citizenship rights. A sociological inquiry into the cultural boundaries, which populist actors try to establish and activate between societal groups, is still a desideratum (Kazin, 1995). In addressing the collapse of the *cordon sanitaire* some studies deal with the consequences arising from the adoption of populist language by the established political parties in terms of the official political culture (Berezin, 2009; Pappas, 2014; Rosenthal & Trost, 2012). Further studies reconstruct how populists try to draw moral boundaries between different communities and so to induce social divisions (Fella & Ruzza, 2009). These contributions point out as many dimensions of the inquiry into populism as could be bundled into a sociological research programme, if this was to focus on the social conflicts that appear in the attempt to establish a cultural hegemony concerning the issue of societal membership (Gramsci, 1992, pp. 233–238). Sociological research on populism could thus examine which influences societal developments exert on the party-political contentions that use the argumentative arsenal of populism.

The fact that to date, despite some important exceptions, there has been little interest in this kind of sociological assessment of populism, however, raises the question whether or not sociology has at its disposal the methodological and theoretical means to develop this kind of research programme. My contribution in this chapter aims to discuss and eventually answer this question in three steps. Firstly, I present a methodological path of research allowing for the establishment of an analytical concept of populism from a sociological perspective. This may be able to explain the social backdrop to and the societal consequences of populism. In a second step, I apply this methodology to the analysis of the specific socio-political reasons for the rise of populism and develop a typological outline for the development of populism solely within the political field. Then, in a third step, based on the results of this assessment, I proceed to an analysis of the societal dynamics that may be considered as the backdrop for the rise of populism and I show the consequences of an unfolding of the populist mobilisation on society as a whole. Finally, I propose a typological definition of the societal phenomenon of populism from the perspective of sociological theory, which can then be refined through empirical research. The main purpose of the analysis is to show that it is indeed possible to provide a consistent sociological definition of populism and that sociology cannot exonerate itself from the task of conducting research in this area on both a theoretical and an empirical level.

The methodological issue

In recent times, the debate on sociological methodology has 'rediscovered' the importance of typological concept-building for improving social research (Kelle & Kluge, 2010). The problem about this debate is that the typological issue is purely considered from an empirical point of view. Following the path of Strauss's Grounded Theory, the method of theoretical sampling and the necessity of establishing comparative case studies to understand social phenomena (Glaser & Strauss, 2012), the question again emerged as to how typological categories can be constructed within inductive social research (Kelle & Kluge, 2010, p. 16). The debate on the construction of empirically founded typologies therefore shows the importance of the methodology of so-called 'typological theory building' for social research. In light of this development, the question arises whether this kind of theoretical concern has ever appeared in sociology before. It is a sign of the current state of amnesia, which characterises the relationship of the social sciences in the context of their historical heritage, that the recourse to sociological theory that should normally occur like an impulse reaction does not play any role in the actual debate. In the cited literature, for instance, the discussion of the type-building methodology in sociology relates in twenty lines the 'impulse' given to type-building in the social sciences of Max Weber's theory of the ideal types. In the same vein, it introduces the phenomenological concept of typology provided by Alfred Schütz (83). Durkheim and Simmel do not appear at all. In what follows, the methodology of typological concept-building is presented as a comparative method producing analytical concepts, which are always the result of a 'grouping process', and in which an object area is arranged into types by means of one or more features (85). The complexity of the theoretical offer, not only of classical sociology, but also of US American sociology after World War II, for instance by Merton, is not taken into account (Merton, 1968). One can speculate at length about the reasons for these relative states of amnesia, starting with the fact that university curricula no longer foresee an education in sociological theory, and ending with considerations about neo-liberal policies for smoothing out the critical potential of the social sciences. Yet, that the debates in empirical methodology do not dare to engage in a critical examination of sociological theory has practical consequences because this attitude gives away the chance to link empirical research and theory building in a relationship of reciprocal fruitfulness. Accordingly, these developments must be countered by retrieval of a theoretical approach to typology building in sociology and by its application to empirical research.

In the following, I will present a general outline of the 'ideal-typical' methodology for the sociological theory building that Max Weber discussed in principle in the essay about the 'objectivity' of the social sciences (Weber, 1949) and then applied to the formulation of his 'basic sociological concepts' (Weber, 2002). Before turning to Weber, a methodological premise, however, is necessary, in order to understand why a typological concept construction, which is not simply the result of a procedure for coding empirical data, is beneficial for conducting research into populism. Since the irresistible expansion of ethnological techniques of inquiry in the social sciences, a sort of common sense has established itself that empirical research should be based on the less possible premises and only develop its concepts empirically. Among others, Weber's ideal-typical methodology also argues against the naiveté of this approach. By entering an empirical field of research, social scientists bring with them a whole host of evidence concerning themselves, the lifeworld and the topic that they are inquiring into, including the knowledge expectations they have towards the field. Consequently, the only method to overcome this bias is to make this precognition as explicit as possible in a methodologically controlled way. Following Weber, this preliminary work must be done typologically, namely, by including the evidence available in the state of art about the research topic and then by selecting the relevant aspects for the perspective of the given research question. These two methodological steps constitute the basis for building sociological ideal types. To return to populism, the relevance of this approach for our topic lies in the fact that it allows the development of a consistent sociological concept of populism, of its emergence and consequences for society, which can be applied as an analytical category to the empirical inquiry into the manifold expressions of the populist phenomenon.

According to Weber, sociologists, as theoretical scientists, develop their analytical categories in three successive methodological steps. First, following the state of art, they gather the knowledge that is already available on a specific topic. Secondly, they assess this knowledge to determine the most obvious traits of a societal phenomenon, and finally, they characterise these traits by ordering them in typologies. To develop analytical categories, sociologists thus select specific aspects of a topic and present them as if they would have already unfolded their development potential down to the last detail, so that sociological categories are called 'ideal types'. Accordingly, they are neither normative categories of how reality should look, nor do they deliver an image of empirical reality, but rather they provide an analytical instrument to assess it. Weber's well-known quote concerning this point argues as follows:

> An ideal type is formed by the one-sided accentuation of one or more points of view and by the synthesis of a great many diffuse, discrete, more or less present and occasionally absent concrete individual phenomena, which are arranged according to those one-sidedly emphasised viewpoints into a unified analytical construct.
>
> (Weber, 1949, p. 90)

Populism: An ideal-typical assessment 51

The heuristic perspective of research, the so-called *Erkenntnisinteresse*, determines the way in which ideal types are constructed by selectively choosing some aspects of empirical reality and presenting them in an accentuated and emphasised form. The effort of building typological categories thus serves the purpose of developing analytical hypotheses that provide a basis, on the one hand, to assess the empirical data, and on the other hand, can be tested empirically. Ideal types allow for the comparison of selected aspects of social reality with what can be considered their limit case of development which is to be expected according to the evidence of the available knowledge on a specific topic. If the empirical assessment of the analytical hypotheses provided by the ideal type construction shows that these do not match the data, the concepts have to be modified by adopting a different, less evident assumption about the course of action. This procedure takes the form of a methodologically guided transition from the more to the less rational, i.e. less rationally evident according to the available knowledge, ideal types of action, following the scale that goes from strategic action (*zweckrational*) to normative action (*wertrational*), to emotional action (*affektuell*) and ending with the simple habitual action (*traditional*) (Weber, 2002). Within empirical reality, for example, no-one will ever encounter *homo economicus* or *homo politicus* per se, but economists, political scientists and sociologists can assess whether a form of empirical behaviour is closer to one or the other because they have knowledge of the two ideal types. Yet, if a particular type of empirical evidence strongly deviates from the expected typological development, sociologists have to examine the character of the deviation and develop new analytical categories that match the specific features of the phenomenon observed.

The recursive cycle of sociological theory building outlined by Weber's ideal-typical methodology can be applied to the most diverse matters of inquiry. Accordingly, the societal backdrop, the rising dynamics and the consequences of populism on society can also be explored, firstly by analysing the available knowledge about the phenomenon, and secondly by linking it in a typological definition, and finally by verifying it in further empirical studies to refine the sociological ideal type of populism. In the following two steps of my chapter, I present the first part of the described process of ideal-typical theory building that – following Weber's methodology – conceptually prepares the approach to new empirical research. In other words, I explore the political and societal aspects of the populist phenomenon as they emerge from the current state of existing research on the topic. I combine then the results of this assessment to suggest a typological definition of populism. The findings of further empirical inquiries, which will be conducted from the starting point of this ideal-typical definition of populism, will be a subject for later and separate studies.

The typology of populism I develop is articulated in two parts and concerns populism as a political and as a societal phenomenon. This distinction is due to the necessity of critically reconstructing the development of the category of populism, as it exists in societal self-interpretation, in order to then differentiate the sociological concept from it. From a theoretical perspective it is evident that the concept of populism has at once a vertical dimension, characterizing the political antagonism between 'people' and 'elites', and a horizontal dimension insisting on the societal discrimination between legitimated and non-legitimated members of the community, may it be seen as people, nation, or state. Yet, these two aspects have to be considered one by one because the label of populism has its first origin in political competition, so that its political, and more apparent meaning tends to overshadow its societal and in a sense more dangerous meaning that aims at shifting definitions of societal exclusion mechanisms. In order to proceed from the historical semantics of populism in socio-political discourse to the building of a sociological concept of populism through an ideal-typical methodology, it is thus necessary to analyse the two occurrences of the term separately. Accordingly, the succession of the different sections of the chapter unfolds from the endeavour to proceed through successive steps from the societal self-interpretation that produces the label of populism to the sociological definition of its analytical concept.

The typology of populism as a political phenomenon

Populism comes to the fore where a crisis of political representation is taking place. This circumstance can be considered as common to all the empirical manifestations of the phenomenon, characterising either political systems that have never been thoroughly democratic or parliamentary democracies that are experiencing a significant crisis of legitimation. Historically, the classical example for the emergence of the populist phenomenon in political systems of uncompleted democracy is given by the rise of Peronism in Argentina (James, 2001). The success of the populist political parties in delegitimised parliamentary democracies can instead be illustrated with reference to the manifold populist takeovers of recent years. These include, among others, the political entrepreneurship of Berlusconi or the Five Star Movement in Italy (Flores d'Arcais, 2001; Iacobini, 2018), of Orbán in Hungary (Lendvai, 2012), Kaczyński in Poland (Łazowski, 2017), Trump in the US (Griffin & Teixeira, 2017), the Brexit advocates in the UK (Clarke et al., 2017), as well as the momentous electoral scores of Marine Le Pen in France and of the xenophobic *Alternative für Deutschland* (AfD) party in Germany (Baltier, 2016; Bebnowski, 2015). Aiming at assessing the current development of the populist phenomenon in Europe and the US, for the purpose of the present analysis my focus is on the development of populism based on the second scenario.

To a greater or lesser extent in the different countries we have mentioned, an important number of members of the political community have the feeling that – it does not matter whether objectively grounded or not – their democratically elected representatives no longer properly represent them. The reasons for this mistrust are related to a combination of different objective and subjective factors that have been and should become the subject of empirical inquiries. As a rule, however, the typical components of the observed legitimation crises can be identified in the following aspects. On the one hand, some people feel that their access to material or symbolic resources is not as secure as they would like it to be, or they are afraid that this will be the case in the future. On the other hand, some people feel that their real or alleged condition of distress is not properly recognised and symbolically taken into account by the rulers. Normally, there is some overlap between these two groups of disappointed members of the political community. The group of the frustrated citizens can be less or more important depending on some particular policies adopted not long ago by the government in office or on contingent events, as could be observed for instance in Germany during the so-called immigration crisis of the summer 2015. These felt or real conditions of distress concerning material or symbolic resources, and the possibly related atmosphere of disorientation and latent fears, constitute the objective factors that can lead to the emergence of populism, but do not suffice to trigger its development, if they are not accompanied by the subjective factors of the populist mobilisation.

Deficiencies in the representation mechanisms have to be considered as a physiological process within all democratic political systems, yet they can significantly facilitate the rise of populism when political entrepreneurs step into their conflict-fraught dynamics, polemically addressing the legitimation crisis of the ruling classes. The kind of political entrepreneurs who embark on the populist adventure have a keen sensibility for the critical side of political representation and exploit it for their own sake, aiming at gaining as much political power as possible in the shortest time. They have something of the mentality of gamblers, so that their behaviour highly disorients political adversaries who are accustomed to playing the political game according to a different set of rules. The pivotal argument that populist political entrepreneurs deploy takes the shape of a violent attack on the legitimately elected political representatives, stigmatising them as an 'illegitimate power elite', exploiting the rest of society for their own ends. In the same move, political entrepreneurs depict the alleged victims of the elite as a coherent, innocent and brave group of people who have no responsibility at all for their current situation of alleged distress. The corresponding narrative wants the people to be a substance that knows neither internal stratification nor conflicts. Finally, the political entrepreneurs organising the populist mobilisation present themselves as the only legitimate representatives of the homogenous people, thus redefining the concept of the people's sovereignty, which is the founding idea of modern democracy. Hence, on the one hand, the slogan of the 'decent people' fighting against the 'corrupt elite' is born, and on the other hand, the process is started of redefining the concept of the people. These are the two main ideal-typical components of populism. Yet, the latter is the most dangerous aspect of the populist mobilisation, leading to an increasing exclusion concerning the societal groups that do not match the populist definition of 'the people'.

By acting in this way, populist political entrepreneurs considerably undermine the accumulated power of the established political parties and jeopardise the legitimate legal procedures that are responsible for allocating political capital in liberal democracies (Bourdieu, 1981). The reaction of the established parties to this threat has to be immediate and very vigorous. Otherwise, in times of a crisis of representation the attacks of the populist political entrepreneurs, stigmatising and delegitimising the democratically elected representatives of the sovereign people can have lethal consequences for the preservation of the accumulated political capital. As a rule, the immediate result of the institutional reaction to the mobilisation of the political entrepreneurs is already the coining of the term 'populism'. In its origin, therefore, the category of populism has to be considered as an instrument of political struggle whose meaning can be summarised as follows. The established political parties argue that the political entrepreneurs attacking their legitimacy have to be seen as 'populists' because they are attempting to delegitimise the regularly elected representatives of the people by designating themselves the only legitimate spokespersons of the people. In fact, however, populists are not legitimate at all because they do not dispose of any parliamentary majority that would entitle them to rule. Taking into account its empirical origin, the term 'populism' thus has to be considered a simple label stigmatising the political entrepreneurs who attack the legitimate elected representatives of the sovereign people as a 'corrupt elite'. The label comes to the fore in the fight for the redistribution of political capital. It is used to counterattack those forces that do not adhere to the institutional rules regulating the political game in liberal democracies, including the principle of the rule of the parliamentary majority.

The sociological analysis of the populist mobilisation could come to the conclusion at this point, following these first elements of its typological assessment, as a phenomenon of the political sphere. On the one hand, it would define populism as a stigmatising label used within the conflict of reciprocal delegitimisation between the established political parties and the upcoming political entrepreneurs organising the populist mobilisation. On the other hand, it would assess populism as the political strategy of the movements and parties that attempt to usurp political capital without submitting themselves to the legal and customary rules, including political culture, regulating its redistribution in parliamentary democracies. To put the matter here in parenthesis, the populist attack against the established rules of the political system concentrates on political culture for specific reasons. Populists try to delegitimise fundamental assumptions concerning racism, anti-Semitism, Islamophobia and so on, to establish new cultural boundaries of exclusion that could be activated to encourage their political ascent. Accordingly, the ideal-typical concept of political populism should include the assessment of its cultural attitude. If a conclusion were put forward here, however, this brief study of populism would lack the most important societal backdrop of the phenomenon. Hence, we need to go beyond the assessment of the socio-political dynamics between established parties and populist challengers. To phrase the matter in Weber's terms, we must move from the ideal-typical assessment of the vertical axis of the phenomenon, which characterises the narrative of the conflict between the elites and the people, and progress to its horizontal axis, so addressing the orders of exclusion that the populist narrative tries to establish to promote tighter social closure (Weber, 2002). This means, in particular, exploring the societal dynamics that the political entrepreneurs attempt to exploit by addressing and redefining the concept of 'the people', so that the further construction of the ideal type of populism implies an inquiry into the societal backdrop of the populist phenomenon. Assessing this aspect of the populist phenomenon is the aim of the third part of my chapter, which will focus more on the objective societal factors that can be seen as the breeding ground for the establishment of populist political entrepreneurship.

The typology of populism as a societal phenomenon

Modern, highly-differentiated societies are not based on a rigid normative frame that is established once and for all in 'phases of effervescence' and then simply reproduced through institutional action or rituality, as Durkheim claims, based on his studies on *The Elementary Forms of Religion* (Durkheim, 2016). On the contrary, normative orders are the result of two different ongoing conflict dynamics (Fitzi, 2015). Firstly, there is the ongoing divergence between the specific logic of the different societal domains and, secondly, the tension between the manifold cultural, ethical, religious and political orientations, coexisting in pluralistic societies. Between economy, religion, politics or science there is a persistent relationship of permanent competition for leadership on social action. In the advanced development stages of complex societies, relationships of colonisation arise between societal domains. To recall two historical extremes of this phenomenon: in one sense, politics may for instance colonise the economy in the societal arrangement of real socialism, or alternatively the economy may colonise politics and the rest of society falls in line with neo-liberalism. Moreover, in advanced migration societies, very different cultural, religious and political stances come together and have to find a *modus vivendi* that allows a common life in peace and is capable of adapting to the ongoing rhythm of sustained societal change. The related latent, sometimes open, conflicts impose a continuous redefinition of the common normative orders of society, which is achieved thanks to the establishment of a provisional societal consensus around specific compromises between different material interests and normative stances.

As a rule, in liberal democracies compromises on societal consensus subsequently become part of the legislation, so that they can be enforced by the administrative machine of modern state bureaucracies. In the second half of the twentieth century, these developments concerned, in particular, the societal arrangements ruling the balance of power between different socioeconomic groups within the industrial relations of production, and thus granted access to citizenship and particularly to social rights mediated by work for a broad majority of the population. The stabilisation of the inclusion mechanisms through social compromise characterised liberal democracies on both sides of the Atlantic, so that the New Deal in the US after the 1929 Wall Street Crash and the construction of the welfare systems in Europe after World War II produced a similar output, in spite of all the differences. The related legal consolidation of the normative orders of society was suggestive of a substantial stability for the institutionalised societal arrangement. Nevertheless, there was no guarantee that the increasing material and normative conflicts characterising the following periods of restrictive neo-liberal remodelling of welfare, as well as the coming economic and political crises would not undermine the established societal consensus and the correlated legislation by also gaining expression in political enterprises. This historical development, which has characterised Western liberal democracies since the Thatcher and Reagan era, still has to become the object of a systematic historical-sociological inquiry that would make a substantial contribution to a better understanding of the backdrop of the current rise of populism (cf. Berezin in this volume).

A negative development of industrial relations, of access to reasonably well-paid jobs and to welfare guarantees, characterised in different forms the recent history of the countries that then experienced an increased populist mobilisation. Depending on the particular societal situation, the existing malaise, however, was more or less visible. Focusing on Europe for instance, it can be observed that, at one end of the scale, in Greece the consequences of the economic and political crisis since the banking crisis of 2008 were so evident that almost all analysts expected the rise of populist parties (Kriesi & Pappas, 2015; Pappas, 2014). At the other end of the scale, 'successful societies' such as Germany showed a different development. Since the wider introduction of more flexible work legislation in 2003, here economic inequality took the shape of a so-called 'two-third society' which made possible the development of a low-wage sector within a wealthy land. The resentments of the socially left behind merged in an explosive mix with the discontent following reunification in the Eastern regions of the country and with classical conservative attitudes, which were no longer handled by the Christian Democrats, since Angela Merkel imposed a shift to the left within her party. This kind of malaise, however, was less visible, because public opinion steadily focused on the economic success of the country and ignored the last third of society, so that analysts again did not expect the rise of a right-wing populist party to emerge as it did.

In the wake of neo-liberal policies of the last forty years, jeopardising the welfare systems in Europe and the New Deal compromise in the US, and weakening the legislation that granted access to citizenship and social rights, all the established criteria for societal membership and for access to social protection were called into question. Accordingly, different social strata today experience or fear social decline and enter into competition for their condition to be acknowledged. These objective factors of societal crisis constitute the privileged breeding ground for the establishment of the populist political entrepreneurship, exploiting the existing and ongoing societal conflicts to plead for a restrictive, pre-legal and pre-political redefinition of the idea of 'the people' as the legitimising basis for the existence of the nation-state and its welfare systems. In a completely short-sighted and counterproductive approach, the populist narrative thus indicates a way for the rescue from the erosion of citizenship in its further restriction for the solely 'genuine members' of the people. For the sake of its ideological debasement, instead of stopping the spiral of tearing down citizenship rights, populism enforces the neo-liberal logic of depriving growing groups of residents within the domain of liberal democracies of their rights. Yet, the populist narrative defining the 'innocent and brave people' as an allegedly ethnical, social, cultural and religious uniform entity who must supposedly be rescued from the domination of the 'parasitic elite' and its 'external allies' manipulates and distorts social reality, but can refer to some objective elements of social malaise. The ability to intercept these really existing or perceived elements of distress and the related feelings of a lack of recognition, as well as the capacity for ideologically transfiguring them, are the decisive skills that populist political entrepreneurs have to master. This is the subjective element that fosters populist mobilisation, yet it cannot lead to success if it does not coincide with the objective preconditions for its upsurge in the material and symbolic conditions of life of different societal groups.

From an historical-sociological point of view, it can be shown that the democratisation of the nation-states and the development of welfare systems after World War II endowed the status of citizens of a national state with a number of different rights and, above all, social citizenship rights. Moreover, an increasingly inclusive interpretation of the citizenship status allowed, to a greater or lesser extent, for access to the same rights also for groups of citizens without 'full' status as nationals, such as foreigners, guest workers, migrants or refugees. These developments were not at all free from conflicts and rejections, as the history of several countries in Europe and in the US shows. Yet, the arrangement of the societal compromise around the welfare or New Deal legislation allowed social groups of workers, migrants and minorities to organise collectively the fight for their rights and to achieve their goals to differing degrees. The massive attack on the welfare systems perpetrated by the neo-liberal deregulation and austerity policies from the 1980s onwards has made it extremely difficult to achieve a societal consensus granting inclusive access to civil, political, social and cultural citizenship rights. Moreover, the fragmentation of post-industrial working relations frustrates the efforts for organising collective paths of fighting for missing rights. Many citizens in various European nation-states, as well as in the US, believe that their access to material or symbolic resources is not as secure as they would like it to be and feel that their real or alleged condition of distress is not sufficiently acknowledged. Consequently, the membership arrangements for the political communities around Europe and, albeit in a different way, in the US, again become the subject of significant societal conflicts.

The resumption of the conflict dynamic that was once stabilised by the Keynesian welfare compromise and ultimately its worsening as a result of the economic or migration crises of the last decade, thus has to be considered as the objective societal backdrop for the rise of the populist mobilisation. Based on this societal matrix, the subjective development factor of populism consisting of the political entrepreneurship of different kinds of demagogues could flourish. Not only do political entrepreneurs attack the ruling elite, but they also exploit the ongoing objective conflicts concerning societal membership to propagate their ideologies, because they know that there is a malaise about the failing redistribution of societal resources. By redefining the concept of the 'people' in a restrictive, compact and exclusive manner, the populist mobilisation deliberately stigmatises specific social groups as competitors for material and symbolic goods. Thus, instead of promoting a campaign to strengthen social rights, populists make legitimate the neo-liberal strategy of restricting the range of citizenship rights by simply claiming to limit access to residual rights for the allegedly native population. The spiral that intensifies the ongoing trend for the erosion of citizenship by establishing stricter criteria of social closure is thus further intensified.

The outcome of the ideal-typical sketch of the relationship between the societal backdrop and the political entrepreneurship of populism is, therefore, that the latter essentially means ideologically motivated and increasing social exclusion, so that it has to be characterised above all as right-wing populism. Accordingly, at this level of the analysis, a brief assessment of the differences between right-wing and left-wing populism must be included in the characterisation of the phenomenon (cf. Priester, 2012). Left-wing populism characterises itself as an open and inclusive variation of the political strategy that plays the 'exploited people' off against the 'corrupt elites', by simultaneously expressing and practising solidarity toward migrants, minorities and the excluded. Despite Laclau's (1977) plea for the populist political strategy as a means of political emancipation, however, the problematic aspect of the left-wing inclusive variation of populism is related to its reverting to the rhetoric of the 'people'. The latter is based on a pre-legal and pre-political conception of societal membership and thereby shifts the focus of the political debate from the legal definitions of citizenship rights, constituting *inter alia* the structure of the welfare systems, into the field of the debate on ethnical and cultural affiliation. By triggering this mechanism, left-wing populism contributes to a shifting of the boundaries of the legitimated political culture, which can then be activated by right-wing populists by redefining who is allowed to belong to the 'people' with the right to access citizenship or welfare services. Consequently, even if not intentionally, left-wing populism prepares and fosters the rise of right-wing populism by undermining the legitimated boundaries of political culture.

To summarise this part of the ideal-typical assessment of populism with a brief assessment of the consequences of the populist mobilisation of society, I would like to draw attention to the following aspects. The restrictive vision of the 'people' characterising right-wing populism implies all the manifold dystopic conceptions of radical nationalism, anti-Europeanism, xenophobia, racism, anti-Semitism and anti-Islamism that are currently studied under the label of populist 'thick' ideologies. These ideological approaches represent as many attempts at restrictively reshaping societal consensus concerning the criteria defining legitimate membership of the nation state as a political and social community. Yet, the question arises as to what their sociological meaning is and therefore what impact they have on society. Restrictively reshaping societal membership implies making social closure more rigid, and thus also the criteria for exclusion and discrimination. Accordingly, the major impact of the populist mobilisation for society as a whole, and ultimately its major risk for democracy, are related to the fact that the populist narrative exerts significant pressure on public opinion with protracted consequences. Irrespective of the circumstances in which populist parties and movements come into office, participate in governments or fail to do so, the populist mobilisation tries to establish restrictive conceptions of social closure within the legitimate political culture. The effects of this process go far beyond the boundaries of the supporters' community, so sustaining the populist parties and movements and reaching the centre of society. Since the established political parties tend to adopt populist shibboleths to score points against their challengers during election campaigns, the restrictive redefinitions of societal membership spread like wildfire in public opinion. Hence, in the worst-case scenario, conceptions of citizenship that are incompatible with a pluralistic and inclusive arrangement of society become part of the legitimate political culture and, ultimately, of the legislation on citizenship rights. This kind of autonomisation processes, turning populist ideologemes into a form of common sense, represent the highest and most dangerous development degree of the phenomenon. They permit further development of the populist mobilisation, so to speak, even beyond the failure of the organised political populist entrepreneurship.

Conclusions

After this brief ideal-typical sketch of the different aspects characterising the objective and subjective emergence mechanisms, the social backdrop and the societal consequences of populism, I would like to conclude by combining them all in a provisional typological definition of populism. This definition, on the one hand, constitutes the ideal-typical synthesis of the different political and societal aspects of the populist phenomenon that were assessed in the preceding part of the chapter. On the other hand, the definition is operatively designed to be applied to further empirical inquiries and to be refined through analysis of the results of the empirical research to come.

Populism, as it must be understood from an ideal-typical sociological point of view, is the political expression of a profound societal crisis that surfaces when a certain number of objective and subjective conditions are fulfilled. The objective conditions of the phenomenon include the fact that the existing and legitimated compromise for the redistribution of material and symbolic societal resources is jeopardised by different types of restrictive policies. The subjective conditions include the circumstance that political entrepreneurs exploit the consequent crisis of societal consensus for the sake of conquering political power; such political actors propagandise their visions for reshaping societal membership on the basis of pre-legal and pre-political criteria. The societal consequences of the crisis that manifests itself in the populist phenomenon are related to stronger acceptance for pre-legal and pre-political redefinitions of the criteria regulating access to citizenship rights. Such criteria are fostered by the populists' mobilisation. Moreover, in a worst-case scenario they might become part of the legitimated political culture and, ultimately, of citizenship legislation.

References

Albertazzi, D., & McDonnell, D. (Eds.). (2008). *Twenty-first century populism: The spectre of Western European democracy*. Basingstoke, UK: Palgrave Macmillan.

Aslanidis, P. (2016). Is populism an ideology? A refutation and a new perspective. *Political Studies*, *64*, 88(104.

Baltier, A. (2016). *Comment devient-on électeur du Front national?*. Paris: Cherche-Midi.

Bebnowski, D. (2015). *Die Alternative für Deutschland: Aufstieg und gesellschaftliche Repräsentanz einer rechten populistischen Partei*. Wiesbaden: Springer VS.

Berezin, M. (2009). *Illiberal politics in neoliberal times: Culture, security and populism in the New Europe*. Cambridge: Cambridge University Press.

Bourdieu, P. (1981). La représentation politique [Éléments pour une théorie du champ politique], *Actes de la recherche en sciences sociales*, 36(37, February/March, *La représentation politique-1*, 3–24.

Canovan, M. (1981). *Populism*. New York: Harcourt Brace Jovanovich.

Clarke, H. D., Goodwin, M. J., & Whiteley, P. (2017). *Brexit: Why Britain voted to leave the European Union*. Cambridge: Cambridge University Press.

Durkheim, É. (2016). *The elementary forms of the religious life*. Dinslaken: Anboco.

Fella, S., & Ruzza, C. (2009). *Re-inventing the Italian right: Territorial politics, populism and 'post-fascism'*. London: Routledge.

Fitzi, G. (2015). *Grenzen des Konsenses. Rekonstruktion einer Theorie transnormativer Vergesellschaftung*. Weilerwist: Velbrück.

Flores d'Arcais, P. (2001). *Macerie. Ascesa e declino di un regime. 1986(2011: il populismo italiano da Craxi a Berlusconi passando per d'Alema*. Roma: Aliberti.

Freeden, M. (1996). *Ideologies and political theory*. Oxford: Clarendon Press.

Gidron, N., & Bonikowski, B. (2013). Varieties of populism: Literature review and research agenda. Working Paper Series, Waterhead Center for International Affairs, Harvard University.

Glaser, B., & Strauss, A. (2012). *The discovery of grounded theory: Strategies for qualitative research*. New Brunswick: Aldine Transaction.

Gramsci, A. (1992). J. A. Buttigieg (Ed.), *Prison notebooks*. New York: Columbia University Press.

Griffin, R., & Teixeira, R. (2017). *The story of Trump's appeal: A portrait of Trump voters*. A Research Report from the Democracy Fund Voter Study Group. Retrieved from www.voterstudygroup.org/publications/2016-elections/story-of-trumps-appeal.

Iacoboni, J. (2018). *L'esperimento: Inchiesta sul Movimento 5 Stelle*. Bari : GLF Editori Laterza.

Ionescu, G., & Gellner, E. (Eds.). (1969). *Populism: Its meanings and national characteristics*. London: Weidenfeld & Nicolson.

James, D. (2001). *Resistance and integration: Peronism and the Argentine working class, 1946–1976*. Cambridge: Cambridge University Press.

Kazin, M. (1995). *The populist persuasion: An American history*. New York: Basic Books.

Kelle, U., & Kluge, S. (2010). *Vom Einzelfall zum Typus. Fallvergleich und Fallkontrastierung in der qualitativen Sozialforschung*. Wiesbaden: VS.

Kriesi, H., & Pappas, T. S. (Eds.). (2015). *European populism in the shadow of the great recession*. Colchester: ECPR Press.

Laclau, E. (1977). *Politics and ideology in Marxist theory: Capitalism, fascism, populism*. London: Humanities Press.

Łazowski, A. (2017). *Time to stop the polish danse macabre*. Brussels: Centre for European Policy Studies.

Lendvai, P. (2012). *Hungary: Between democracy and authoritarianism*. London: Hurst & Company.

Mény, Y., & Surel, Y. (2002). *Democracies and the populist challenge*. New York: Palgrave.
Merton, R. K. (1968). *Social theory and social structure* (enlarged ed.). New York and London: The Free Press.
Moffit, B. (2016). *The global rise of populism: Performance, political style, and representation*. Stanford, CA: Stanford University Press.
Mudde, C. (2007). *Populist radical right parties in Europe*. Cambridge: Cambridge University Press.
Mudde, C., & Rovira Kaltwasser, C. (Eds.). (2012). *Populism in Europe and the Americas*. Cambridge: Cambridge University Press.
Müller, J.-W. (2016). *What is populism?*. Philadelphia, PA: University of Pennsylvania Press.
Panizza, F. (2005). *Populism and the mirror of democracy*. London: Verso.
Pappas, T. S. (2014). *Populism and crisis politics in Greece*. New York: Palgrave Macmillan.
Pasquino, G. (2005). *Populism and democracy*. Bologna: The Johns Hopkins University Bologna Center.
Priester, K. (2007). *Populismus. Historische und aktuelle Erscheinungsformen*. Frankfurt and New York: Campus.
Priester, K. (2012). *Rechter und linker Populismus. Annäherung an ein Chamäleon*. Frankfurt and New York: Campus.
Puhle, H. J. (1986). Was ist Populismus?. In H. Dubiel (Ed.), *Populismus und Aufklärung* (pp. 12–32). Frankfurt am Main: Suhrkamp.
Rosenthal, L., & Trost, C. (2012). *Steep: The precipitous rise of the tea party*. Berkeley, CA: University of California Press.
Taggart, P. (2000). *Populism*. Buckingham: Open University Press.
Urbinati, N. (2014). *Democracy disfigured: Opinion, truth, and the people*. Cambridge: Harvard University Press.
Weber, M. (1949). 'Objectivity' in social science and social policy. In M. Weber (Ed.), *The methodology of the social sciences* (pp. 50–112). Glencoe: The Free Press.
Weber, M. (2002). *Basic concepts in sociology*. New York: Citadel Press.
Wodak, R. (2015). *The politics of fear: What right-wing populist discourses mean*. London: Sage.

4 How to define populism?
Reflections on a contested concept and its (mis)use in the social sciences

Cristóbal Rovira Kaltwasser

Introduction

Academics and pundits alike who are interested in populism commonly start their analyses by paraphrasing the first sentence of Marx and Engels' *Communist Manifesto*: a spectre is haunting Europe – the spectre of populism.[1] However, the spectre of communism was arguably much more concrete than the current spectre of populism. This is related to the absence of scholarly agreement on how to define populism. In contrast, the meaning of communism is relatively clear: it alludes to either a specific mode of production in which a classless society becomes real and/or an ideology with specific characteristics that set it clearly apart from democratic socialism and that was employed by different types of communist party organisations during the twentieth century (Brown, 2014). In the case of populism, many scholars have adopted such a broad definition that it is impossible to grasp what populism really is. Take, for instance, the following conceptual clarification advanced by Pierre-André Taguieff:

> Populism is a *dimension* of political action, susceptible to syncretism with all forms of movements and all types of governments. Thus a single party dictatorship can legitimate itself by populist means, while a liberal-pluralist democracy does not rule out the possibility of a seizure of power by a populist leader through normal voting procedures. Whether dimension or style rather than ideology or form of mobilisation, populism is so elastic and indeterminate as to discourage all attempts at a rigorous definition.
>
> (Taguieff, 1995, p. 25)

Not surprisingly, in light of such broad definitions, a few authors have proposed avoiding the term altogether (Ignazi, 2000). Yet, how can we explain why populism is such a contested concept in the social sciences? Without the intention of offering a definitive answer to this question, I would like to develop two arguments which are helpful for thinking more thoroughly about the contested nature of the concept of populism. These arguments can be categorised as normative concerns and academic parochialism. The first point is relatively obvious. Most of those who are interested in populism assume that populism is something bad. For example, there is a tendency to take for granted that populism in Europe is about adopting an agenda centred on anti-immigration (Betz, 1994), while in Latin America populism is about promoting irresponsible economic policies (Dornbusch & Edwards, 1991). To make things even more complicated, some scholars take the opposite view and argue that populism is essentially something good. As Ernesto Laclau (2005) maintains, populism can be thought of as a mechanism by which excluded sections of society can organise themselves to confront the establishment to pursue political and socioeconomic integration.

The very existence of these contradictory views permeates the debate on populism, leading the discussion about the meaning of the term to become a normative rather than a conceptual dispute. Otherwise stated, those who are interested in studying populism tend to adopt a normative position according to which populist forces can be judged. The problem is that if scholars are more worried about judging than understanding populism, researching the topic turns out to be a relatively futile exercise – if we know beforehand that populism is something good or bad, the outcome of the research will of course corroborate our intellectual presumption. Otherwise stated, scholars should try to work with a clear definition of populism in order to study empirically under what conditions populist forces work as a threat to or a corrective for democracy. Fortunately, in the last few years scholars have started to undertake empirical research on the positive and negative consequences of populism on democracy (Houle & Kenny, 2018; Huber & Schimpf, 2016; Mudde & Rovira Kaltwasser, 2012; Rovira Kaltwasser, 2012).

Academic parochialism is the second reason why populism is such a contested concept within the realm of social sciences. This term is used here to denote a common problem in the scholarship on populism: the absence of dialogue between epistemic communities undertaking research in different countries and world regions. This is a real pitfall, because most authors are prone to assume that 'their' case study represents the most genuine example of populism. Consequently, there is a tendency to propose definitions of populism that are useful for analysing one specific experience but are problematic for studying populism across time and places. By way of illustration, whereas specialists of the French National Front (FN) and the Italian Northern League (LN) are prone to assuming that populism necessarily involves xenophobic attitudes (Berezin, 2009), scholars of the U.S. populist movement of the nineteenth century normally think that grassroots networks should be considered a defining attribute of populism (Postel, 2007), and those who analyse the Peronist party in Argentina are inclined to argue that populism is inevitably related to the promotion of clientelism (Levitsky, 2003).

The very rise of Donald Trump in the US has reinforced this trend, as academics and pundits alike are trying to grasp 'Trumpism' without necessarily taking into account the existing scholarship on populism. However, when it comes to analysing populism there is no need to reinvent the wheel, since there is a significant amount of research that should be employed and built upon (Rovira Kaltwasser et al., 2017). In fact, scholars have started to advance cross-national and cross-regional research on populist forces (De la Torre, 2014; Moffitt, 2016; Mudde & Rovira Kaltwasser, 2012, 2013a, 2017). This is a welcome development, because it allows us to better understand the defining attributes of populism as well as additional attributes – secondary categories in the language of Sartori (1970) – that permit the identification of subtypes of populism that are prevalent in certain countries and world regions.

Pleading for a minimal definition of populism

As I have argued elsewhere in more detail (Rovira Kaltwasser, 2012), the best way to deal with the contested nature of the term populism is to work with a *minimal* definition. The great advantage of minimal definitions is that they force us to identify the main characteristics – or to use more a sophisticated jargon, the necessary and sufficient criteria – of the phenomenon under consideration. Only by advancing a minimal definition it is possible to confront Sartori's (1970; Collier & Gering, 2009) dilemma of the inversely proportional relation between the intension and extension of concepts: the more defining attributes a concept has, that is greater *intension*, the fewer instances it encompasses, that is more limited *extension*. This means that the identification of the defining attributes of the object of study leads to the formulation of a minimal concept that can 'travel' well: it can be used for analysing many different cases across the world. For instance, although there is an ongoing debate about how to define democracy, there is growing academic consensus that, at a minimum, the term democracy refers to the periodic realisation of free and fair elections (Coppedge et al., 2011).

Fortunately, the scholarly debate on populism is slowly advancing in the direction of proposing a minimal definition of the concept. In fact, some authors stress the importance of conceiving of populism as a phenomenon with clear boundaries that can and should be studied empirically in comparative terms. Mudde's (2004) and Weyland's (2001) propositions are crucial in this regard, since they advance minimal definitions of populism that have become very influential in the European and Latin American debates, respectively. According to Mudde, populism should be conceived of as:

> a thin-centred ideology that considers society to be ultimately separated into two homogenous and antagonistic groups, 'the pure people' versus 'the corrupt elite', and which argues that politics should be an expression of the *volonté générale* (general will) of the people.
>
> (Mudde, 2004, p. 543)

Weyland, in turn, defines populism as 'as a political strategy through which a personalist leader seeks or exercises government power based on direct, unmediated, uninstitutionalised support from large numbers of mostly unorganized followers' (Weyland, 2001, p. 14). Although it is true that both definitions point out similar features, they differ in one important aspect: while Mudde underlines that populism is first and foremost a specific set of ideas, Weyland stresses that populism is essentially a method whereby a leader tries to establish a direct relationship with disorganised constituencies (Rovira Kaltwasser, 2011). In other words, the defining attributes of populism are of an ideological/discursive nature for Mudde and of an institutional/organisational nature for Weyland. After this brief clarification, the obvious question is which of these two definitions is more plausible and useful for undertaking comparative research on populism.

Building upon previously performed research (Mudde & Rovira Kaltwasser, 2012, 2013a, 2013b, 2014; Rovira Kaltwasser 2014a, 2014b), I would like to argue briefly why I consider Mudde's conceptual approach more useful than Weyland's definition. In fact, the approach advanced by Mudde is part of a broader theoretical framework that conceives of populism as an ideational phenomenon (Hawkins, 2009, 2010; Hawkins & Rovira Kaltwasser, 2017; Mudde & Rovira Kaltwasser, 2017; Stavrakakis & Katsambekis, 2014). While it is true that scholars sympathetic to the ideational approach do not agree on the specific genus that should be employed, such as discourse, frame, thin-centred ideology, worldview, and so forth, all of them are of the opinion that populism is first and foremost a specific set of ideas that is characterised by the moral and Manichean distinction between 'the people' and 'the elite'. Given that Mudde's conceptualisation is probably dominant within the ideational approach, I will use it as a yardstick for comparison with the one proposed by Weyland. In more concrete terms, I am interested in showing that Mudde's conceptualisation has three significant advantages over Weyland's for the realisation of comparative studies on populism. Let's analyse each of them in detail.

The *first* advantage of Mudde's approach is that it allows us to observe both the demand and supply side of populist politics. In effect, the very definition of populism as an ideology or discourse permits us to grasp that the phenomenon is not only and necessarily about a skilful leader who is able to mobilise the masses. Populism can emerge and take root only if there are persons who share the populist set of ideas, and in consequence, do believe that there is 'a corrupt elite' that is acting against the will of 'the pure people'. Put another way, to study populism in depth, it is necessary to take into account both the mass and the elite level. This is something Weyland's definition gives little attention to, since it focuses on the leader and his capacity to obtain support from large constituencies. However, there are cases in which the populist ideology can be widespread amongst certain social sectors, but no leader is able to successfully exploit this. In consequence, the emergence and electoral fortune of populist forces is not necessarily related to the rise of a strong and charismatic leader (Mudde & Rovira Kaltwasser, 2014). Even though the latter can certainly facilitate the emergence of populist forces, they are also the product of constituencies that have moral and rational motives for adhering to the Manichean distinction.

Not by chance, scholars have started to explore the demand for populism by examining mass surveys and proposing special items to measure populist attitudes (Akkerman, Mudde & Zaslove, 2014; Hawkins, Riding & Mudde, 2012). Although more research is certainly needed, preliminary findings reveal that populist sentiments are relatively widespread across the population. Nevertheless, it seems that populist attitudes are normally dormant: they become activated only under specific circumstances and usually for a limited segment of the electorate, which has the impression that established political parties have been acting against the will of 'the people'. For instance, van Hauwaert and van Kessel (2018) find that populist attitudes in Europe not only help to explain support for populist parties, but also moderate the effect of issue positions on the support for populist parties. In addition, Meléndez and Rovira Kaltwasser (2017) identify that partisans tend to reject populism, while those holding high levels of populist attitudes are prone to repudiating mainstream political parties and thus advance an anti-establishment political identity.

The *second* advantage of the ideational approach lies in the proposition of clear conceptual boundaries. In fact, the definition advanced by Mudde points out that there are two direct opposites of populism: elitism and pluralism. Elitism is also based on the Manichean distinction between 'the people' and 'the elite', but has a mirror image of the morality. In other words, elitists believe that the people are dishonest and vulgar, while the elites are superior in cultural, intellectual and moral terms. Looking at the contemporary world, technocracy is a clear example of elitist thinking that is at odds with populism. After all, technocrats are of the opinion that, given that 'the people' can be easily mobilised by demagogues, it is better that experts take the most important decisions. However, technocracy is just one illustration of a longstanding tradition that looks upon the demos with fear and that, due to recent political events such as the Brexit referendum and the triumph of Trump, has enjoyed a resurgence. As Sheri Berman has recently indicated, not a few decision makers 'seek to wall off as many political and policy questions as possible from the influence of uninformed, ignorant voters and instead place them in the hand of experts' (Berman, 2017, p. 37).

Pluralism, in turn, offers a view about society which is totally different to that of elitism and populism. Instead of thinking about a moral distinction between the homogeneous people and the elite, pluralism assumes that societies are composed of several social groups with different ideas and interests (Plattner, 2010). Hence, pluralism takes for granted that it is impossible to generate something like a 'general will' of the people. The latter is seen as a construction through which despots are enabled to commit atrocities in the name of the people. This means that those who adhere to pluralism are normally inclined to think of popular sovereignty as a dynamic and open-ended process rather than a fixed and unified will of the people (Ochoa Espejo, 2011). An important consequence of this approach lies in the impossibility of knowing for sure what the wishes of the electorate are. By contrast, populist forces always claim that they represent the true will of the people and thus nobody has the legitimacy to oppose them (Müller, 2016, pp. 25–33).

There is a *third* advantage of the ideational approach in general and of Mudde's definition in particular, namely that it permits us to understand the flexibility and malleability of the populist discourse. This is related to the fact that both 'the corrupt elite' and 'the pure people' are essentially empty vessels which are framed in very different ways in past and present manifestations of populism. Seen in this light, one should not assume that all populist forces are equal. While populism is always about making the Manichean distinction between 'the people' and 'the elite', the latter two adopt different meanings depending on the socio-economic and socio-political context in which the populist actors operate. This means that we can distinguish subtypes of populism, in which different understandings of who belongs to the people and the elite are developed. For instance, most contemporary populist forces in Europe tend to be exclusionary due to their nativist interpretation of 'the pure people', while most current populist forces in Latin America are inclined to be inclusionary because of the identification of 'the pure people' with the socioeconomic underdog (Mudde & Rovira Kaltwasser, 2013a). Nevertheless, the Great Recession has transformed political dynamics in Europe and therefore we are witnessing the emergence of inclusionary forms of populism in countries that have been deeply affected by the economic crisis (Stavrakakis & Katsambekis, 2014).

Moreover, although populist forces are always anti-establishment, they do not share a common idea of who is part of the vilified elite. Populist leaders and followers can develop a more or less explicit alliance with sectors of the establishment (such as business groups, media moguls, the military) with the aim of winning support for the promotion of specific reforms. There is no better example of this than Donald Trump in the US, a billionaire who has used his private wealth to finance political campaigning and spares no effort in employing populist rhetoric to attack those elite sectors at odds with his own political views. This ambivalent relationship between populist forces and elite sectors can also be seen in contemporary Europe. For instance, populist radical right parties had a positive view of the European Union during the 1990s, but they started to change this opinion after the Great Recession and the more recent refugee crisis. Today, almost all populist radical right parties show increasing levels of Euroscepticism and are at the forefront of demanding referenda for withdrawing from the European Union, which is depicted as an undemocratic institution controlled by a fraudulent elite (Pirro & van Kessel, 2017). Even in the case of Latin America, one can see that populist actors are not always prone to attacking the establishment as a whole. As Kenneth Roberts (2006) has convincingly argued, this tends to happen when populists advance radical policy proposals resisted by the elite. Under these circumstances, populist forces will mobilise the masses and organise grassroots constituencies to secure the political resources to counterweight entrenched power structures.

What is populism not?

After having laid out the advantages of Mudde's minimal concept over Weyland's, it is time to turn our attention to a number of common misunderstandings that crop up when defining and reflecting on populism. According to the ideational approach presented and defended above, it is not difficult to show that populism is often conflated with other phenomena that only in some cases go hand in hand with it. This means that it is important to disentangle features that in different national/regional contexts tend to appear with populism but are not necessarily inherent to it. Without the intention of developing a detailed and definitive list of misunderstandings, I think one should consider at least four issues: clientelism, charismatic leadership, economic policies and xenophobia. Let's briefly analyse each of them.

Clientelism

Analyses of populism focused on poor and/or economically underdeveloped regions as Latin America are inclined to depict populist forces as examples of clientelism. However, clientelism is a phenomenon that also occurs in rich societies such as Austria or Japan, and there are abundant examples of parties that are anything but populist and have developed clientelistic networks, as in the old Tory party in the UK and the more recent 'Unión Demócrata Independiente' in Chile. In fact, in many places the history of clientelism is linked to traditional parties controlled by landlords who have been able to construct elitist rather than populist political machines by mobilising voters under their control. As Herbert Kitschelt and Steven Wilkinson (2007) have argued, clientelism is a particular mode of exchange between electoral constituencies and politicians, in which voters obtain some goods such as direct payments or privileged access to employment, goods and services for their support of a patron or party. Hence, it is evident that clientelism and populism are two different phenomena: while the former refers to a specific type of interaction between political leaders and the electorate, the latter alludes to a particular ideology or discourse, which is based on the Manichean distinction between 'the people' and 'the elite' and the very idea that politics is about enacting popular sovereignty.

Charismatic leadership

Many scholars take for granted that populism cannot emerge without the existence of a strong and charismatic leader. However, the populist worldview is shared by many persons regardless of the existence of a leader able to make use of this worldview. As Michael Kazin (1995) has shown for the US, populism can sometimes be a leaderless movement. There is no better example of this than the contemporary Tea Party movement, which instead of being commanded by a strong and charismatic leader seems to be driven by various networks of activists, some of which have vast leverage to develop programmatic proposals that are not necessarily shared by the leaders of the Republican Party (Formisano, 2012; Skocpol & Williamson, 2012). Moreover, there are many charismatic leaders who are pluralist and thus repudiate the populist ideology, such as Barack Obama in the US, Nelson Mandela in South Africa and so forth. This means that charisma and populism are two different phenomena. Given that the formation of a new political vehicle profits from a charismatic leader able to attract votes, it is not a coincidence that many electorally successful manifestations of populism tend to rely on charismatic figures. But the controversial nature of these figures usually hinders the development of a proper party organisation that is well-structured and capable of recruiting professional activists. In consequence, the relationship between charisma and populism is more complicated than many scholars think (Mudde & Rovira Kaltwasser, 2014).

Economic policies

Not a few scholars have argued that the electoral appeal of populist forces is related to the defence and/or implementation of a specific type of economic policies. For instance, Kitschelt (1997) postulates that the 'winning formula' of European populist radical right parties consists in combining the promotion of neo-liberal reforms with an anti-immigration discourse. By contrast, Rüdiger Dornbusch and Sebastian Edwards (1991) maintain that Latin American populism should be characterised as an economic approach that emphasises growth and income redistribution, and deemphasises the risks of not only inflation and deficit finance but also external constraints. More recently, Edwards (2010) has categorised the governments of Hugo Chávez in Venezuela, Rafael Correa in Ecuador and Evo Morales in Bolivia as 'populist' due to the implementation of unsustainable macroeconomic policies, while Acemoglu, Egorov and Sonin have argued that populism should be thought of as 'the implementation of policies receiving support from a significant fraction of the population, but ultimately hurting the economic interests of this majority' (Acemoglu, Egorov & Sonin, 2013, p. 2). Nevertheless, any cross-regional comparison of populist forces reveals that, at the end of the day, economic issues and/or specific social policies are not a *defining* attribute of populism. Regardless of their adherence to the populist set of ideas, many politicians are inclined to advance certain economic proposals that are quite irresponsible, simplistic and radical. Just to propose an example, even though few would categorise George W. Bush in the US or Raul Alfonsín in Argentina as populist leaders, there is little doubt that their economic policies were anything but responsible.

Xenophobia

The European debate on populism is centred on the rise of anti-immigrant parties, which because of their xenophobic tendencies are often depicted as neo-fascist organisations. While there is little doubt that European radical right parties are indeed against immigration and multiculturalism, this is not related to their populism, but rather to their nativism – a xenophobic version of nationalism – according to which the state should be inhabited only by members of the native group, and non-native, hence alien, people and values are perceived as threatening the nation-state (Mudde, 2007). Interestingly, as the relationship between populism and nativism can be traced back in history (Betz, 2017), it would be wrong to assume that the combination of the two just appeared with the rise of populist radical right parties in Europe. Additionally, it is worth noting that precisely due to their adherence to the populist ideology European populist radical right parties are different from the old or traditional European radical right: while the former are (nominally) democratic, though at odds with some aspects of *liberal* democracy, the latter are simply anti-democratic and support the formation of an authoritarian government (Mudde, 2010). Further, leftist populist forces not characterised by xenophobic attitudes do exist in some European nations (March, 2011) and the economic crisis that Europe is experiencing today has paved the way for the emergence of leftist populist forces such as Podemos in Spain and Syriza in Greece (Kioupkiolis, 2016; Stavrakakis & Katsambekis, 2014). Moreover, a xenophobic outlook is not a common attribute of the different manifestations of Latin American populism, since populist forces in this region normally adopt an inclusionary approach – they are interested in integrating those who are discriminated against, in particular the very poor.

In summary, any comparison between different cases of populism across the world gives evidence that Paul Taggart (2000) is right in stating that populism inevitably has a chameleonic nature. In effect, the chameleonic nature of populism arises from the fact that it often enters marriages of convenience with other sets of ideas, which are crucial for the development of political projects that are appealing to the electorate. Nevertheless, this additional set of ideas should not be considered defining attributes of populism, but rather devices that are used in different cases to attract the interest of social groups. Ultimately, this is why 'there is no Populist International; no canon of key populist texts or calendars of significant moments; and the icons of populism are of local rather than universal appeal' (Stanley, 2008: 100). This should not distract us, however, from the fact that all manifestations of populism share not only the Manichean distinction between the pure people and the corrupt elite, but also a particular conception of politics that is akin to Rousseau's idea that nothing should trump the principle of popular sovereignty.

Subtypes of populism according to their organisational features

As I already mentioned, the ideational approach to populism is increasingly becoming dominant, particularly in the political science literature. This is a substantial improvement in our scholarship because it allows us to generate cumulative knowledge, foster academic dialogue and conduct cross-national and cross-regional research. However, the growing consensus on an ideational definition has made scholars less aware of an issue stressed by Weyland (2001) in particular, and the scholarship on Latin American populism in general (Hawkins & Rovira Kaltwasser, 2017a, 2017b): the relevance of organisational features. An important peculiarity of populist forces is that they usually rely on strong leaders, who centralise power and thanks to their charisma can mobilise large segments of the electorate. Nevertheless, it is also true that populist parties can survive without their leaders and one can think also about the existence of populist social movements (Aslanidis, 2016, 2017). Therefore, it is worth asking ourselves which organisational features are employed by populist forces (Heinisch & Mazzoleni, 2016).

How to define populism? 71

There are two reasons why we should pay more attention to the organisational dynamics behind populism. On the one hand, by looking at their organisational features it is possible to better understand the electoral success and failure of populist forces. For instance, research on populist radical right parties in Europe has shown that their electoral fortunes are closely related to their capacity to develop professional cadres, maintain links with civil society groups and advance strong institutional settings (Art, 2007, 2011; Mudde, 2007). Nothing precludes populist parties from being initially controlled by a strong and charismatic leader but eventually developing different factions and administrative bodies that not only limit the founding leader's influence but also end up replacing him.

On the other hand, organisational attributes can also be used as secondary features to distinguish subtypes of populism. In other words, populist forces are different not only because of their divergent framings of 'the pure people' versus 'the corrupt elites', but also because of their adoption of dissimilar types of organisational attributes. Although it is true that populism is first and foremost a set of ideas, by examining how these ideas are used by actors who employ distinctive organisational dynamics, one can better understand the formation of populist forces of different kinds. For example, Evo Morales in Bolivia can be considered a case of bottom-up populism (Madrid, 2008), the Austrian Freedom Party should be seen as an instance of top-down populism (Heinisch, 2008), and the Tea Party in the US is a case of populism that combines bottom-up and top-down dynamics (Formisano, 2012). Not by coincidence, Roberts (2006) argues – against Weyland – that populism can indeed lead to the formation of strong institutional structures, which are able to build organised constituencies with a clear and durable identity. There is no better example of this than Peronism in Argentina. As Steven Levitsky (2003) and Pierre Ostiguy (2009) have demonstrated, despite various programmatic transformations over time, the Peronist party has maintained a common identity, undergone relevant leadership changes and continued to successfully court a significant part of the Argentine electorate.

How should we construct a typology of subtypes of populism according to their organisational features? As I have argued elsewhere in more detail (Mudde & Rovira Kaltwasser, 2017, pp. 42–61), by looking at the different cases of populism across time and space, it is possible to identify three *ideal types*: personalist populist leaders, populist political parties and populist social movements. All these political forces employ the populist set of ideas, but they have different organisational attributes. It is worth noting that some of these ideal types are more prevalent in certain world regions than in others, something that in turn is related to the existence of different institutional settings, as for example presidential versus parliamentary systems. Moreover, as we will argue, each of these ideal types tends to have different effects on the democratic regime.

When reading about populism, the *first* thing that comes to mind is the rise of personalist leaders who resort to the populist ideology to project themselves as the only legitimate representatives of the people. This kind of leader tries to develop a direct link with the electorate and is therefore normally at odds with the development of intermediary organisations. One can find various examples of this pattern of leadership in Latin America, such as in the cases of Juan Domingo Perón in Argentina and Alberto Fujimori in Peru, two populist leaders characterised by showing little respect for democratic procedures – while Perón had little tolerance for the opposition, Fujimori closed the parliament. In fact, populist leadership of a personalist character usually tends to concentrate a great amount of power, which has rather perverse effects on democracy. Given that the populist leader in government is keen on ruling without constraints, those institutions that can hold the arbitrariness of the executive power accountable come under threat. The cases of Hugo Chávez and Nicolás Maduro in Venezuela are clear examples of how personalist populist figures can end up eliminating democratic spaces and lead to the consolidation of a competitive-authoritarian regime (Hawkins, 2016; Mainwaring, 2012).

The *second* option lies in the formation of political parties that rely on a populist discourse to represent the ideas and interests of (particular segments of) the electorate. To gain a foothold in the electoral arena, populist parties usually seek to politicise certain issues that deliberately or not have been omitted by established political forces. Populist political actors can construct political organisations with clear rules and build an electoral stronghold at the local or regional level from where they then try to expand their influence throughout the national territory. In contemporary Europe, one can identify a large number of populist political parties, the vast majority of which pursue a radical right agenda (Mudde, 2007, 2013). These parties not only argue that it is necessary to curtail immigration and that immigrants already in the country must assimilate with the national culture, but also maintain that the elites in power are allies of the foreign population that arrives in Europe. The usual argument is to point out that the business community benefits from immigration as this contributes to keeping wages low. For their part, political elites are supposedly seeking to win new voters by incorporating immigrants who, when benefitting from the welfare state, will end up supporting the established parties.

Finally, under certain circumstances, social movements can make use of the populist discourse. This pattern of mobilisation is somewhat unusual, as social movements generally seek to mobilise a particular segment of society, such as students, workers, or women (Aslanidis, 2016). What is unique about a populist social movement is that it is based on a frame that distinguishes between 'the pure people' and 'the corrupt elite' with the aim of bringing together all those citizens who are angry about the current political situation (Aslanidis, 2017). Normally these social movements are rather transient, but they can have a major impact on a country's political agenda and can even contribute to bringing to life new political leaders. For example, as a result of the financial crisis in 2008, the United States experienced the emergence of two populist social movements: on the one hand, the Tea Party with a radical right agenda that was later picked up partly by Donald Trump and, on the other hand, Occupy Wall Street with a radical left-wing programme that later had a major influence on the candidacy of Bernie Sanders (Judis, 2016).

Future lines of inquiry

As stated at the beginning of this chapter, the great advantage of working with a minimal definition of populism is that it permits us to advance a comparative research agenda. By identifying the common core of different manifestations of populism, it becomes possible not only to contrast them, but also to distinguish them from other features, such as clientelism, economic policies, charisma and xenophobia that regularly occur with populism but are not defining properties of it. In consequence, the recognition of the necessary and sufficient attributes of populism paves the way for the development of new lines of inquiry that have not been addressed properly yet, or that been answered only by taking into consideration a small amount of cases in one specific world region. Although this is not the place to offer a detailed overview of the elements that a comparative research agenda on populism could include, I would like to finish by pointing out three potential avenues of further study.

First, one of the topics that has received increasing academic and media attention is the ambivalent relationship between populism and democracy. Not baselessly, academics and pundits alike are worried about the rise of populist forces, which once in power are inclined to undertake political reforms at odds with key elements of the liberal democratic regime. However, it is also true that populist leaders and parties are able to speak for certain constituencies that do not feel represented by the political establishment (Arditi, 2004, 2005). Whether we like it or not, populism certainly has a democratising impetus, because it questions whether those who are in power are governing in favour of the majority or are rather interested in preserving the interests of a minority (Rovira Kaltwasser, 2014b). The undemocratic side of populism comes to the fore when it starts to disrespect the rules of public contestation and ends up fostering the creation of an uneven playing field between incumbents and opposition. Do populist forces lead to the formation of (competitive) authoritarian regimes or do they rather promote a democratisation of democracy? This is a relevant question that can and should be answered by undertaking empirical research, which should be comparative enough to draw some conclusions that are not specific to only one particular country or region. For instance, it would be relevant to investigate whether inclusionary or exclusionary populist forces have different effects on a democratic regime (Mudde & Rovira Kaltwasser, 2013a). At the same time, scholars should examine whether populism has a specific impact on each of the different stages of the democratisation process, that is, liberalisation, transition and consolidation (Mudde & Rovira Kaltwasser, 2017: 86–93).

Second, given that there is increasing concern about the negative effects of populism on the democratic system, it is important to study how we should deal with populist forces. Although some authors have done some studies on strategies for coping with political extremism in general (Downs, 2012) and the European far-right in particular (Eatwell & Mudde, 2004), there is a real research gap when it comes to understanding what policies are best suited to dealing with populism per se. Future comparative research on this subject could begin by taking into account two main actors: mainstream political parties and supranational institutions (Rovira Kaltwasser & Taggart, 2016). One the one hand, mainstream political parties play an important role, since they must implicitly or explicitly decide how to relate with populist forces. While the options range from full cooperation to frontal confrontation, there is probably no 'one size fits all approach' (Rovira Kaltwasser, 2017). Depending on the political agenda and radicalism of the populist forces, it might be appropriate to establish some level of dialogue with them or try to ostracise them. On the other hand, little has been written about the role that supranational institutions such as the European Union and the Organisation of American States can play when it comes to dealing with the rise of populist forces. Because both supranational institutions contain a democratic clause, they have legal and political mechanisms to monitor if populists-in-power are undertaking reforms leading to a deterioration of the rule of law. However, as Müller (2013) and Legler, Lean and Boniface (2007) have argued about the European Union and the Organisation of American States respectively, it seems that neither of these supranational organisations is well-equipped to cope with the challenges to democracy raised by populism.

Last, but not least, instead of assuming that populist actors misrepresent 'the people', future research should try to elucidate the mode of political representation advanced by populist leaders and followers. In fact, authors have maintained that populism is 'hostile to representative politics' (Taggart, 2002: 66), constitutes 'pseudo-representation' (Alonso, Keane & Merkel, 2011, p. 66), and should be conceived of as a 'perverse inversion of the ideals and procedures of representative democracy' (Rosanvallon, 2008, p. 265). While it is true that populist forces are usually at odds with the political establishment as well as unelected bodies, they are not against representation per se, but rather want to see their own representatives in power. Put another way, it is flawed to suppose that populists misrepresent 'the people' – whether we like it or not, they do represent certain constituencies. In order to gain new insights into the complex relationship between populism and political representation, it would be relevant to take into consideration new theoretical discussions (Rehfeld, 2005; Saward, 2006) that reveal that political representation is not only about institutions designed to connect the will of the people with the decisions of political actors – it is also about the very process of defining who 'we, the people' are. This means that political representation is *constitutive*: it enables the formation of constituencies and thus can play a foundational role (Brito Viera & Runciman, 2008). This is particularly evident in the case of populism. After all, populist leaders, parties and movements normally give voice to groups that do not feel represented by the political establishment.

Note

1 The author would like to acknowledge support from the Chilean National Fund for Scientific and Technological Development (FONDECYT project 1180020) and the Center for Social Conflict and Cohesion Studies (COES, CONICYT/FONDAP/ 15130009).

References

Acemoglu, D., Egerov, G., & Sonin, K. (2013). A political theory of populism. *The Quarterly Journal of Economics, 128*(2), 771–805.

Akkerman, A., Mudde, C., & Zaslove, A. (2014). How populist are the people? Measuring populist attitudes in voters. *Comparative Political Studies, 47*(9), 1324–1353.

Alonso, S., Keane, J., & Merkel, W. (2011). Editor's introduction: Rethinking the future of representative democracy. In S. Alonso, J. Keane, & W. Merkel (Eds.), *The future of representative democracy* (pp. 1–22). Cambridge: Cambridge University Press.

Arditi, B. (2004). Populism as a spectre of democracy: A response to Canovan. *Political Studies, 52*(1), 135–143.

Arditi, B. (2005). Populism as an internal periphery of democratic politics. In F. Panizza (Ed.), *Populism and the mirror of democracy* (pp. 72–98). London: Verso.

Art, D. (2007). Reacting to the radical right lessons from Germany and Austria. *Party Politics, 13*(3), 331–349.

Art, D. (2011). *Inside the radical right: The development of anti-immigrant parties in Western Europe*. New York: Cambridge University Press.

Aslanidis, P. (2016). Populist social movements of the great recession. *Mobilization: An International Quarterly, 21*(3), 301–321.

Aslanidis, P. (2017). Populism and social Movements. In C. Rovira Kaltwasser, P. Taggart, P. Ochoa Espejo, & P. Ostiguy (Eds.), *The Oxford handbook of populism* (pp. 305–325). New York: Oxford University Press.

Berezin, M. (2009). *Illiberal politics in neoliberal times: Culture, security, and populism in New Europe*. New York: Cambridge University Press.

Berman, S. (2017). The pipe dream of undemocratic liberalism. *Journal of Democracy, 28*(3), 29–38.

Betz, H. (1994). *Radical right-wing populism in Western Europe*. New York: Palgrave Macmillan.

Betz, H. (2017). Nativism across time and space. *Swiss Political Science Review, 23*(4), 335–353.

Brito Viera, M., & Runciman, D. (2008). *Representation*. Cambridge: Polity Press.

Brown, A. (2014). Communism. In M. Freeden, M. Stears & L. Tower Sargent (Eds.), *The Oxford handbook of political ideologies* (pp. 364–384). Oxford: Oxford University Press.

Collier, D., & Gerring, J. (Eds.). (2009). *Concepts and method in the social science: The tradition of Giovanni Sartori*. New York: Routledge.

Coppedge, M., Gerring, J., Altman, D., & Bernhard, M. (2011). Conceptualizing and measuring democracy: A new approach. *Perspectives on Politics, 9*(2), 247–367.

De la Torre, C. (Ed.). (2014). *The promise and perils of populism: Global perspectives*. Lexington, KY: University of Kentucky Press.

Dornbusch, R., & Edwards, S. (Eds.). (1991). *The macroeconomics of populism in Latin America*. Chicago and London: The Chicago University Press.

Downs, W. M. (2012). *Political extremism in democracies: Combating intolerance*. Basingstoke, UK: Palgrave Macmillan.

Eatwell, R., & Mudde, C. (Eds.). (2004). *Western democracies and the new extreme right challenge*. London: Routledge.

Edwards, S. (2010). *Left behind: Latin America and the false promise of populism*. Chicago, IL: University of Chicago Press.

Formisano, R. (2012). *The tea party*. Baltimore, MD: Johns Hopkins University Press.
Hawkins, K. (2009). Is Chávez populist? Measuring populist discourse in comparative perspective. *Comparative Political Studies*, *42*(8), 1040–1067.
Hawkins, K. (2010). *Venezuela's chavismo and populism in comparative perspective*. Cambridge: Cambridge University Press.
Hawkins, K. (2016). Responding to radical populism: Chavismo in Venezuela. *Democratization*, *23*(2), 242–262.
Hawkins, K., Riding, S., & Mudde, C. (2012). Measuring populist attitudes. Working Paper Series on Political Concepts, No. 55, ECPR Committee on Concepts and Methods.
Hawkins, K., & Rovira Kaltwasser, C. (2017a). The ideational approach to populism. *Latin American Research Review*, *52*(4), 513–528.
Hawkins, K., & Rovira Kaltwasser, C. (2017b). What the (Ideational) Study of Populism Can Teach Us, and What it Can't. *Swiss Political Science Review*, *23*(4), 526–542.
Heinisch, R. (2008). Austria: The structure and agency of Austrian populism. In D. Albertazzi & D. McDonnell (Eds.), *Twenty-first century populism: The spectre of Western European democracy* (pp. 67–83). Basingstoke, UK: Palgrave Macmillan.
Heinisch, R., & Mazzoleni, O. (Eds.). (2016). *Understanding populist party organisation: The radical right in Western Europe*. Basingstoke, UK: Palgrave Macmillan.
Houle, C., & Kenny, P. D. (2018). The political and economic consequences of populist rule in Latin America. *Government & Opposition*, *53*(2), 256–287.
Huber, R. A., & Schimpf, C. H. (2016). Friend or foe? Testing the influence of populism on democratic quality in Latin America. *Political Studies*, *64*(4), 872–889.
Ignazi, P. (2000). *Extreme right parties in Western Europe*. Oxford: Oxford University Press.
Judis, J. (2016). *The populist explosion: How the great recession transformed American and European Politics*. New York: Columbia Global Reports.
Kazin, M. (1995). *The populist persuasion: An American history* (revised ed.). Ithaca and London: Cornell University Press.
Kioupkioilis, A. (2016). Podemos: The ambiguous promises of left-wing populism in contemporary Spain. *Journal of Political Ideologies*, *21*(2), 99–120.
Kitschelt, H. (in collaboration with A. J. McGann). (1997). *The radical right in Western Europe: A comparative analysis*. Ann Arbor, MI: The University of Michigan Press.
Kitschelt, H., & Wilkinson, S. (2007). Citizen-politician linkages: An introduction. In H. Kitschelt & S. Wilkinson (Eds.), *Patrons, clients, and policies: Patterns of democratic accountability and political competition* (pp. 1–49). New York: Cambridge University Press.
Laclau, E. (2005). *On populist reason*. London: Verso.
Legler, T., Lean, S. F., & Boniface, D. S. (Eds.). (2007). *Promoting democracy in the Americas*. Baltimore, MD: Johns Hopkins University Press.
Levitsky, S. (2003). *Transforming labor-based parties in Latin America: Argentine peronism in comparative perspective*. Cambridge: Cambridge University Press.
Madrid, R. (2008). The rise of ethnopopulism in Latin America. *World Politics*, *60*(3), 475–508.
Mainwaring, S. (2012). From representative democracy to participatory competitive authoritarianism: Hugo Chávez and Venezuelan politics. *Perspectives on Politics*, *10*(4), 955–967.
March, L. (2011). *Radical left parties in Europe*. London: Routledge.

Meléndez, C., & Rovira Kaltwasser, C. (2017). Political identities: The missing link in the study of populism. *Party Politics*. Retrieved from http://journals.sagepub.com/doi/abs/10.1177/1354068817741287.

Moffitt, B. (2016). *The global rise of populism: Performance, political style, and representation*. Stanford, CA: Stanford University Press.

Mudde, C. (2004). The populist Zeitgeist. *Government and Opposition*, *39*(4), 541–563.

Mudde, C. (2007). *Populist radical right parties in Europe*. Cambridge: Cambridge University Press.

Mudde, C. (2010). The populist radical right: A pathological normalcy. *West European Politics*, *33*(6), 1167–1186.

Mudde, C. (2013). Three decades of populist radical right parties in Western Europe: So what?. *European Journal of Political Research*, *52*(1), 1–19.

Mudde, C., & Rovira Kaltwasser, C. (Eds.). (2012). *Populism in Europe and the Americas: Threat or corrective for democracy?*. Cambridge: Cambridge University Press.

Mudde, C., & Rovira Kaltwasser, C. (2013a). Exclusionary vs. inclusionary populism: Comparing contemporary Europe and Latin America. *Government and Opposition*, *48*(2), 147–174.

Mudde, C., & Rovira Kaltwasser, C. (2013b). Populism. In M. Freeden, M. Stears, & L. Tower Sargent (Eds.), *The Oxford handbook of political ideologies* (pp. 491–512). Oxford: Oxford University Press.

Mudde, C., & Rovira Kaltwasser, C. (2014). Populism and political leadership. In R. A. W. Rhodes & P. Hart (Eds.), *The Oxford handbook of political leadership* (pp. 376–388). Oxford: Oxford University Press.

Mudde, C., & Rovira Kaltwasser, C. (2017). *Populism: A very short introduction*. New York: Oxford University Press.

Müller, J.-W. (2013). Safeguarding democracy inside the EU: Brussels and the future of liberal order. *Transatlantic Academy Paper Series*, No. 3.

Müller, J. W. (2016). *What is populism?*. Philadelphia, PA: Pennsylvania University Press.

Ochoa Espejo, P. (2011). *The time of popular sovereignty*. University Park, PA: Pennsylvania University Press.

Ostiguy, P. (2009). Argentina's double political spectrum: Party system, political identities, and strategies, 1944–2007. Working Paper No. 361, Kellogg.

Pirro, A. L. P., & van Kessel, S. (2017). United in opposition? The populist radical right's EU-pessimism in times of crisis. *Journal of European Integration*, *39*(4), 405–420.

Plattner, M. F. (2010). Populism, pluralism, and liberal democracy. *Journal of Democracy*, *21*(1), 83–90.

Postel, C. (2007). *The populist vision*. Oxford: Oxford University Press.

Rehfeld, A. (2005). *The concept of constituency: Political representation, democratic legitimacy, and institutional design*. Cambridge: Cambridge University Press.

Roberts, K. (2006). Populism, political conflict, and grass-roots organization in Latin America. *Comparative Politics*, *38*(2), 127–148.

Rossanvallon, P. (2008). *Counter-democracy: Politics in an age of distrust*. New York: Cambridge University Press.

Rovira Kaltwasser, C. (2011). Skizze einer vergleichenden Forschungsagenda zum Populismus. *Totalitarismus und Demokratie*, *8*(2), 251–271.

Rovira Kaltwasser, C. (2012). The ambivalence of populism: Threat and corrective for democracy. *Democratization*, *19*(2), 184–208.

Rovira Kaltwasser, C. (2014a). Latin American populism: Some conceptual and normative lessons. *Constellations*, *22*(4), 494–504.

Rovira Kaltwasser, C. (2014b). The responses of populism to Dahl's democratic dilemmas. *Political Studies*, *62*(3), 470–487.

Rovira Kaltwasser, C. (2017). Populism and the question of how to respond to it. In C. Rovira Kaltwasser, P. Taggart, P. Ochoa Espejo & P. Ostiguy (Eds.), *The Oxford handbook of populism* (pp. 489–507). New York: Oxford University Press.

Rovira Kaltwasser, C., & Taggart, P. (2016). Dealing with populists in government: A framework for analysis. *Democratization*, *23*(2), 201–220.

Rovira Kaltwasser, C., Taggart, P., Ochoa Espejo, P., & Ostiguy, P. (2017). Populism: An overview of the concept and state of the art. In C. Rovira Kaltwasser, P. Taggart, P. Ochoa Espejo, & P. Ostiguy (Eds.), *The Oxford Handbook of Populism* (pp. 1–24). New York: Oxford University Press.

Sartori, G. (1970). Concept misformation in comparative politics. *American Political Science Review*, *64*(4), 1033–1053.

Saward, M. (2006). The representative claim. *Contemporary Political Theory*, *5*(3), 297–318.

Skocpol, T., & Williamson, V. (2012). *The tea party and the remaking of republican conservatism*. Oxford: Oxford University Press.

Stanley, B. (2008). The thin ideology of populism. *Journal of Political Ideologies*, *13*(1), 95–110.

Stavrakakis, Y., & Katsambekis, G. (2014). Left-wing populism in the European periphery: The case of SYRIZA. *Journal of Political Ideologies*, *19*(2), 119–142.

Taggart, P. (2000). *Populism*. London: Open University Press.

Taggart, P. (2002). Populism and the pathology of representative politics. In Y. Mény & Y. Surel (Eds.), *Democracies and the populist challenge* (pp. 62–80). Basingstoke, UK: Palgrave Macmillan.

Taguieff, P. (1995). Political science confronts populism. *Telos*, *103*, 9–44.

van Hauwaert, S. M., & van Kessel, S. (2018). Beyond protest and discontent: A cross-national analysis of the effect of populist attitudes and issue positions on populist party support. *European Journal of Political Research*, *57*(1), 68–92.

Weyland, K. (2001). Clarifying a contested concept: Populism in the study of Latin American politics. *Comparative Politics,* *34*(1), 1–22.

5 Populism and 'unpolitics'

Paul Taggart

Introduction

There is now something of a consolidation in the study of populism. This is at a time when there is clear upsurge in populism as a political force across the world, from Europe, to Latin America, the US and Asia. There is no full agreement on a definition, but the upsurge in the sheer volume of work on populism has come along with some more patterning of that work. One of the most dominant themes has been the consideration of populism as ideology (Hawkins & Rovira Kaltwasser, 2017; Taggart, 2000). There is a now an extensive body of scholarship, both conceptual and empirical, that uses populism as an ideology. While we have some convergence here, and it is a welcome convergence, the elements that make up that consensus have omitted and elided over the relationship of populism to politics.

This chapter argues that we need to re-insert a fuller sense of populism's relationship to politics into the definition of populism. To do this, I suggest that populism has, at its core, an implicit assertion of what I will term 'unpolitics'. And it is the confrontation of this unpolitics with the functioning of representative politics that makes populism so potent and so provocative to contemporary representative democracy.

This chapter is structured in the following way. First, I offer a literature review to try and back up the case that the element of politics has dropped out of the consideration of populism. The chapter then offers a definition of unpolitics that contrasts it with other related concepts, and then the chapter considers three different implications of unpolitics for populism. This chapter is designed as a think piece. It is consciously non-empirical in the sense of looking at particular instances of populism but I am attempting to make a (hesitant) wider point about how to study populism in general.

Populism as ideology

It will be a relief to hear that this paper is not another that seeks to engage in the practice of definitions of populism, but I do want to make three observations about what the definitional debate shows us. First, I would say that Cas Mudde's (rightly) influential definition points us to the primary elements of populism, and they are a series of concepts. According to Mudde, populism is 'an ideology that considers society to be ultimately separated into two homogeneous and antagonistic groups, "the pure people" versus "the corrupt elite", and which argues that politics should be an expression of the volonté générale (general will) of the people' (Mudde, 2004, p. 543). The people-centredness is clearly there. And this aspect has had plenty of academic attention (Canovan, 2005; Ochoa Espejo, 2012; Stavrakakis, 2014). Similarly, the opposition to elites is well established.

Politics for populists is, however, reduced in this definition to being an expression of one of the most oblique concepts in political theory. However, we can make this more accessible by seeing the importance of the general will as embodied in the populist emphasis on popular sovereignty (Canovan, 1999, 2004). This focus is really about populism as a feature of democracy rather than politics. Certainly it is true that populism emphasises popular sovereignty and the will of majority as an enabling component of democracy that has become constrained. Populism also plays up popular sovereignty, but plays down the other features of democracy that emphasise constraint, such as the rights and rule of law. So this emphasis is a good one and one that is a core feature of populism. It also goes a long way to explaining why the manifestation of populism is so problematic for democracy, as it challenges it from within (Mény & Surel, 2002).

The weakness of this element of the definition is that is misses the more fundamental ambivalence about politics itself which populism derives from. It is from this ambivalence to politics that the corruption of Mudde's 'corrupt elites' comes from. The elites are not inherently corrupt but rather are corrupted by being involved in politics. For populist thinking the steady state model is one where most citizens get on with their own lives and avoid politics and where those that are involved in politics will inherently be unrepresentative and will, more importantly, inevitably be corrupted by any sustained political activity. Simply asserting the general will is not enough to fully describe the populist sense of politics. And I would argue it goes deeper than this – it misses the unpolitics of populism.

The second observation is that populism can give rise to a series of secondary features. These are factors that are not universal. Not all populists demonstrate these features but they occur commonly enough for us to suggest that they have some association with populism. I am going to call these 'tropes'. Ben Stanley has talked about the populist playbook and this is a very similar idea – that there are a set of resources that populists can and do call upon but which are chosen in response to a particular context so are not always mobilised. The thin-centredness of populism as an ideology explains why we have to be prepared to see populism as an ideology which may give rise to features that are symptomatic of its core elements but which are themselves not necessary and sufficient for us to identify them as universal features of populism (Freeden, 2017; Stanley, 2008; Taggart, 2000).

The three core features of populism lie then in its people centredness, its antipathy towards elites and, I am suggesting here, a particular conception of politics which I am calling 'unpolitics'. The tropes can be considered secondary features of populism but all stem from unpolitics. But before we consider these, it is important to try to define and clarify what I mean by unpolitics.

Definition and differentiation of unpolitics

Unpolitics is not the same as anti-politics or being apolitical. I am defining unpolitics here as the repudiation of politics as the process for resolving conflict. It is both negative in the sense of rejecting key elements of politics (settlements, corruption and conspiracies) but also positive in the sense of tending to celebrate or resort to other forms of activity (e.g. war, religion) but staying within a democratic frame of reference.

It is clearly not apolitical, as populism can lead to full engagement in politics. The only way in which it could potentially be seen as apolitical is in the idea that populists are only 'reluctantly' political – that unconventional populist leaders will often claim to be in politics as a temporary measure to fix a crisis. The narrative of populism has as one of its core features the idea that right-thinking, virtuous and ordinary people are those that it is appealing to and it is these sorts of people who are normally non-political. Politics is a degenerative activity and these people just normally like to get on with their lives, earn a living and avoid the political world. That is why the 'silent majority' is silent. It has chosen to not have a voice as it has chosen to not be political. However, it is the emergence of a sense of crisis that mobilises this constituency to rise up and start to become actively engaged in politics (as populist actors) or active supporters of those actors engaged in politics (as a populist constituency).

Unpolitics is not the same as the rejection of politics or anti-politics. There are two points here. First, that it is not anti-politics in the sense that anti-politics is revolutionary. Populism's power is in being within the realms of reformism and stopping short of revolution. It works within the boundaries of existing democratic politics. As soon as it steps outside those boundaries it becomes authoritarian, revolutionary but most decidedly not populist. The second point is that it is also not without politics or apolitical. At its core it may have a hankering for a world without politics, but populism is driven to engagement with politics but in a way that is at odds with that politics. This is partly why populism is always so challenging a phenomenon for those who are either systematically engaged in, or engaged by, politics as an activity. The disjuncture between unpolitics and politics is what makes populism often so spectacular and so perplexing to students of politics.

The nature of populist tropes

The three tropes that follow from unpolitics are features that often, but not always, are apparent in populism. I am admittedly being rather broad-brush here and this is not an empirical survey of the presence of these tropes. Rather what I am seeking to do is to see if these broad brushstrokes paint a picture of some of the more opaque aspects of populism.

Politics as war

In the classic von Clausewitz ([1832–1834] 1984, p. 87) definition, 'War is merely the continuation of policy by other means' but what I want so suggest here is that for populists there is a strong undertone of politics being the continuation of war by other means. What I mean here is that the repudiation of politics by populists means that when they engage in political activity the tone, tools and metaphors that they adopt can have more in common with war than with the practice of politics. This also goes some way to explaining the appeal of populists to their constituencies, even at times of apparent chaos and confusion.

The war metaphor for populists can be seen in three key ways. First, it can be seen in polarisation. The binary nature of politics for populists is frequently noted. For some populism has been termed bifurcatory or as Manichean (Hawkins, 2010). It seems almost self-evident to suggest that there is something of a relationship between polarisation and the emergence of populism. But what is not as clear is whether polarisation is the cause or the effect of populism. The framing of politics by populists is more important as a cause than as an effect of polarisation.

The second implication of the war trope for populists is the neglect of rights. What is striking about populists is that the trenchant assertion that they are there to champion those who have been neglected and who are the majority is almost never cast in terms of rights. The war metaphor implies that the enemy are very much an enemy in everything. The elite are essentially to be opposed and these must be a complete defeat. For populism, the war trope justifies the suspension of rights, just as might be expected in the situation of states going to war.

The emphasis for populism is on wars and not battles. Populism views politics as on-going conflict. It is for this reason that I am identifying a war and not a battle trope. For populists, defeat in any one battle does not signify defeat. Indeed, populists can often claim that defeat is evidence of the superior resources of the enemy but this is itself vindication of the populist cause. It is almost the case that success and failure in elections can be equal grist to the populist mill. Populism's power can be to use defeat as a source of effective mobilisation.

Politics as religion

To suggest a parallel between populism and religion is nothing novel. We can see it implicit in the work of Hawkins (2010) and explicit in the idea of missionary politics in Zúquete (2007). Historically, we can also see strong religious parallels in the early populists. The clearest case is of the Russian *narodniki* whose movement had all the elements of evangelising, conversion and proselyting that we might expect with a religious movement (Venturi, [1960] 1983).

In practice, identifying a parallel with religion or a quasi-religious (Taggart, 2000) aspect to populism is rather vague. For those manifestations of populism without an explicit link to religion, then, we need to be clearer on *how* this putative link might manifest itself. I would suggest that there are three ways we can see this trope: in terms of charismatic leadership, in the emphasis on the virtue of the people and in a tendency to evangelise.

The *first* manifestation of the religious trope can be seen in that way that populism is often associated with, or can itself celebrate, charismatic leadership (see Barr, 2009; Taggart, 2000, pp. 100–103). There is sometimes a tendency to talk about populism as always being associated with charismatic leadership. We need to be precise here about the meaning of charisma and to take it to mean something more than just personalistic leadership. The leadership of someone like Chavez is about not only his personal qualities but also lies in him alone embodying the people. (The Trump case does not work well here.) We need to go back to the Weberian idea of charisma implying being touched by God. This idea means that authority attaches not to office or to tradition but to the individual alone.

Looking at examples of the contemporary populist radical right in Europe, there is certainly a strong association between powerful individual leaders and the parties that they lead (Van der Brug & Mughan, 2007) and the same holds true for some Latin American cases (see Weyland, 2003). But there is nothing inherent in populism that means it inevitably tends to charismatic leadership. Populists in the nineteenth century in the US and in Russia did not have charismatic leaders. They were both cases of bottom-up mass movements without clear leaders. The religious parallel is instructive here. The idea from religion of a messiah or a prophet as sent by God is something that does not occur with regularity. With religion the importance of a God-given representation comes about only occasionally and the presence of such figures can imply the need to the reinstate the virtue of the people, to move them back on to a track that is more in accord with God. For populists, the charismatic leadership claim is very much that a sense of crisis (Taggart, 2000) brings about the need for extraordinary leadership. The unpolitics is clear in that often those extraordinary individuals come from outside conventional politics. Businessmen and billionaires are more attractive to populists than established conventional politicians. The 'gift of grace' of such figures is that their extraordinariness is what enables them to lead, or to channel, the ordinariness of their constituency. Whether it is Berlusconi, Babis, Trump or Perot, populist leaders of this ilk flaunt their exceptionality as a paradoxical mark of their connection to the ordinariness of their constituency. And even when populist leaders are not from outside conventional politics, they often use the socio-cultural norms of the 'low' (Ostiguy, 2017) to ram home how they can transgress conventional political norms, even if they have not, in practice, crossed over into politics from 'outside'.

The *second* way we can see the religious parallel is in the virtue of the people. As Edward Shils (1956) observed, an aspect of populism is the inversion of virtue: virtue coming not from detachment or from learning or study, but rather virtue as inherent within the people. In a sense then, the populist narrative of a virtuous people is a parallel for the people as being blessed. The reason that populists eschew experts, theories and intellectuals is that wisdom does not come from learning or from books. Rather it comes from ordinariness and innocence. There are strong religious parallels with the idea either of a 'chosen people' or that we are all God's children.

The *third* aspect of populism that can link with its religious parallel is the tendency to evangelise. Think here of the co-operative movements that underlay the US populists in the 1870s and 1880s (Goodwyn, 1976). There was a strong element of education as these farmers sought to spread ideas about how they might operate collectively to overcome the atomisation and powerlessness that they felt in the face of money, political and railroad interests. And we see that idea of spreading truth also important in the *narodniki*. There was in both movements a strong theme of learning. For the US populists, the co-operative movement placed a great emphasis on spreading its message through teaching and instruction. This was linked to learning about how to operate as a collective agrarian enterprise to free the farmers from their dependence on the banks and railroads. But it inevitably spilled into teaching and learning about politics (Goodwyn, 1976).

Politics as conspiracy theory

The third trope that we can identify in populism is in the tendency towards conspiracy theory. The assertion here is that populists will often tend towards a diagnosis of the present condition that verges on, or is characterised by, being a conspiracy theory (Castanho Silva, Vegetti & Littvay, 2017). This stems from the propensity to see the elite as corrupt and conspiratorial and as unrepresentative of the people. The prevalence of this situation then implies that there is agency at work – that it is a design.

The key elements of a conspiracy theory are that power is being wielded by the powerful in a collusive way with a deliberate element of secrecy (Sunstein & Vermeule, 2009). As Fenster (1999) notes, conspiracy theories are theories of power and so they are more than casual empirical assertions. This means that the populist resort to conspiracy theories is more fundamental that a claim about a case. It also amounts to a claim about politics. It may be about politics at national level but it also may feed into wider global conspiracies.

Conspiracy theories simplify complexity. They provide an over-arching explanation for what might seem difficult or even impossible to otherwise fully explain. It may be that politics is conducted via the active collusion of the powerful in their own interests and with an element of secrecy. However, we are not concerned here with the veracity of the claims of populists but rather in the tendency to resort to conspiracies as an explanation. The need for a simple explanation is indicative of the unpolitics of populism. For Castanho Silva, Vegetti & Littvay (2017), conspiracy provides not simplicity but also a powerful narrative.

The allusion to collusion in populism is also very natural. An opposition to an elite or an 'establishment' will naturally lead to the assumption that this grouping is somehow unified in not only ends but means. Although an elite/establishment may be either heterogeneous or pluralistic, it is a useful rallying cry of populism to try and to tar them all with the same brush. The eliding of terms such as liberal/cosmopolitan/metropolitan are often attempts to frame elites in a unitary, and negative, way for populists. In some sense the monism that is inherent in the populist conception of the people and the heartland from which they derive is here mirrored in their view of those that are not 'the people'.

Conclusion

I have tried to show that the concept of unpolitics is a useful one to unpack some of the aspects of populism. I have argued that underlying populism as an ideology is a very profound and fundamental ambivalence about politics such that it implicitly celebrates or is drawn to unpolitics. In practice this means that populists will often, but not always, be pulled into narratives and ways of thinking associated with activities divergent from politics, namely war, religion and conspiracy theories. I have identified these as tropes, as tendencies that can occur and which taken together or separately imply a predilection for unpolitics over politics. The effect of these tropes can be powerful.

Politics as practice is about settlement. Settlements are changing sets of norms about ideas, rules and justice that shape politics at any given time in any given location. They are inherently dynamic. These can be both wider settlements about the nature of politics in a nation/state or they can be far more micro and can relate to a policy area of an issue of political contention. These settlements shape who the winners and losers are, and shape the nature of political competition. They are, however, dynamic and by no means immutable, and so much of politics takes place with settlements and therefore knowing the shape of (or where to look for) existing settlements will provide a fuller picture.

Populism tends to relish unsettling politics. Populism seeks unsettlements. Pierre Ostiguy (2017) talks about this as populism 'flaunting the low'. By this he means that populism revels in its transgression of norms. This is why populism is both disruptive and celebratory in its unsettling of its opponents. The other effect of populism's unsettlements is that it has the effect of lumping together its opponents. By forcing all opponents to contest populism on two levels – by countering the policies/issues/positions and by simultaneously defending the norms that are being transgressed in the manner in which these positions are put, populism conflates differences between opposition and also emphasises its own distance from this falsely conflated grouping.

The purpose of identifying these tropes is not to use them to categorise cases of populism. They are not useful for doing this because these tropes are neither necessary nor sufficient for classification as populism. Rather the identification of these tropes is meant to help us (or perhaps only me) to unpack populism: to point to the unpolitical core of populism.

Of course, I am aware that one objection to my argument may be that I am equating politics itself with either liberalism or representative democratic politics. There is a difficulty in separating understandings of politics in the contemporary world from understandings of liberal democracy and representative politics. Of course, other forms of politics exist and even flourish (Geddes, 1999) but it is difficult to disentangle politics from its liberal and representative forms. More prosaically, I would also suggest that populism is only a feature in liberal and representative political contexts.

The urge to unpolitics and its power in general is a source of the effectiveness of populism in contemporary politics. There is nothing new however in either populism or its unpolitics. The prevalence of contemporary populism then means that we need to address what it is that makes unpolitics so palatable and politics so unpalatable to so many at this juncture. The success of populism and the celebration of unpolitics represents perhaps a particular failing of politics at a particular time.

References

Barr, R. R. (2009). Populists, outsiders and anti-establishment politics. *Party Politics*, *15*(1), 29–48.
Canovan, M. (1999). Trust the people! Populism and the two faces of democracy. *Political Studies*, *47*(1), 2–16.
Canovan, M. (2004). Populism for political theorists?. *Journal of Political Ideologies*, *9*(3), 241–252.
Canovan, M. (2005). *The people*. Cambridge: Polity.
Castanho Silva, B., Vegetti, F., & Littvay, L. (2017). The elite is up to something: Exploring the relation between populism and belief in conspiracy theories. *Swiss Political Science Review*, *23*(4), 423–443.
Fenster, M. (1999) *Conspiracy theories: Secrecy and power in American culture*. Minneapolis, MN: University of Minnesota Press.
Freeden, M. (2017). After the Brexit referendum: Revisiting populism as an ideology. *Journal of Political Ideologies*, *22*(1), 1–11.
Geddes, B. (1999). What do we know about democratization after twenty years?. *Annual Review of Political Science*, *2*(1), 115–144.
Goodwyn, L. (1976). *Democratic promise: The populist moment in America*. New York: Oxford University Press.
Hawkins, K. A. (2010). *Venezuela's Chavismo and populism in comparative perspective*. Cambridge: Cambridge University Press.
Hawkins, K. A., & Rovira Kaltwasser, C. (2017). What the (ideational) study of populism can teach us, and what it can't. *Swiss Political Science Review*, *23*(4), 526–542.
Mény, Y., & Surel, Y. (2002). The constitutive ambiguity of populism. In Y. Mény & Y. Surel (Eds.), *Democracies and the populist challenge* (pp. 1–21). London: Palgrave Macmillan.
Mudde, C. (2004). The populist zeitgeist. *Government and Opposition*, *39*(4), 541–563.
Ochoa Espejo, P. (2012). Paradoxes of popular sovereignty: A view from Spanish America. *The Journal of Politics*, *74*(4), 1053–1065.
Ostiguy, P. (2017). A Socio-cultural approach. In C. Rovira Kaltwasser, P. Taggart, P. Ochoa Espejo, & P. Ostiguy (Eds.), *The Oxford handbook of populism* (pp. 73–97). Oxford: Oxford University Press.
Shils, E. A. (1956). *The torment of secrecy: The background and consequences of American security policies*. London: Heinemann.
Stanley, B. (2008). The thin ideology of populism. *Journal of Political Ideologies*, *13*(1), 95–110.
Stavrakakis, Y. (2014). The return of 'the people': Populism and anti-populism in the shadow of the European crisis. *Constellations*, *21*(4), 505–517.
Sunstein, C. R., & Vermeule, A. (2009). Conspiracy theories: Causes and cures. *Journal of Political Philosophy*, *17*(2), 202–227.
Taggart, P. (2000). *Populism*. Buckingham: Open University Press.

van der Brug, W., & Mughan, A. (2007). Charisma, leader effects and support for right-wing populist parties. *Party Politics*, *13*(1), 29–51.
Venturi, F. ([1960] 1983). *Roots of revolution: A history of the populist and socialist movements in nineteenth century Russia.* Chicago, IL: University of Chicago Press.
von Clausewitz, C. ([1832–1834] 1984). *On war,* translated by M. Howard & P. Paret. Princeton, NJ: Princeton University Press.
Weyland, K. (2003). Economic voting reconsidered: Crisis and charisma in the election of Hugo Chávez. *Comparative Political Studies*, *36*(7), 822–848.
Zúquete, J. P. (2007). *Missionary politics in contemporary Europe.* Syracuse, NY: Syracuse University Press.

Part II
Theoretical approaches

6 'We the people'

Liberal and organic populism, and the politics of social closure

Jürgen Mackert

Introduction

It has repeatedly been remarked that the debate on populism has so far been dominated by political science, concentrating mainly on its subject matters such as politics, party and electoral systems, the distinction of right-wing populism and left-wing populism and so forth. From a sociological perspective, there is an obvious lack of linking the social phenomenon 'populism' to wider strands of theoretical reasoning. In this chapter, I want to contribute to such endeavours (see Berezin, Snow & Bernatzky, and McCarthy in this volume) by suggesting a genetically informed conceptualisation and systematisation of 'populism' and by analysing dynamics of populism from the perspective of closure theory.

I argue that populism is an early form of any kind of modern democratic politics and characteristic both for the period before a democratic upheaval as well as for the early development of democratic systems. Being a constitutive element of politics at the beginning of the democratic age, populism reflects deep social segregations and fissures. In this context, early 'democratic' politics as they unfolded in the two great democratic revolutions either sought to defend privileges by keeping 'the people' away from the franchise and, of course, from political power, or to reorganise the distribution of wealth and life-chances in favour of the exploited and humiliated. Thus, I try to defend a continuity thesis by arguing that from the beginning of the modern democratic age until today, populism has always been a constitutive and intrinsic element of any kind of democratic politics. Populist politics – which I conceive as highly socially exclusionary political strategies – can be (re)activated under certain conditions of societal crisis in order to promote a fierce politics of exclusion. While in former times the conflict may have been one of ruler vs. subjects that today resonates in the populist formulation of an opposition of 'the corrupt elite' and 'the pure people' (Mudde, 2004), the pluralisation of social cleavages and fault lines has complicated the populist field. Today, in liberal-democratic societies we see populist constructions of social boundaries multiplying, now covering a broad range of vertical and horizontal social or cultural fault lines in society (Brubaker in this volume) that may be activated in political contestations. Populists' strategies of social exclusion thus re-accentuate many of the fundamental conflicts that characterise liberal-democratic societies, such as citizens vs. migrants, old vs. young, urban vs. rural, wealthy vs. poor, Christian vs. Muslim as well as conflicts about sexual orientation, same-sex marriage and so forth, thereby putting categories of people against each other. All of this has only little in common with the high ideals of democratic reasoning, civilised debate and Western values that so regularly are claimed to be the leading principles of Western politics. Rather, as I will show, the boundaries between 'democratic politics' and 'populist politics' are fluent, as today we see a wide *field of populism* emerging in once liberal-democratic Western societies.

This chapter joins the recent debate by conceiving of populism as a constitutive though pre-democratic political strategy in democratic regimes that justifies its radical exclusionary demands in 'the name of the people'. In developed liberal democracies this strategy can be revitalised according to fundamental reorganisations of democratic society's politico-economic foundations and display various tactics. Understood in this way populism cannot be separated from major ideologies such as liberalism, liberal democracy, the idea of the 'sovereignty of the people', and the concept of 'We the people' that are at the core of the legitimation of modern democracy. In what follows, I suggest a *historically* informed *analytical* approach that may help to promote and redirect *comparative* empirical research on today's manifestations of populism. First, based on two conceptions of 'the people' I distinguish two versions of the phenomenon. Second, I contextualise the rise of populism within the two great democratic revolutions. Third, with regard to analysis, I propose to analyse populism using the instruments of the theory of social closure; fourth, this enables me to distinguish tactics of populism's exclusionary politics, which allows for comparative analyses.

The rise of democracy and populism – a genetic view

Populism in Western societies originates in the two great democratic revolutions, albeit differently, and remains an intrinsic part of democratic societies throughout the centuries. In historical perspective, it has played its role repeatedly, yet over long periods turned into a kind of deactivated mode. Nevertheless, in the face of deep societal crises, political actors can reactivate this strategy. In an early contribution to the problem of the radical right for American democracy, Seymour Martin Lipset has made an argument at least with regard to the lower classes:

> The lack of an aristocratic tradition in American politics, which is related in large part to our early adoption of universal male suffrage, helped to prevent the emergence of a moderate rhetoric in political life. Almost from the start of democratic politics in America, the political machines were led by professional politicians, many of who, were of lower middle class or even poorer origins, who had to appeal to a relatively uneducated electorate. This led to the development of a campaign style in which any tactic that would win votes was legitimate.
>
> (Lipset, 1955, p. 180)

Lipset's argument quite obviously breathes an aristocratic spirit itself. Yet, there is no reason to assume that aristocracy with its refined manners was the spearhead of democracy. Rather, for all classes the transformation to democracy impelled the invention of democratic rules and procedures and the development of a 'democratic habitus' for 'civilised' political behaviour that both are results of long learning processes in societies. Of course, the preconditions were distributed unequally across the social classes of any single society (Eder, 1991), but this did not make aristocrats or the bourgeoisie fervent proponents of democracy. People of higher status who were used to ruling had to learn to adjust to arguing and giving reasons for their political interests while the working class had to learn to use the mandate and ways of organising around political ideas when they finally won the universal male suffrage, as pointed out by T.H. Marshall (1950).[1]

The revolutionary and violent ways of giving birth to early democratic forms of politics show that 'the initial framework in which democratically legitimated power is to be created is not enacted democratically' (Linz, 1996, p. 10) and, as Claus Offe (1998) added, that a democratic regime cannot be established by the use of democratic means. I follow this line of reasoning by pushing the Linz/Offe argument a bit further. If it is convincing that neither the democratic framework nor the democratic regime itself can be established by democratic means, it then becomes simply implausible to assume that democratic politics would emerge rapidly after violent or revolutionary upheaval had ended. Rather, in a long process, all political actors had to learn and get used to procedures that worked as a framework to balance contradictory interests, to accept rules and regulations of decision-making, to accept being outvoted and so forth. Democratic civility, as we see today in populists' racist, anti-Muslim or misogynist outbursts, can never be taken for granted.

To argue this way rejects two familiar but implausible ideas. First, neither the French Revolution nor the American Revolution instantaneously realised the idea of democracy in a modern conception of the idea. Rather, both regimes institutionalised populist regimes that only gradually could be transformed into democracies. What had been fought out violently by violent revolutionary processes (Tilly, 2002) only opened the perspective for democratic regimes to emerge slowly over time. In the short term, winners and losers of revolutionary transformation were certainly still in a belligerent state of mind. How should democracy immediately emerge from this situation?

Second, there is good reason to assume that because of the deep social distortions before democratic revolutions and because of the collective experiences in violent revolutionary struggles the subsequent hostile attitudes within society promoted not democratic consensus but highly exclusionary strategies. Thus, populism preceded the emergence of democratic politics and it played a critical role in its formation.

One of the major consequences of the two great democratic revolutions were populist struggles over different definitions of 'the people', to be sure a deeply 'undemocratic' means that is in no way reminiscent of civilised deliberation and decision-making. Democratic debate in today's sense only developed gradually over time and during processes of an emerging public sphere and establishment of institutions of representative democracy. Therefore, apart from sheer violence, a politics of pitting people, statuses or classes against one another has been an important obstetrician of the two first democracies, during both the French and the American revolution, that re-emerges after society's transformation in the form of still (pre-)democratic populism.

Two conceptions of 'the people'

As it is with the rise of modern democracy that 'the people' are addressed for the first time as the very subject that at once legitimates authority and in whose name it is exercised, initial steps toward a sociological conceptualisation of populism start here, as both social phenomena refer fundamentally to 'the people'. In order to elaborate on *how* they are intrinsically linked and how this came about in the historical process, I follow Michael Mann (2005) whose main argument is clearcut:

> Democracy means rule by the people. But in modern times *the people* has come to mean two things. The first is what the Greek meant by their word *demos*. This means the ordinary people, the mass of the population. So democracy is rule by the ordinary people, the mass of the population. But in our civilization the people also means 'nation' or another Greek term, *ethnos*, an ethnic group – a people that shares a common culture and sense of heritage, distinct from other peoples. But if the people is to rule in its own nation-state, and if the people is defined in ethnic terms, then its ethnic unity may outweigh the kind of citizen diversity that is central to democracy.
>
> (Mann, 2005, p. 3)

The distinction between *demos* and *ethnos* serves as the starting point for distinguishing a liberal and an organic version of democracy that allows understanding of two different conceptions of democracy.

The liberal and organic versions of democracy

Mann argues that in the face of the different meanings of *demos* and *ethnos,* two different conceptions of 'the people' can be distinguished: 'a *stratified* and an *organic* people' (Mann, 2005, p. 55). While the first stresses *differences within the people*, the state's duty is to mediate between their different interests; the latter views the *people as an organic whole*, as indivisible.

The *liberal* version of 'We the people' that emerged in North-western Europe stresses individual and human rights but more recently also 'the rights and regulations of groups' (56). Social class played the most critical role due to the emerging capitalist class system, thereby creating a socially stratified people. Inevitably, the dominance of class created well-known rifts in modern societies, such as left versus right, or religious versus secular (56). Finally, age and gender followed as critical dimensions of inclusion in the sections of society that were entitled to vote. Yet this did not create a people as an organic whole since class, age, and gender all point to ongoing stratifications in society.

The *organic* version of 'We the people' emerged in Central Europe, given the dominance of empires (Austria, Russia, and Turkey) with a culturally diverse populace. In this context critical developments allowed nationalist movements to override class movements. Aspirations to democracy appeared later when the view that the people as a whole should rule had become common; the state as bearer of a moral project defended a specific conception of 'the good life', and multi-ethnic populations were predominant in the existing empires. Thus, social classes were at once ethnically impregnated. As 'subordinate classes began to demand political representation, this became entwined with imperial versus proletarian conflicts' (62). Consequently, we can see the same process at the other end of the social hierarchy:

Disprivileged elites initially claimed representative rights only for themselves, as in the Northwest earlier. But faced with pressure from below, they began to speak in the name of 'the whole' people against the imperial ethnicity and its local clients. (62)

Against the background of this historic perspective, that allows one to distinguish two conceptions of democracy on the basis of two different conceptions of 'We the people', it becomes obvious that it makes no sense to conceive populism as a pre-modern phenomenon if we want to come to terms with how it operates today. It is only when the people begin to play a critical role in politics that they can be addressed by populism. This does not happen until a context of modern democracy emerges that addresses the people and draws their legitimation by referring to a hypothetical common will.

This nexus means that populism cannot be conceived as a political or social reaction against democratic politics within developed democratic systems. Rather, populism comes first. It not only precedes modern democracy, but it also serves as a critical aspect of its foundation because 'the people' become the addressee of politics long before democratic institutions and procedures are in place. Thus, populism not only precedes modern democratic deliberation; rather, it paves its way and turns into a constitutive feature of democracy.

'We the people' in the great democratic revolutions

During the French Revolution that propagated the modern core values of 'liberty, equality and brotherhood', the revolutionaries, including Jean-Paul Marat who turned out to be the most radical and bloodthirsty and at once the self-declared '*ami du peuple*', usually addressed 'the people' in their speeches, circular letters, or publications. One might say that they spoke in the name of approximately 98 percent of the French who belonged to the extremely heterogeneous and powerless third estate. The foundation of American democracy is no less based on explicit populist convictions, albeit in a different way. When the Founding Fathers met to proclaim the famous 'We the people', unlike the French revolutionaries, they addressed only a small proportion of the people. Only 55 white men, all of them representatives of the highest social rank, property owners, some of them even slaveholders, claimed to be those who should rule in the name of the people. In fact, this conception of democratic rule does not really fit modern ideas of democratic equality since the 'Founding Fathers did not mean to include women, slaves, and Native Americans. Most of them did not want to include white men who lacked property, though they were pushed towards this by the revolutionary process surging around them' (Mann, 2005, p. 56).

Although both versions of democracy are *speaking on behalf of the people* with regard to the important democratic ideal of equality, there are significant differences. During the French Revolution, the revolutionaries developed radical ideas of equality in the name of the utmost part of the people belonging to the lower estates and, in fact, they demanded replacing the privileges of the few with equal rights for all. Contrary to this emphatic idea of democracy, the Founding Fathers imposed a very specific conception of all men being equal that defended possession and higher rank as a God-given natural and legitimate foundation of democracy.

Both democratic revolutions referred to the *problem of inequality* – the first taking it as the very reason for upheaval, the latter concealing it. However, they both propagated *highly exclusive models of 'democracy'* by either excluding a small group, finally sending them to the guillotine, or by excluding the vast majority from political participation. Thus, in a sense, both democratic revolutions were based on exploiting the idea of 'the people'. However, while to this day the American model sticks to its allegedly revolutionary idea of possessive individualism as the very core of its version of modern democracy (Macpherson, 1967), the French revolutionary example changed. Ultimately, it followed the Western European model and developed a system that accepts both considerable social inequality and the unequal distribution of wealth by at once, providing services through the institutions of the welfare state.

However, this is only part of the story. In both democratic revolutions, not only did social inequality and, consequently, internal social stratification play a critical role but also strategies of argumentation and patterns of justification resulting from a conception of the people as a whole. Brubaker (1992) has shown that the French Revolution not only declared the rights of man and the citizen but also reinforced the boundaries with France's neighbouring nations and states, thereby constructing a French people that as a whole distanced itself from 'the other' on the grounds of nationalist sentiments. While this may still seem to be in line with ideas of the French Revolution, we can see how easily French colonialism was able to refer to this distinction and oppose 'the French' and 'the uncivilised'.

As far as the American Revolution is concerned, this is no less obvious. When the American Founding Fathers presumed to speak on behalf of all Americans, in fact they were representing a privileged group against the background of a *socially highly stratified* American people. However, as the country was in fact settled by Native Americans, Thomas Jefferson was easily able to use different tactics

'We the people' 97

by addressing the people as a whole that he now interpreted *organically*. A slave owner himself, on the subject of the conflicts between the new settlers and the legitimate inhabitants of the continent, he simply declared to be even ready to commit genocide:

> If ever we are constrained to lift the hatchet against any tribe, we shall never lay it down till that tribe is *exterminated*, or driven beyond the Mississippi. ... In war, they will kill some of *us*; we shall *destroy* all of *them*.
> (Thomas Jefferson, cited in Mann, 2005, p. 70)[2]

Following Mann's convincing historical arguments about the emergence of the different conceptions of 'We the people' I suggest distinguishing between different versions of populism.

Liberal and organic populism

There are two forms of *liberal populism*: economic and cultural, reflecting the deep division within liberalism itself (Hirschman, 1977; Macpherson, 1977). On the one hand, *economic liberal populism* today is pursued by those who profit from neo-liberal economics by enjoying tax cuts, tax loopholes, as so on. This form of liberal populism focuses on struggles for redistribution and is aimed directly at those who suffer from neo-liberalism's propagating an anti-social – at times social Darwinist – conception of society. On the other hand, as a strategy used by those who believe that pluralisation in modern democratic societies has gone too far, *cultural liberal populism* targets individual rights, cultural pluralism, and religious heterogeneity and the recognition, respect, or tolerance of cultural and religious minorities. At times, this form of populism is no less social Darwinist as this strategy not only exposes the problems of difference but either claims clear-cut hierarchies of skin colour, religion, gender, descent and so on, or argues in favour of their subjugation or even eradication. *Organic populism*, in contrast, is radically *essentialist* in character. The conception of the people as an ethnic whole leaves virtually no room for rational discourse but aims directly at marginalising or expelling those who disturb the alleged unity of a people.

Organic populism and cultural liberal populism overlap as minorities in all guises are under threat of becoming the target of these strategies. However, the latter tends to be extreme and more at risk of developing into life threatening strategies against those who are not accepted to be part of the people. In fact, there is a critical difference between populist debate about the veil, mosques, or religious practices such as circumcision that emerges against an *internal* 'other', and calls for driving all Muslims out of the United States, France, the UK, Germany, and Hungary referring to some 'other' that should allegedly be *outside* the community.

We can see both forms (and three versions) of populism as *political strategies for purity*. From this perspective, regardless of whether it is in its organic or liberal form – populism is the first step toward unleashing the 'dark side of democracy' that need not necessarily develop into violent action against minorities or, generally, 'the other'. Populism as a political strategy is therefore *highly exclusionary* toward those who, in the view of its proponents, do not belong to either conception of 'the people'. However, it is at once *highly inclusive* in the sense of aiming to construct a coherent 'we'. This reference to the *theory of social closure* needs further elaboration as it helps to reveal the complex ways in which populism operates.

Populism as a political strategy: the politics of social closure

What does it mean to view populism as a deliberate exclusionary strategy? As both conceptions of 'We the people' under certain circumstances trigger exclusionary populist strategies, it may be a fruitful sociological contribution to the debate on populism to analyse them against the background of the 'theory of social closure' (Mackert, 2012; Murphy, 1984; 1988; Parkin, 1974; 1979; Weber, [1922] 1978). First, in both cases – be it *internal* social stratification or the clear demarcation of the whole people against the *external* 'other' (that, unfortunately, may also live within this people's society, for instance, as religious minorities) – *boundaries* have to be drawn, *identities* have to be defined, and *communities* have to be built. Second, as neither form of society or community can be built or exist without enacting processes of social closure, populist strategies necessarily operate as exclusionary in defining who is 'in' and who is 'out', albeit differently, depending on the conception of 'We the people' that dominates their strategies.

Basic elements of social closure: boundaries, identity, and community

Regardless of whether the criterion is being a member of a social category, stratum or class, or of an allegedly organic whole, populism draws clear-cut *boundaries* between those who are in and those who are out. Drawing boundaries has symbolic, social, and at times spatial dimensions that all serve to create identities and, consequently, communities by defining those who belong to 'the people' and those who do not, thereby creating a dividing line between 'us' and 'them'.

Following Lamont and Molnár, we can define *symbolic boundaries* as 'conceptual distinctions made by social actors to categorize objects, people, practices, and even time and space' (Lamont & Molnár, 2002, p. 168). Both versions of populism necessarily draw this type of interpersonal boundaries as they make it possible to categorise those who are different from 'the people'. This happens with processes of social pluralisation that refer to the social stratification of a modern society as well as with their religious, ethnic, or cultural heterogenisation. On the one hand, populism may mobilise against poor, homeless, or rich people; on the other hand, it may construct a boundary that separates sexual minorities, proponents of same-sex marriage, Jews or Muslims, or those with specific lifestyles that do not fit into a clear-cut worldview. In this sense, populist strategies aim at classifying people in order to create categories by which they can be sorted. In a certain sense, these interpersonal symbolic classifications materialize in *social boundaries* that make them socially powerful and effective, as they are 'objectified forms of social differences manifested in unequal access to and unequal distribution of resources (material and nonmaterial) and social opportunities' (168).

As soon as populist praxis and discourse succeed in promoting a kind of *implicit consent* that symbolic boundaries are valid, they can be turned into identifiable patterns of social exclusion, racial or ethnic segregation, religious separation, all of these being boundaries that become relevant with regard to the allocation of resources, life chances, and citizenship rights. Then, populists' critical questions include the following. What kind of rights should certain groups have? What resources should they have? Are their members equals or perhaps second-class citizens? Social boundaries within societies along the lines of social class, strata, milieus, religion, race, ethnicity, gender, and so on then become decisive.

Finally, *spatial boundaries* are the most familiar form of boundaries as they refer to the sovereign border of a national state: 'Borders provide most individuals with a concrete, local, and powerful experience of state, for this is the site where citizenship is strongly enforced (through passport checks, for instance)' (183). In fact, from its origins in the course of the democratic revolutions, populism in both its conceptions has been a national project to date. Thus, sovereign borders play a crucial role in populist strategies. Denying people entry to a sovereign territory or expelling them for various reasons, guaranteeing the safety of national borders by policing them strictly is a basic element of all populist strategies, and in part, with regard to Europe, it explains populists' anti-European stance.

How does this drawing of boundaries refer to identities and community? Being a relational process, the creation of *identity* depends on constructions of 'us' and 'them' that normally go hand in hand with ideas of superiority or even supremacy. All kinds of criteria may play a role in a group believing itself to be superior, be it knowledge (Merton, 1972), possession of property, or rightfully holding positions of power (Scotson & Elias, 1994). Alexander and Smith have shown how these ideas about oneself and others are generalised in the discourse of civil society, creating a clear hierarchy between constructed identities (Alexander & Smith, 1993). Thus, analysing populism in the context of closure theory leads us directly to the main mechanism of creating identities – 'storytelling' (Tilly, 2005). This social mechanism reveals how populists speak about themselves and those they do not perceive as 'true' members of a modern democracy and how they see the relations between themselves and 'the others'. Storytelling is the social process of constructing identities that are organized hierarchically, thus interpreting the distinction between identities, that is, 'us' and 'them', ultimately with serious consequences.

Therefore, processes of social closure referring to different forms of boundaries and allowing for the construction of identities are also crucial for building a *community*. Wimmer (2008) has convincingly shown how, for example, ethnic boundaries are generated by classification struggles between actors, while Hardin, referring to conflicts between social groups, has stressed the significance of exclusionary codes in coming to terms with the dynamics at work. Contrary to universalistic norms, exclusionary norms require a certain degree of group separation. Therefore, 'norms of exclusion' also operate as norms of inclusion, separating both groups from one another (Hardin, 1995). One might say that populists today refer to a universalistic norm in modern democracies, that is, citizenship, thus reinterpreting it in a particularistic sense by using its exclusionary side to deprive constructed non-members from rights, resources, and protection (Walzer, 1983). Against the background of these three analytically distinguishable dimensions of social closure, their relevance for a proper conceptualisation of populism is obvious.

Populism: strategies of social closure

Analysing populism from the perspective of the theory of social closure means seeing it as a political strategy that aims at creating a national community by defining and excluding those who by definition do not belong to it. It develops in contexts of asymmetric opportunity structures advantageous for those who intentionally – and therefore strategically – deploy them in order to push exclusionary politics. Following a clear-cut programme, populism is targeted at the vulnerable in a society, such as Muslims in the face of Islamist terrorism, women in the face of quotas that threaten the dominant position of white men in companies, banks, politics, and so on, or the young in the face of the greying of Western societies. Populism has at least three addressees: first, 'the people', depending on how they are defined, and whom the proponents see as their supporters; second, established politicians whom they claim do not represent the will of the 'people' they constructed; and, third, the vulnerable, who, in a weak and inferior position, have very few opportunities to oppose populist strategies. If, based on this general definition of what it means to view populism as a strategy, we move on to further conceptualising it in the context of closure theory, we see that populism turns out to be a more complex phenomenon.

Following Max Weber's initial definition, social closure is the fundamental process of both 'communal' (*Vergemeinschaftung*) and 'associative' relationships (*Vergesellschaftung*), neither of which would be possible without social closure (Weber, [1922] 1978). Thus, conceiving populism as a strategy of social closure means understanding it as being opposed to any conception of an 'open society' in the sense of being democratic and pluralistic, the consequence being a 'closed society'. Such a society can be called 'closed' against outsiders insofar as, 'according to its subjective meaning and its binding rules, participation of certain persons is *excluded, limited,* or *subjected to conditions*' (43; emphasis added). Weber's concept turns out to be particularly interesting sociologically because considering the feasible extents of exclusion allows for different effects and degrees of populist strategies.

Further, both *openness* and *closeness* may be motivated traditionally, affectually, or rationally in terms of values or expediency (Weber, [1922] 1978). Weber argued that it was the aim of processes of social closure to minimise competitors for economic opportunities, rights, and resources. Populism argues precisely along these lines – although often implicitly – thereby referring to 'some externally identifiable characteristic of another group of (actual or potential) competitors – race, language, religion, local or social origin, descent, residence etc. – as a pretext for attempting their exclusion' (342).

Unfortunately, Weber's concept of social closure remained somewhat rudimentary, particularly as he almost neglected to refer to those being excluded, such as the targets of populism.[3] This important step towards conceptualising social closure as a political process by systematically considering these reactions and elaborating the Weberian approach was taken by Frank Parkin (1974), who developed a kind of general concept that allows an understanding of all kinds of power relations in society (Mackert, 2012).

With regard to populism, it is important to note that Parkin conceptualised social closure as the interplay of strategies of social *exclusion*, enforced by those who attempted to reserve rights, resources, and privileges for their own group. Conversely, those suffering from being excluded had the option of using strategies of *usurpation*, thus endeavouring to be included again, to be able to participate, to enjoy the same rights, to have a fair share of resources, and so on.[4] Extending the concept in this way transformed social closure from a narrow concept into a general approach for the analysis of all kinds of power relations in societies. However, for the debate on populism as a strategy of social closure from Parkin's numerous elaborations, there are two elements that are critical as they allow us to come to terms with different social phenomena, among them populism, in a new way.

First, Parkin stresses the critical role of the state in modern societies with regard to closure struggles, thereby pointing to a critical weakness in Weber's claim, namely, that closure may take *any* trait of a social group to enforce that very group's exclusion. Rather, Parkin argues that any exclusion of social groups takes up this group's legal subordination that has been enacted by the state:

> In all known instances where racial, religious, linguistic, or sex characteristics have been seized upon for closure purposes the group in question has already at some time been defined as legally inferior by the state. Ethnic subordination, to take the commonest case, has normally occurred as a result of territorial conquest or the forced migration of populations creating a subcategory of second-class citizens within the nation-state.
>
> (Parkin, 1979, pp. 95–96)

If we think about this claim in relation to populism, we see that the modern liberal-democratic state cannot be conceptualised simply as the counterpart to populism. Quite the contrary, democratic politics and state activities are part of emerging populist strategies as they both prepare the ground for it to flourish.

Second, we have to elaborate on Parkin's argument that in advanced capitalist societies not only private property but also credentialism operate as dominant strategies of closure. While Parkin, in order to overcome Marxist orthodoxy, saw both criteria as equally important and decisive for powerful exclusion, it was Raymond Murphy who disagreed with this argument and who offered his own conception in that he differentiated between *principal*, *derivative*, and *contingent* forms of exclusion (Murphy, 1984, pp. 555–557; Murphy, 1988).[5] This is an important critique but in order to come to terms with populism, I propose following the ideas of both Parkin and Murphy but introduce different terms here. I argue that populism as a strategy employs different versions of exclusionary politics that we can define as *dominant*, *secondary*, and *third* forms. To sum up the advantages of conceiving populism as a strategy of social closure, we can list at least five critical aspects:

- Populism by exerting social closure refers to spatial boundaries and constructs symbolic boundaries that turn out to be effective as social boundaries
- Making reference to and creating different types of boundaries, populism generates identities and communities by excluding clearly defined social groups
- Populism as a political strategy exerts different degrees of exclusion and can be distinguished according to the different types of underlying motivation
- Exclusionary politics of the democratic state lay the ground for the rise of populism that profits from precedent stigmatisation or legal subordination of different groups of the population
- As populism comes in two versions, liberal (economic and cultural) and organic, these employ different dominant forms. This distinction between dominant forms has to be complemented by secondary and third forms that can all come into play whenever populism implements politics of closure.

Populism as highly variable and context-sensitive

Conceiving populism as a political strategy against the background of closure theory allows us to dispel much of the confusion about the phenomenon itself. In order to have a clear picture, we can look at some figures that may help us coming to terms with the variability and context-sensitivity of populism.

Figure 6.1 presents organic and liberal populism as bend points on a continuum. Using the criteria 'homogeneity' and 'internal social stratification', we can distinguish between both versions of populism but at the same time it becomes obvious that populists in both camps need not restrict their tactics only to the critical aspect of the form of populism they strategically pursue. Rather, the figure makes it obvious that organic and liberal populism are not mutually exclusive as populist strategies. On this continuum, we can imagine various ways of combining them, one being more dominant than another. If we look at Marine Le Pen's recent strategy of addressing the French nation as a whole in order to stop migration, while resorting to the economic liberal version of populism when discussing problems of poverty, we see the variability of adopting populist strategies and employing them tactically with regard to specific topics, aims, or addressees.

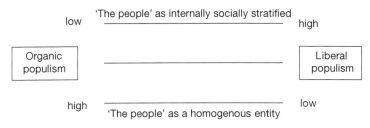

Figure 6.1 The continuum of manifestations of the two versions of populism

Figure 6.2 refers exclusively to the two versions of liberal populism. Again, we have a continuum that is characterized by economic liberal populism and cultural liberal populism as endpoints that only refer to extreme forms of liberal populism. While we can find a combination of both strategies in almost any democratic party, it becomes most obvious in liberal parties, as this differentiation makes it conceivable that liberalism is in itself a contradictory political program. While in times of embedded liberalism, liberal parties may have succeeded in performing a kind of balancing act by demanding economic liberties while at the same time making strong pleas for the basic civil rights of the individual, inclusion and pluralism, this is no longer possible today. After more than three decades of neoliberal transformation not only of the globe but also of classic liberal parties, we see that there is not much left besides the program of possessive liberalism.

On the grounds of these distinctions and the idea of seeing pure forms of populism only as the extreme on a continuum, Figure 6.3 presents the field of populist politics as a *heuristic concept* that allows us to understand why – to this day – populism is also a (possible) strategy to be used by democratic parties that are apparently interested in and leaning toward inclusionary politics. If we take 'social democracy' as an umbrella term that covers various forms of democratic politics, it is clear that by moving away from their noble objective to pursue politics of social inclusion, the 'social democrats' necessarily enter the field of populist politics.

Contrasting the two (basic) versions of populism ('exclusionary' political strategies and social democracy as an ideally 'inclusivist' form of politics), we see

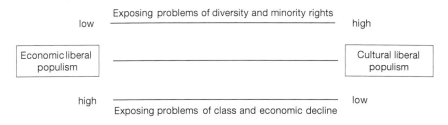

Figure 6.2 The continuum of manifestations of liberal populism

104 Jürgen Mackert

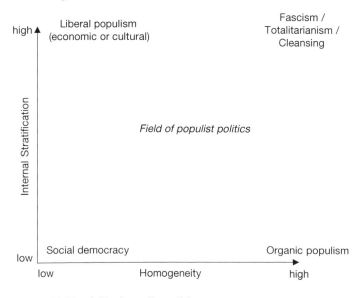

Figure 6.3 The field of populist politics

a broad field of potentially populist politics within which dominant, secondary, and third forms of closure politics can be pursued. Tony Blair and Gerhard Schröder's (1998) *Third Ways* is a case in point. By blaming the victims of the consequences of their neo-liberal politics, they both used the strategy of economic liberal populism, stressing internal social stratification by either forcing individuals to be self-reliant or exposing the unemployed to severe attacks by insulting them and criticising them for spending their lives in the hammock of the welfare state, at the expense of the hard-working middle-classes. With their politics, they both moved from the area of social democracy up toward a form of liberal economic populism. This leads us to the final point as we need to take a closer look at the tactics of combining all possible forms of exclusionary populist politics.

Tactics of adopting dominant, secondary and third strategies

This possibility of combining strategies as critical tactics of populism appears to be one of the main reasons why it is so difficult to come to terms with the allegedly 'chameleonic character' of populism. By looking at the ways in which populist parties or leaders employ these tactics, the theory of social closure shows that they are not just an amalgamation of strategies but that we can differentiate between them by distinguishing between dominant, secondary, and third strategies. Looking at Donald Trump's electoral campaign makes the argument plausible:

Given that the US represents a thoroughly liberal democracy, Trump's populism is essentially an *economic liberal populism* that takes up economic misery as the *dominant strategy*. This strategy makes it possible to mobilise a desperate white lower-middle class, angry white men confronted with flagging industry who do not see any future in their current jobs and who feel they have been left behind by politics. Obviously, they have proven to be unable to keep up with the pace of social change. They are suffering from the consequences of a globalised economy that Trump then cites as the very reason why jobs are being lost and this serves as the lynchpin for announcing the need to 'make America great again'.

As the economic descent of the white working class goes hand in hand with its social insignificance and an assumed cultural marginalisation, *cultural liberal populism* comes into play and operates as a *secondary strategy*: the perceived loss of masculinity (Roose, 2017) and the assumed dominance and gaining of rights by women and many cultural groups. This strategy aims at scandalising the loss of white male supremacy in the face of a growing religious heterogeneity, particularly the presence of Islam, and social pluralism, including issues such as women's rights, same-sex marriage, and rights for sexual minorities.

There are also references to *organic populism* as a *third strategy* that comes into play by opposing the American people as a whole against the Mexicans, who as a group are defamed as illegals, rapists, or individuals living at the expense of Americans – without any reference to the people's internal stratification.

The tactics of intermingling these three forms of populism amount to a politics of closure. Trump's campaign has proven to be highly exclusionary, using economic liberal, cultural liberal, and organic populism to construct boundaries, create identities and communities that operate by opposing a constructed 'us' against a constructed 'them' – but as becomes evident from the different strategies, this happened in multiple ways. A *dominant economic liberal populist form* opposes typical losers of economic change against those who profit from it, that is, Wall Street. It is irrelevant that Trump himself is a millionaire as he gives the white working-class a voice that they urgently need in the fight for jobs. By focusing on this group, *cultural liberal populism* as a *secondary populist form* opposes and defends traditional masculinity against women and people of different sexual orientations.

Hope – ironically a core concept of Obama's campaign in 2008 but now being directed at another section of the population – plays a crucial role here, as 'making America great again' not only means bringing jobs back to a desperate group of voters but also restoring clear-cut symbolic boundaries between men and women and the social roles they have to play. As this type of social model implies a conservative worldview, cultural liberal populism also opposes white workers against immigrants, Muslims, Jews, gays and lesbians to create more social boundaries. Finally, playing the card of *organic populism* as the *third populist form* by citing the Mexican border as a problem to be addressed adds a spatial boundary to the mix. This allows Trump to create an inclusionary conception of a homogenous American people that has to be protected from a purported Mexican invasion. Here, extreme exclusion is propagated as the alleged solution to many problems.

Of course, Trump's campaign was easily able to pick up on a long-lasting tradition of legal subordination of, for example, Latin American immigrants who are denied the opportunity of naturalisation although they contribute to the US economy to a considerable extent. As closure theory shows, populism does not emerge from nowhere but, as a constitutive feature of democracy, it can be activated, one trigger being the legal subordination of minorities in a democratic system that has itself been fundamentally transformed by both neo-liberalism and – in the European case – de-democratisation in the classic sense by Europeanisation (Münch, 2017).

Yet there is also another side to the story. White working-class men have been neglected by mainstream politics for decades, deprived of their jobs and future hopes, estranged from unions that have been under enormous pressure for a long time now, and they have been facing profound cultural challenges calling into question their cultural values. Now they have proven to be the very group that turned the tables. Thus, it becomes obvious that democratic politics would have been wise not to subjugate and misjudge a considerable section of the population. In a way, considering the decades-long decline of the white working-class only shows that democracy always necessarily has a populist element to it, as this group was left behind by democratic politics, no less than Blacks or the poor victims of Hurricane Katrina (Somers, 2008). As I argued above, in a historical perspective, populism precedes institutionalised democratic politics that aims at social inclusion. Yet, after democracy has been established, populism does not just disappear completely. It remains an element of democracy that, under conditions and contexts that no longer adhere to the aim of developing inclusion in societies, in supranational entities such as the European Union, or on a global scale with regard to the effects of both geo-politics and/or world trade, can still be activated and become dominant. Even if it were only targeted against refugees and the wretched of the earth, this would still hold true.

Conclusion

Recent research on populism has brought forth many interesting findings on its effects on democratic political systems, its effects on both governments and the electorate, its being conceptualized as an ideology, and so forth. Yet the social sciences have so far neglected both a historical view and a comparative perspective on the social phenomenon. In this article, I have attempted to develop both. First, I suggested seeing populism as a constitutive part of modern democracy that preceded institutionalised democratic politics, which still had to be developed after the two great democratic revolutions. Second, I proposed an analytical frame of two versions (albeit three forms) of populism, each characterised by specific dynamics of exclusion that allow us to construct a social space in which political manifestations of populism can be located.

This call to open the debate on populism for sociological as well as comparative historical research would enable a deeper understanding of the *longue durée* of populism in the history of modern democracy, the causes that can still trigger it to this day, and a deeper understanding of the different manifestations of the phenomenon we see now that cannot adequately be captured by political-normative concepts such as left-wing or right-wing populism.

Notes

1 However, Marshall only refers to the latter aspect. To him, as for liberals in general, from Jeremy Bentham and John Stuart Mill to their successors, it seems to be self-evident that the noble man knows how to behave democratically.
2 We now know that the Mississippi was not the frontier that protected Native Americans from being almost completely extinguished by genocide by white settlers. However, Jefferson's populist discourse and announced practice show that populist strategies, regardless of which conception of 'We the people' they are based on, can both serve as a starting point and prepare the ground for a development toward genocide.
3 Weber only referred to the excluded by arguing that exclusion 'may provoke a corresponding reaction on the part of those against whom it is directed'; see Weber, [1922] 1978, p. 342.
4 This article does not focus on the options or possible strategies of the victims of populism. Closure theory can certainly be related to this, too, but as I am interested primarily in coming to terms with how populism can be understood and how it operates, I restrict my discussion to those who enact closure. However, according to my definition of populism as inherently exclusionary, 'left-wing populism' is a misnomer in established democratic systems. Rather, this type of politics is oriented toward economic inclusion and should be seen as a counter strategy to socio-economic exclusion.
5 Again, I will not go deeper into Murphy's highly interesting analysis as I am only concerned with reconstructing the general foundations of closure theory that helps us to come to terms with populism as a strategy.

References

Abbott, A. (2001). *Time matters: On theory and method*. Chicago, IL: The University of Chicago Press.

Alexander, J. C., & Smith, P. (1993). The discourse of American civil society: A new proposal for cultural studies. *Theory and Society, 22*(2), 151–207.

Blair, T., & Schröder, G. (1998). *Europe: A third way/Die Neue Mitte*. South Africa: Friedrich Ebert Foundation.

Brown, W. (2003). Neo-liberalism and the end of liberal democracy. *Theory and Event, 7*. Retrieved from https://muse.jhu.edu/article/48659.

Brown, W. (2015). *Undoing the demos: Neoliberalism's stealth revolution*. Cambridge and London: Zone Books.

Brown, W. (2016). Sacrificial citizenship: Neoliberalism, human capital, and austerity politics. *Constellations, 23*(1), 3–14.

Brubaker, R. (1992). *Citizenship and nationhood in France and Germany*. Harvard, MA: Harvard University Press.

Eder, K. (1991). *Geschichte als Lernprozeß? Zur Pathogenese politischer Modernität in Deutschland*. Frankfurt am Main: Suhrkamp.

Hardin, R. (1995). *One for all: The logic of group conflict*. Princeton, NJ: Princeton University Press.

Hirschman, A. O. (1977). *The passion and the interests: Political arguments for capitalism before its triumph*. Princeton, NJ: Princeton University Press.

Lamont, M., & Molnár, V. (2002). The study of boundaries in the social sciences. *Annual Review of Sociology, 28*, 167–195.

Linz, J. J. (1996). *Democratization and types of democracy: New tasks for comparativists*. Mimeo, NY: Yale University.

Mackert, J. (2012). Social closure. In J. Manza (Ed.), *Oxford bibliographies online*. Oxford: Oxford University Press.

Mackert, J., & Turner, B. S. (2017). Citizenship and its boundaries. In J. Mackert & B. S. Turner (Eds.), *The transformation of citizenship. Volume 2: Boundaries of inclusion and exclusion* (pp. 1–14). London: Routledge.

Macpherson, C. B. (1967). *The political theory of possessive individualism: Hobbes to Locke*. Oxford: Oxford University Press.

Macpherson, C. B. (1977). *The life and times of liberal democracy*. Oxford: Oxford University Press.

Mair, P. (2013). *Ruling the void: The hollowing of Western democracy*. London: Verso.

Mann, M. (2005). *The dark side of democracy: Explaining ethnic cleansing*. Cambridge: Cambridge University Press.

Marshall, T. H. (1950). Citizenship and social class. In T. H. Marshall (Ed.), *Citizenship and social class and other essays* (pp. 1–85). Cambridge: Cambridge University Press.

Merton, R. K. (1972). Insiders and outsiders: A chapter in the sociology of knowledge. *American Journal of Sociology*, 78(1), 9–47.

Münch, R. (2017). European citizenship between cosmopolitan outlook and national solidarities. In J. Mackert & B.S. Turner (Eds.), *The transformation of citizenship. Volume 2: Boundaries of inclusion and exclusion* (pp. 169–191). London: Routledge.

Murphy, R. (1984). The structure of closure: A critique and development of the theories of Weber, Collins and Parkin. *British Journal of Sociology*, 35(4), 547–567.

Murphy, R. (1988). *Social closure: The theory of monopolization and exclusion*. Oxford: Clarendon Press.

Offe, C. (1998). 'Homogeneity' and constitutional democracy: Coping with identity conflicts through group rights. *The Journal of Political Philosophy*, 6(2), 113–141.

Parkin, F. (1974). Strategies of social closure in class formation. In F. Parkin (Ed.), *The social analysis of class structure* (pp. 1–18). London: Tavistock.

Parkin, F. (1979). *Marxism and class theory: A bourgeois critique*. London: Tavistock.

Roose, J. M. (2017). Citizenship, masculinities and political populism: Preliminary considerations in the context of contemporary social challenges. In J. Mackert & B. S. Turner (Eds.), *The transformation of citizenship. Volume 2: Boundaries of inclusion and exclusion* (pp. 56–76). London: Routledge.

Scotson, J. L., & Elias, N. (1994). *The established and the outsiders: A sociological enquiry into community problems*. London and Thousand Oaks: Sage.

Somers, M. R. (2008). *Genealogies of citizenship: Markets, statelessness, and the right to have rights*. Cambridge: Cambridge University Press.

Tilly, C. (2000). Processes and mechanisms of democratization. *Sociological Theory*, 18(1), 1–16.

Tilly, C. (2005). *Identities, boundaries and social ties*. Boulder, CO: Paradigm.

Vogl, J. (2014). The sovereignty effect: Market and power in the economic regime. *Qui Parle: Critical Humanities and Social Sciences*, 23(1), 125–155.

Walzer, M. (1983). *Spheres of justice: A defense of pluralism and equality*. New York: Basic Books.

Weber, M. ([1922] 1978). In G. Roth & C. Wittich (Eds.), *Economy and society: An outline of interpretive sociology*. Berkeley, CA: University of California Press.

Weber, M. ([1920] 2001)). *The protestant ethic and the spirit of capitalism*. London and New York: Routledge.

Wimmer, A. (2008). The making and unmaking of ethnic boundaries: A multilevel process theory. *American Journal of Sociology*, 113(4), 970–1022.

7 Past is prologue
Electoral events of spring 2012 and the old 'new' nationalism in post-security Europe

Mabel Berezin

Introduction

In April 2012, the French Socialist Party candidate, François Hollande came in first in the first round of the Presidential election. Two weeks later, French citizens elected Hollande their President. As only the second Socialist since François Mitterrand's 1985 election to obtain the presidency, Hollande's victory set off a night of celebration on the streets of Paris. The dark side of the Left's victory was the third-place finish of Marine Le Pen, the Presidential candidate of the National Front – France's long-standing right nationalist party. On the same day as the second round of the French Presidential election, a neo-Nazi party the *Golden Dawn* appeared virtually out of nowhere to become contenders for seats in the Greek parliament.

In between the French and Greek elections, the Dutch Prime Minister dissolved Parliament and called for new elections. The Dutch dissolution, less noticed than the French or Greek results in the international press, was important because it appeared to signal the end of political influence for Geert Wilders – the anti-Islamic, Eurosceptic head of the right nationalist Freedom Party (*Partij voor de Vrijheid*, PVV). Alarmed headlines such as: 'Golden Dawn and the Rise of Fascism'; 'Europe on the Verge of a Nervous Breakdown; Are we on the brink of repeating the catastrophe of the 1930s?' or 'Hitler Who?' began to emerge in the international press.

By spring 2012, three years of economic crisis and austerity had generated anti-Europe sentiment among ordinary citizens and contributed to what politicians, pundits and even social scientists described as a surprising electoral presence of the populist nationalist right. The recidivist nationalist political parties that dominated the spring 2012 electoral events shared a desire to exit the Eurozone and to turn the clock back on, if not the entire post-war period, much that had occurred after 1979 when the post-war social contract along with post-war prosperity began to unravel (Eichengreen, 2007). From the avowedly neo-Nazi Greek *Golden Dawn* to the French *National Front*, parties of various nationalist and conservative stripes promote a backward- rather than forward-looking vision across Europe.

In spring 2012, the Euro was heading towards its umpteenth crisis since the May 2010 bailout talks began. Unemployment was at 11.4 per cent for adults and 23 per cent for youth (job seekers under age 25) in the Eurozone (Eurostat, 2017). Public expectations that the June 2012 European summit that produced a 'Compact for Jobs and Growth' would offer workable solutions to the crisis were low (EUCO, 2012a). The spring 2012 national elections forced politicians and citizens to question whether the Euro was sustainable. In addition, these elections shattered European and global public perceptions that the Eurozone occupied a forward-looking and democratic collective political space. The escalating European sovereign debt crisis challenged the hope of a Europe of 'common values' and dream of a 'constitutional patriotism' (Müller, 2007) that would provide the economic union with a scaffold of civic solidarity.

This chapter argues that fault lines and *lacunae* in the European project as it evolved, since the 1992 Maastricht Treaty that promoted accelerated integration, have provided a powerful opening for the nationalist right to give voice to existent, albeit submerged, collective nationalist ideas and feelings. The elections of spring 2012 constituted a moment that focused public attention on the nationalist right and the defects in the European project. Spring 2012 was also a moment that looking back from the vantage point of today constituted a prologue to electoral events of 2016 and 2017.

The electoral and communicative salience of the European right is the collateral damage of multiple ensuing crises – debt, security, refugee. But in spring 2012, debt and austerity were the salient issues (Blyth, 2013; Kriesi, 2014). The sovereign debt crisis fuelled an unprecedented discussion in the European public sphere that linked economics, culture and morality (Fourcade et al., 2013). Multiple voices addressing multiple publics contributed to this discussion. The nationalist right was a particularly noisy and prominent participant in the public discussion and used the moment of crisis to make electoral gains and to advance its own positions.

This chapter takes as its starting point the spring elections of 2012 and focuses on the period between 2010 and 2012 – the years during which the European debt crisis heated up. The salience of the European nationalist right is a trans-European phenomenon with specific national iterations. This chapter discusses the phenomenon as a whole and marshals evidence from specific instances of the right where appropriate. The chapter's method is narrative and historical – meaning that it pays attention to temporality and sequence as it maps events. The evidence that the chapter deploys to support its claims consists of election results, policy statements, newspaper accounts and political propaganda.

The chapter proceeds in four sections: first, it discusses elections as events; second it maps the electoral salience of the nationalist right and shows the correlation between the rise of the right in five countries and the progress of the debt crisis; third, it examines multiple responses to the debt crisis across a range of public voices. Lastly, the chapter identifies three institutional factors that created a favourable climate for the nationalist right to thrive sufficiently under the policy and media radar screen, so as to appear to have emerged out of nowhere. These institutional factors are: conflicting visions of the meaning of Europe; the durability of the nation-state; and a radical shift in the form and content of security.

Elections as events: focusing collective attention

The political crisis brewing in contemporary Europe coupled with the attendant insertion of right parties into mainstream political processes has deep roots in the *longue durée* of post-war political history more broadly, and European integration history more narrowly. Elections are more than simply temporal occurrences that provide grist for the mill of political statistics and public opinion polls. Recent literature on the intersection of politics and culture (Berezin, 2012; Sewell, 1996; Wagner-Pacifici, 2010) has identified events as *loci* of political meaning.

Sewell defines a historical event as '(1) a ramified sequence of occurrences that (2) is recognized as notable by contemporaries, and that (3) results in a durable transformation of structures' (Sewell, 1996, p. 844). His theory of *events* has several characteristics. Events are the subject of narrative and are recognised as significant when they occur. Events reveal 'heightened emotion'; collective creativity; take ritual form and most importantly – generate more events. For example, Sewell treats the storming of the Bastille as a unitary event that was pivotal to the series of events that constituted the French Revolution. His story of the Bastille depends heavily upon sequencing, but he also uses 'thick description' to embed his analysis in its cultural particularity. His richly contextualised narrative underscores the importance of collective perception, performance and emotion.

Sewell is interested in identifying events that change the course of history. Arguably there are many events, such as elections, that occur and recur in political life that are not as iconic as the storming of the Bastille and that still have importance within a nationally constituted political space. Few events result in a 'durable transformation of structures' (844); but many events, such as elections, are capable of altering collective perceptions. In the realm of politics, *what matters* is as crucial for analysis as *what happened*. Why does meaning suffuse some events more than others? Implicit cultural and political knowledge assigns importance to some events and not others.

Events re-calibrated as 'social facts' serve as conduits to implicit political and cultural meaning. Emile Durkheim described 'social facts' as 'ways of acting, thinking, and feeling that present the noteworthy property of existing outside the individual consciousness' (Durkheim [1895] 1964, p. 2). Social facts include collective phenomena – the law, the economy, the unemployment rate, or in the context of this chapter, elections – as well as the individual and collective perception of them. Thus, Durkheim argues that a 'social fact' is a structural and a psychological fact that goes beyond structure. He labels this combination of material and mental phenomena as 'social currents' and describes them as 'the great movements of enthusiasm, indignation, and pity in a crowd do not originate in any one of the particular individual consciousnesses. They come to each one of us from without and can carry us away in spite of ourselves' (4–5).

It is a short analytic leap from a *social fact* to a *political fact*. Within the realm of cultural analysis, political facts, rather than politics or the polity per se, are social facts that combine emotional valence, collective perception, institutional arrangements – and implicit cultural knowledge. Drawing upon Sewell and Durkheim, Berezin reformulates events as *'templates of possibility that collectivities experience as political facts'* – bounded temporal phenomena that permit publics – 'to see relations and interconnections that link to broader macro and micro level social processes' (Berezin, 2012, p. 620). In this formulation, events are important for *what* they force publics and analysts to imagine – and these imaginings may generate hope as well as fear, comfort as well as threat.

Events speak to collective resonance, present possibilities, and offer visions of possible paths – even if those paths are *not* pursued. *Events* speak to futurity. They make manifest what *might* happen, rather than predict what *will* happen. Public political events, such as the spring 2012 elections, engage the collective imagination and have the capacity to alter public perceptions that *may* in the future alter political actions. Because they make manifest the possible, they have the power to engage collective emotions from fear to collective euphoria and the range of emotions that lay in between these polarities.

Elections, such as the elections of spring 2012, recalibrated as events provide a powerful interpretive lens on political significance. In this context, history and temporality matter. The political landscape upon which extreme nationalist politics emerged extends back to the 1970s and the unravelling of the post-war social contract. In this view, the electoral events of spring 2012 are transition points signalling the end of one stage of a process and the beginning of another.

The European nationalist right from post war to the debt crisis

The elections of spring 2012 solidified and accentuated recidivist nationalist trends that had been part of the European landscape for decades. Political parties that academics today categorize as nationalist and/or right had been in existence since at least the 1970s and some go back further. For example, the Swiss People's Party (SVP) began in 1918. Other parties, such as the Austrian Freedom Party (FPÖ) and Italy's Italian Social Movement Party (MSI) were outgrowths of World War II. The MSI became the National Alliance (AN) in 1995 and has since moved centre right.

Until recently, these parties were more significant for their perceptual impact than their electoral salience, as they rarely became part of governing coalitions. Initially, political analysts focused on the right challenge to social democracy (see Kitschelt, 1995) as opposed to its ethnocentrism or xenophobia which has engaged a newer cohort of analysts (Bale, 2012; Betz, 1994; Mudde, 2007). In general, with some exceptions (Art, 2011; Berezin, 2009), these scholars take a party-centric approach to the study of the right that does not focus upon the historical context in which parties emerged and grew attractive to citizens.

National specificities characterise right parties, yet trans-European generalities are identifiable. The trajectory of right-party salience maps onto shifts in European political economy and European Union development. 'Left-over' right parties such as the MSI in Italy, and agrarian conservatives such as the Danish Progress Party (FP) as well as the newly formed National Front dominated a long post-war period that ended in 1989. In the years between the 1973 Arab oil embargo and the beginning of neo-liberalism in the 1980s, the right had little electoral salience. In the 1990s, the right became more visible, principally but not exclusively around issues of immigration.

The French National Front is a benchmark right party for social scientists. Jean-Marie Le Pen founded the National Front in 1972. Its original animus was directed against Marxists and it had anti-Semitic tendencies. In the 1980s, the National Front became identified as the leading anti-immigrant and xenophobic party in Europe. Restriction of immigration within European national states began in the post-war period and accelerated in the 1960s and 70s when non-European nationals entered the migrant stream.[1] Immigration policy within Europe was built on a post-war European commitment to human rights. Freedom to immigrate and the right to seek asylum were built into Articles 13 and 14 of the UN's 1948 *Declaration of Human Rights*. The moral obligation attached to the right to immigrate encouraged nation-states to move quietly as they began to control the flow of immigration and to tighten borders in the 1980s. While nation-states were designing restrictions on immigration, the European right, led most notably by Jean-Marie Le Pen in France, began its noisy chorus of anti-immigrant rhetoric. Anti-immigrant sentiment and xenophobia became the calling card of the vocal right. For this reason, early social science analysis of the right (Schain, 1996) began with immigration and immigrants as a major causal factor and either ignored or under-emphasised other causal narratives.

The emphasis upon immigration distracted attention from the fact beginning in the late 1990s, the right has increasingly made European integration one of its issues (Berezin, 2009). Immigration may be necessary but it is not sufficient to explain the contemporary salience of the right. As early as 1998, Jean Marie Le Pen in France made Europe the target of his attacks (99–111). In 2002 when Jean-Marie Le Pen came in second place in the first round of the French Presidential election, Europe and its potential dangers occupied a large part of the National Front's political platform. By 2002, even French left parties began what seemed a quixotic and recidivist attack on the accelerating European project that promised benefits for all.

A trans-continental Euro-scepticism, which has increased in recent years as the debt crisis and austerity policies continue, carries an aura of respectability and legitimacy that xenophobia did not. A political party can be anti-Europe without carrying the social and political stigma of being against a person or group. This anti-Europe sentiment that was fuelling the nationalist right hit forcibly in 2005, when both France and the Netherlands within weeks of each other rejected the draft European constitution in popular referenda (167–195).

Strong nationalist tendencies that did not support the continued expansion of Europe and were opposed to European Monetary Union bubbled beneath the surface of European integration. These right voices began to dominate after 2000 and the electoral salience of the right increased. From 2009 when the sovereign debt crisis emerged in response to the first Greek crisis, right parties began to move upward in polls. In some instances, they became part of governing coalitions. Upward movement occurred in countries that one would not expect, such as Sweden and Finland. While this analysis is centred on what used to be Western Europe, recent political developments in Hungary and Poland suggest that the former Eastern Europe has not been immune to this tendency.

In the years between 2009 and spring 2012, there were 16 Parliamentary elections in what was Western Europe. Among these elections, results in Sweden, the Netherlands, Finland and Greece, as well as the French parliamentary and presidential election stand out either because they defy expectations or because they enforce underlying trends. Figure 7.1 maps these trends in these five nation-states and illustrates the right's ascendance is temporarily coincident with the expansion of European Union in the 1990s.[2] The graph traces the showing of the right in national parliamentary elections, beginning in 1970. The vertical bars represent periods in European political and economic development. With the exception of the National Front, which begins to ascend in the mid-1980s, the other right parties do not start to achieve electoral salience until after the year 2000, and the big jump occurs after 2010. These five cases were abstracted from a larger database that mapped these trends for a total of fifteen national-states. For reasons of visual clarity, we limited Figure 7.1 to the five nation states that drew

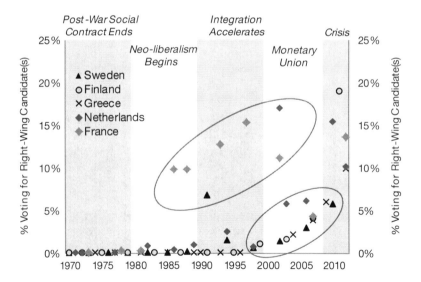

Figure 7.1 Trajectory of right electoral salience 1970–2012; selected countries
Source: Mackie and Rose (1991) and NSD (2017).

particular attention between 2010 and 2012. The overall trajectory does not depart from the trends that Figure 7.1 maps.

On June 9, 2010, Geert Wilder's PVV came in third place with 15.45 per cent of the vote in the Dutch parliamentary elections. In this election Wilders, who is known for his support of free market capitalism and his virulent campaign against Islam in the Netherlands, earned a place for himself and his party in the Dutch governing coalition. On September 19, 2010 a Swedish right populist party, the *Swedish Democrats*, received 5.7 per cent of the vote, which made the party eligible for a seat in the Congress. The Swedish Democrats decorated their campaign mailings with blue and yellow flowers – the colours of the Swedish flag. 'Safety and Tradition' was their motto. 'Give us Sweden back!' was their *cri de coeur*. On April 2011, the Finnish populist party *True Finns* received 19 per cent of the vote in the Parliamentary Election. This percentage provides a sharp contrast to the 4.1 per cent that they received in the 2007 Parliamentary election. In 2011, the *True Finns* received the same percentage of votes as the Social Democrats (19 per cent) and a percentage point less than the Liberal Conservatives (20 per cent).

The 2012 Greek parliamentary elections held on the same day as the second round of the French presidential election initially received minor attention in international media. Greece was waiting for a bailout and struggling with its national iteration of austerity. By the day of the election, the central question in Greece was whether the Socialist party (*PASOK*) would oust the *New Democracy* austerity-focused/Germany-friendly centre right ruling party in Greece. The Greek elections defied expectations as citizens voted against mainstream parties and supported extreme left and extreme right anti-austerity and anti-Europe parties. The extreme left Syriza party received 16.8 per cent of the vote in the first electoral round and polled second behind *New Democracy*.

The avowedly neo-Nazi *Golden Dawn* party polled 7 per cent of the vote – enough to make it a contender in the second-round elections held on June 17. The success of the *Golden Dawn* served to focus the attention of European policy makers and the media on the second round of the Greek parliamentary elections. On June 17, 2012, the *Golden Dawn* polled 6.9 per cent of the vote and acquired 18 seats in the 300-member Greek Parliament. The *Golden Dawn* with harsh Neo-Nazi symbols and a violent anti-immigrant and anti-Europe agenda even managed to oust *LAOS* – the long-standing Greek right party (Dinas & Lamprini, 2013).

Templates of possibility: crisis and beyond

The sovereign debt crisis generated a large discussion in the public sphere. Social and political actors of all sorts gave voice to various public imaginaries in the period between spring 2010 and 2012, as well as the months that followed. Deploying the terms developed in the second section of this chapter, we ask, what *templates of possibility* did the crisis events generate. What visions of futurity emerged in the European public sphere? The chapter examines three different voices and their publics: first, the right nationalist party leaders themselves;

second, the European intellectuals and media; and lastly, the ordinary national citizen as represented in voting and popular protest.

Hoping for success: political rhetoric becomes economic rhetoric

In the years between 2010 and 2012, the nationalist right began to view the ongoing sovereign debt crisis with its attendant unpopular austerity policies as a political opening. In the space of those two years, parties began to shift the orientation of their political communications from issues of solely of national identity to issues of economics. During this period, right nationalists began sounding similar to classic left politicians in their defence of the people and the working classes and accelerating their attacks on European Union politicians and policies (Berezin, 2011). The absence of a viable left alternative has opened up a rhetorical space for nationalists to give voice to traditional left concerns. Marine Le Pen is a master of this strategy.[3] The European left and centre right share increasingly similar, if not identical, positions on European integration and generally support with some modification neoliberalism as an economic strategy.

The rhetorical strategies of right nationalist politicians are increasingly economic in orientation. Timo Soini the Finnish leader of the populist True Finns writing in the *Wall Street Journal* on May 9, 2011 explained why he did not support bailing out Europe's failing nations. He writes:

> At the risk of being accused of populism, we'll begin with the obvious: it is not the little guy who benefits. He is being milked and lied to in order to keep the insolvent system running. . . . I was raised to know that genocidal war must never again be visited on our continent and I came to understand the values and principles that originally motivated the establishment of what became the European Union. This Europe, this vision, was one that offered the people of Finland and all of Europe the gift of peace founded on democracy, freedom and justice. This is a Europe worth having, so it is with great distress that I see this project being put in jeopardy by a political elite who would sacrifice the interests of Europe's ordinary people in order to protect certain corporate interests.
>
> (Soini, 2011)

In April 2012, Dutch politician Geert Wilders learned that his 2010 victory was not as substantial as he thought. Wilders refused to support the right centrist government's decision to adopt austerity and save the Euro. His resistance to the governing coalition of which he was a part generated a parliamentary crisis and on April 25, the Queen dissolved the Dutch Parliament. Wilders thought that his party's success in the June 2010 elections and his place in the governing coalition had earned him a right to resist. He overplayed his hand and overestimated his popularity. In the September 12 Dutch election, Wilders and his party received a 10.08 per cent vote share and did not earn seats in the new governing coalition.

Wilders maintained an active public presence. On June 9, 2013, he addressed a conference on 'Europe's Last Stand' sponsored by the conservative think tank, the *American Freedom Alliance* in Los Angeles, California. Wilders' speech, 'The Resurgence of National Pride and the Future of Europe' identified 'three things' that 'ordinary people' in Europe 'want': politicians to solve the 'problem of Islamization'; to 'restore national sovereignty'; and 'they do not want their money to be used to pay for mistakes made elsewhere' (Wilders, 2013a). On November 21, 2013, writing in the *Wall Street Journal*, Wilders identified the 'Euro crisis' as the key to what he describes as the 'resurgence of European Patriotism' (Wilders, 2013b). Citing Ronald Reagan as his hero and denying the label of extremism, Wilders notes:

> Next May [date of European Parliamentary elections], all over Europe, voters will rebel at the ballot box. They will reject the supranational experiment of the European Union. They will cast their votes for a restoration of national sovereignty. They are not extremists, they are democrats.
>
> (Wilders, 2013b)

On January 21, 2014, the Dutch newspaper *De Telegraaf* reported a poll that showed Wilders' party gaining public support and likely to be part of a governing coalition if election were called at that point. In February 2014, Wilders commissioned a report, *NExit: Assessing the Economic Impact of the Netherlands Leaving the European Union* (Capital Economics, 2014). By March 2017, Wilders managed to come in second in the Parliamentary Elections to obtain 5 additional seats for his party.

Electoral trends suggest that nationalist and economic claims had resonance among European citizens. Marine Le Pen resurrected the National Front after its 2007 Presidential and parliamentary defeats. Marine Le Pen used rhetoric similar to Wilders in the run up to the 2012 French Presidential election (Berezin, 2013). She based her campaign on France exiting the Eurozone, generalised Europhobia coupled with Islamophobia, and a pledge to protect French industry and workers (Berezin, 2013). Marine Le Pen put a new slogan on her Google website: 'Solidarity with the victims of fiscal injustice and eurosterity!' She created a new logo that said: 'No to fiscal injustice!' The image in the colours of the French flag exchange the 'e' at the end of the French spelling of fiscal with a Euro sign (Le Pen, 2013).

On May 5, 2012, Hollande won the presidency but the significant election results came in two weeks earlier, on April 22 during the first round of the two-tiered French voting system. Marine Le Pen, leader of the National Front came in third place. With 17.9 per cent of the first-round vote, Le Pen trailed Hollande and sitting French president Nicolas Sarkozy, who virtually tied each other with 28 per cent and 27 per cent of the vote respectively.

Le Pen captured a larger portion of the vote than Jean-Luc Mélenchon's hastily assembled Left Front (Front de Gauche, 2011) coalition. She outperformed her father, Jean Marie Le Pen, in his 2002 first round 'victory' where he only polled

16 per cent. Mélenchon's platform was not all that dissimilar from that of Marine Le Pen. The official 2012 program of the Left Front, entitled *Human First* (*L'humain d'abord*) – as a counterpoint to the National Front's familiar *France First* logo – called for France to abandon the Treaty of Lisbon and to construct another Europe. The programme identified the European Central Bank as 'an obstacle to ending the crisis.' The extreme left is no friendlier to the Eurozone than the extreme right. If one adds the vote totals for Le Pen and Mélenchon in the first round, the candidates from both extremes of the political spectrum in France polled more than either Hollande or Sarkozy. The 'victory' of the extremes in 2012 was indicative, for anyone who cared to look, of the massive rejection of mainstream politicians in the 2017 French Presidential election. In 2017, political outsiders Le Pen, Mélenchon and the winner Emmanuel Macron dominated the electoral space.

Fearing dissolution and the return of the 1930s

After the spring 2012 elections, academics, journalists and various public intellectuals began to consider the possible disintegration of the Eurozone and to draw explicit connections between intractable economic issues and the rise of recidivist nationalism. The shock of the Greek elections, the continuing failure on the part of European leaders to negotiate a solution to the debt crisis, and the unpopularity of the bailouts of defaulting members in Germany and northern Europe focused public attention and generated a new line of political commentary that began to consolidate in early summer 2012. The public commentary had two prongs: first, that the strength of the right was a surprising development and would possibly initiate a replay of the 1930s; and second, that the crisis of the Eurozone was becoming a political, as well as economic, problem.

By 2013, it was common to find headlines in global media such as a *New York Times* editorial that shouted: 'Europe's Populist Backlash' and warned that the 'politics of populist anger are on the march across Europe' (*New York Times*, 2013). In spring 2009 when the European crisis first began, few academics or commentators viewed the crisis as potentially challenging to democratic practices or sentiments. In general, commentators on the European sovereign debt crisis addressed its economic consequences and paid little or no attention to its political consequences. Amartya Sen writing in the *Guardian* in July 2011, when the Greek crisis was heating up, was among the first public intellectuals to draw the connection between the crisis and challenges to democracy.[4] A *LexisNexis* search of international English language newspapers between the years 2000 to 2013 confirmed that the return of fascism was becoming a concern of the global media. Beginning in 2009, there was a steady up-tick in articles that contain 'fascism' and 'rise and/or return' in their headlines.[5]

European leaders began to warn that the Eurozone must be held together to contain nationalist and populist backlash. Two examples from prominent European officials illustrate the point. On April 25, 2012, three days after the first round of the French presidential election, Herman Van Rompuy, President of the European

Council in an address to the Romanian parliament warned that the European integration must be preserved to hold off

> threats to democracy. . . . We politicians must work hard to convince people that this [a united Europe] is possible. . . . This is a challenge, as election results and opinion polls all over Europe confirm. Nationalist and extremist movements are on the rise; many of them blame 'Brussels' for bad news.
> (EUCO, 2012b)

On September 12, 2012, Italian Prime Minister Mario Monti, speaking at the Ambrosetti Forum on Lake Como proposed a special European summit to confront growing populism in the face of the continent's financial crisis.

> We are in a *dangerous phase*. . . . It is paradoxical and sad that in a phase in which one was hoping to complete the integration instead there is forming a dangerous counter-phenomenon ['angry populism'] that aims at the disintegration.
> (The European House Ambrosetti, 2012 – emphasis added)

Monti himself became a casualty of 'angry populism'. An economist, Monti had assumed the role of Prime Minister of Italy in November 2011 when Silvio Berlusconi's third government collapsed. Italians perceived Monti as Angela Merkel's choice which did not help his government. Monti ran for Prime Minister in February 2012 but his pro-Europe, pro-austerity and pro-growth policies were widely unpopular with Italians. His coalition came in fourth in the popular vote behind the discredited Silvio Berlusconi and the singer turned politician Beppe Grillo, whose 5-Star Movement was against all forms of pre-existing political coalitions.[6]

Imagining nothing

In his last book, the late political scientist Peter Mair described contemporary European politics as *Ruling the Void* (Mair, 2013), which captures the spirit of the European public and citizenry. The social psychologist Nico Frijda (1993) has devised the analytic category 'mood' to capture 'climate'. Volatility characterises the European political climate – volatility of institutional and extra-institutional popular politics and volatility of collective response (Mair, 2013, pp. 29–34). It is this volatility that is more evocative of the 1930s than any specific events.

Volatility is manifesting itself in fear, anger, uncertainty, depression and distrust. Indices of ill health and even increases in suicide rates in crisis-stricken countries such as Spain, Italy and Greece provide evidence of collective despair (Stuckler & Basu, 2013). Increasing rates of youth unemployment, as high as 50 per cent in Greece and in Sweden 30 per cent, contribute to the prevailing mood of hopelessness (OECD, 2012).

120 *Mabel Berezin*

Party salience, as represented in voting results, even volatile ones, are institutional responses to the erosion of security that might have been imaginary in the 1980s and 90s but has become very real in the new century – with the sovereign debt crisis being at the core of this. Extra-institutional responses, such as trans-European protests against austerity, are evocative of the 1930s.

For example, in October 2010, the French Socialist Party organised a grand march through the centre of Paris and strikes in public services to protest the raising of the retirement age. The official party organisers gave out stickers with sayings such as 'retirement is life, not survival' and '60 years is freedom'. Plastered on street posts throughout central Paris were posters that a youth group called the *New Anticapitalist Party* designed and distributed. The posters displayed a picture of Sarkozy and Francois Hollande on a 500 Euro note. Referring to the politicians and the bank note, the poster proclaimed in bold letters 'GET OUT!' (Dehors): 'Because they are worth nothing'.

Social disenfranchisement is most acutely felt among European youth. Kaldor and Selchow (2012) studied youth protest across Europe. They identified a phenomenon which they labelled 'Subterranean Politics' by which they meant *ad hoc* protest around social issues that rose up and captured cross-cutting constituencies of youth that had no strong institutional base. *Occupy Wall Street* would be one genre of this type of protest but groups such as the Pirate Party would be another. According to Kaldor and Selchow, their most surprising finding was that European youth had no interest in European Union policy or politics and did not see it as relevant to their concerns. Since 2012, the movements of the dis-enfranchised have only grown. In addition to Mélenchon's political success, there has been the 'movement of the squares' in France and Spain.

From the ballot box to the streets, the volatility of the European political mood state coupled with the almost anomic quality to European youth protest are more evocative of the political mood of the 1930s than any specific policies or statistics can capture.

Why did the nationalist right begin to resonate among European publics?

So far, this chapter has focused upon the correlation between the general salience of the national right as evidenced in electoral gains and the European sovereign debt crisis. This section explores the institutional factors that support a collective retreat to nationalist sentiment and which have contributed to the upward trajectory of the nationalist right. These factors are: competing and conflicting visions of what Europe is and does, and the practical consequences of that conflict; the institutional durability of the nation-state; and lastly, the shift in the locus of security.

What does 'Europe' mean? Conflicting visions

Europe in theory and practice is a terrain of conflicting visions and multiple stories.[7] The meaning of Europe is very much dependent upon who is speaking and to whom. Given that Europe is a set of institutional and governing arrangements, these different visions pose practical as well as theoretical problems. The Europe that politicians and intellectuals speak of today is distant from the original post-war European peace project. In response to the current crisis, some European politicians have tried to strategically invoke the past. For example, on September 22, 2012, French President François Hollande and his German counterpart Angela Merkel attended a ceremony in Ludwigshafen, Germany to mark the fiftieth anniversary of Charles de Gaulle's speech on reconciliation to German youth. Hollande invoked the traditional post-war vision of Europe when he said, 'Europe is not simply institutions, procedures, juridical texts – they are necessary. Europe, generation after generation, is the most beautiful political project that we can imagine together' (Elysée, 2012 – translation M.B.).

In the 1990s, the traditionalist vision of Europe as a post-war peace project began to recede in response to political and social changes. The fall of Eastern Europe made war and peace less of an issue, and globalisation and privatisation made markets and trans-border cooperation more of an issue. These two phenomena led to a growing neo-liberal and bureaucratic vision often coded in popular discourse as 'Brussels', and a competing and more idealistic vision that focused on creating a single European identity.

Both visions had academic champions. Political scientists (see Moravcsik, 1997) tend to elaborate the neo-liberal and institutional vision of Europe. Public intellectuals and left leaning politicians more often espouse the idealistic vision of Europe. The public discourse and writings of German philosopher Jürgen Habermas elegantly espouse the idealistic vision. As a sequel to his 2009 book, *Europe: The Faltering Project*, (Habermas, 2009), he published *The Crisis of the European Union* (Habermas, 2012) that argued for the necessity of a 'constitutional project' for Europe. In summer 2012, Habermas engaged in a policy debate that first appeared in *Frankfurter Allgemeine Zeitung* on the necessity of organising a broad public debate on the re-organisation of the European polity. He followed up on these ideas in April 2103 when he gave a lecture in Leuven entitled, 'Democracy, Solidarity and the European Crisis'. While the political science approach to Europe does not factor in social issues and immigration, the Habermasian approach is often understood as a defence of multiculturalism.

Both analytic approaches inhabit different mental worlds, as do the conflicting visions of Europe that they represent. Listening to realists and idealists on the subject of European Union politics (not that they are often in the same room together!), it is difficult to understand that they are discussing the same political entity. Both realists and idealists fail to take into account that 'Europe' writ large has never been popular among ordinary people. The well-known low voter turnout figures for EU parliament elections – figures which have been declining over time; as well as the failure to pass a European constitution in any of the nation-states where it was submitted to a popular, as opposed to a parliamentary, referendum attests to the weak appeal that the ideal of Europe has for citizens of various national states.

Lack of popular support would make Europeanisation no different from other nineteenth century nationalist projects where peasants had to become Frenchmen (Weber, 1976). What is salient about the European project is how ineffective the European identity project has been among ordinary, not elite citizens.[8] The 2015 Greek debt crisis made it clear how reluctant citizens were to bail out citizens of debtor countries and made it clear how little today's national citizens view themselves as part of a common European project. As the World War II generation passes on and the post-war generation ages, the living memory of World War II fades and along with it, the argument for a European peace project.

As the traditionalist argument for European Union and solidarity wanes, the neo-liberal and idealist versions remain – but hardly in robust form. The sovereign debt crisis tarnishes the neo-liberal solutions to global competitiveness and social well-being. The idealist version is often connected to the incorporation of immigrant groups across Europe. Events such as the May 2013 riots in the suburbs of Stockholm, among others, and terrorist events in French and Germany in the years between 2015 and today have made the right-wing argument that some immigrants are not capable of incorporation compelling at the same time that austerity worsened their material conditions. The landscape of completing claims and visions that dominate the European project make for benign confusion in the absence of crisis, but become seriously undermining of the entire project when faced with the stress of first, debt and later, terror and refugees.

The nation-state: a durable institution

It is a truism of the Euro crisis to point out that the EU created a currency union (EMU) but neglected to create viable regulatory systems or political institutions to buttress it. On one level, a failure of institutional design plagues the entire EU project. Throughout Europe, policy is often decided at the national level and there are many contradictions built into the system. For example, one cannot be a citizen of Europe and carry an EU passport unless one is first a citizen of a member state. Talk of European federalism continually emerges; yet, the obstacles to such a step are large.

On September 2, 2013, Daniel Cohn-Bendit, founder of the German Green Party and member of the European Parliament, with Felix Marquardt, wrote an op-ed for the *New York Times* in which he argued that the 'Fix for Europe' resided in 'People Power'. Adopting a pragmatic tone, Cohn-Bendit and Marquardt proclaimed that,

> we need a Pan-European effort to determine Europe's best practices in every field and adopt them across the Continent.... [Europe] will change only when European-minded politicians who are elected to national offices agree to transfer power to truly European institutions.
>
> (Cohn-Bendit & Marquardt, 2013)

Less than a week after this article appeared, Vaclav Klaus, former President of the Czech Republic, published an article on his web-site entitled 'Democrats of Europe, wake up!' in which he denounced Cohn-Bendit's and Marquardt's ideas. Klaus, known for his active Euroscepticism defends the nation-state as a safeguard of European democracy. He accuses the authors of as naively supporting expansion of Europe, which Klaus describes as a 'totalitarian ideology coated with modern paint' (Klaus, 2013).

The ascendant European nationalist right suggests that arguments such as Klaus presented had greater resonance for ordinary citizens. In times of prosperity and growth, it was relatively easy for policy makers to overlook the lack of interest in European parliamentary elections and the distrust of moving to a European constitution. When the constitution was rejected by popular referenda in 2005 in both France and the Netherlands, scholars and politicians attributed its rejection to temporary glitches in national politics rather than any deeper distrust of the constitutional project.

The *Global Attitudes Project* of the Pew Research Center monitors public opinion in Europe on an annual basis. In a report released on May 29, 2012, 'European Unity on the Rocks', Pew Research Center (2012) researchers found, as their title suggested, that the European project was wobbly but still fundamentally intact. In Pew's 2012 report, they found among the eight countries that they surveyed a median 60 per cent favourability rating towards the 'European Project'. There was wide variability among national states surveyed – with a 68 per cent favourability rating in Germany, and not surprisingly a 37 per cent favourability rating in Greece. A year later in Pew's May 2013 survey, the median favourability rating had dropped to 45 per cent. Support for Europe dropped in all countries, but the steepest drop occurred in France where favourability went from 60 per cent to 41per cent – a loss of 19 percentage points. The title of Pew's 2013 report, 'The New Sick Man of Europe: The European Union', captured the dreary statistics that the document contained and did not augur well for Europe's future.

A central problem facing Europe is the durability of the nation-state as a political institution. At its core, the Europe that began with Maastricht in 1992 sought to build solidarity based upon a community of interest rather than a community of culture – albeit a community of constructed culture. Ernest Renan's ([1882] 1992, p. 9) warning that a 'Zollverein [customs union] is never a fatherland' was equally applicable to the contemporary European project as it was to nineteenth century France and Prussia.

Nation-states are durable political institutions because they wed culture to politics and economics. Nation-states are material objects embedded in geographical space and territorially bound. As Poggi (1979) elegantly argues, states adjudicate risk for their members by providing physical protection and social security. *National experience*, the point where collective and individual biography intersect, interrogates the past to produce the future, is a crucial by-product of the activities that citizens perform in common and the materiality of the state.[9] *Experience*, individual and collective, does not simply float unanchored in social and political space. As Parsons ([1942] 1954, p. 147) observed in his discussion of propaganda, institutions anchor experience since they define expectations. Thus, institutions are a necessary but not sufficient dimension of political cultural analysis. Culture and politics come together in national institutions that bind individuals together in national communities of meaning. Citizenship is the legal institution that defines the boundaries of belonging (Brubaker, 1992), but it is not the only institution. Schools, religion, military conscription, and common language engage citizens in the collective practice of belonging. In short, the European project has not offered any alternative to date that attenuates the durability of national cultures and national states.

When security ends

Europeanisation, which is often a code word for neo-liberalism and globalisation, particularly among nationalist politicians, threatens to shift the locus of security from the state to the market. Before the financial crisis, such distinctions and tropes presented themselves in the public sphere as the fear-mongering of extremist politicians. The crisis, with the constant public discussion of debt and bail-outs coupled with rising youth unemployment across Europe, has lent more than a patina of reality to nationalist claims.

The expanded EU project that we can date to the 1992 Maastricht treaty was a project of *plenty, not* of *scarcity*, and scarcity is emerging on a global scale. Scarcity in a trans-national polity such as EU threatens the practical security (social welfare, linguistic and cultural similarity) that the European nation-states guaranteed in the post-war period. The old forms of security are weakening if not entirely disappearing in Europe and elsewhere, and creating a *post-security polity where scarcity not plenty is the norm;* and marketisation takes precedence over re-distribution. The collective reaction to the *post-security polity* is that national protection over-rides European solidarity and promotes a resurgence of a nationalist centre or right depending on the historical specificity of the individual national state.

The global financial crisis was the first crisis to exacerbate economic fissures and cultural fault lines in the European project and brought into focus institutional problems that nations formerly adjudicated. The sovereign debt crisis forced Europe to recalibrate itself as a *post-security polity*. Nation-states, the bedrock of pre-EU Europe, institutionalised a form of 'practical security' that lent collective emotional security to citizens. Political security was located in citizenship laws and internal and external defence ministries. National social welfare systems produced economic security and social solidarity as a by-product. Linguistic, educational and even religious policies created cultural security because they enforced assumptions, if not realities, of similarity and identity. In contrast to the 'old' Europe where security, solidarity and identity were guaranteed, the *post-security polity* privileges markets, fosters austerity that threatens solidarity, and supports multicultural inclusion at the expense of nationalist exclusion.

Past is prologue

In the aftermath of the Paris Peace meetings in 1919, John Maynard Keynes observed:

> The bankruptcy and decay of Europe, if we allow it to proceed, will affect everyone in the long-run, but perhaps not in a way that is striking or immediate. This has one fortunate side. We may still have time to reconsider our courses and to view the world with new eyes. For the immediate future, events are taking charge, and the near destiny of Europe is no longer in the hands of any man. *The events of the coming year will not be shaped by the deliberate acts of statesmen, but by the hidden currents, flowing continually beneath the surface of political history, of which no one can predict the outcome.* In one way only we influence these hidden currents, – by setting in motion those forces of instruction and imagination which change *opinion.*
> (Keynes, [1919] 1920, p. 165, emphasis added)

The 'hidden currents' of 2012 and beyond were no doubt different than when Keynes wrote. But, events are compelling and Keynes' warning is well taken. The confluence of events, the sovereign debt crisis first, followed by the Paris terror attacks and refugee crisis of 2015, combined with a volatile political mood, provided an empty space which set the stage for the elections of 2016 and 2017. Right-wing political parties challenged democracy by looking backward to enforce a political form, the national state which despite its durability might have been better suited to the nineteenth and twentieth centuries than to the twenty-first century.

This chapter argued that the elections of 2012 were a collateral damage from the sovereign debt crisis that exacerbated fault lines in the European project. Europe and the Eurozone were never solely economic issues. Europe, the Europe that evolved institutionally and culturally in the 1980s and 1990s, was a fragile and fissured political and cultural entity. The European sovereign debt crisis served as an initial 'tipping point' that exposed cracks in the European infrastructure as well as its shaky foundation. In 2010, the first wave of the global financial crisis hit Europe. National primacy became increasingly salient for ordinary citizens and a sea change in the electoral fortunes of the nationalistic right followed.

Events are *templates of possibility* (Berezin, 2012, p. 620) that focus analytic, as well as collective, attention. Events shift the unit of analysis from political actors, whether voters or party operatives, to events that marked salient moments in collective national perceptions. Events as political facts lend analytic rigor to the cultural analysis of politics. Events are *templates of possibility* for agents.

Many events led to the elections of spring 2012, the sovereign debt crisis and the electoral salience of the old 'new' nationalism. But without the fixity of 'spring 2012', it would be difficult to proceed with an analysis that crosses temporal boundaries and anticipates the crises of 2015 and beyond. By viewing the elections of spring 2012 analytically as events, we are able to place them in a broader historical context as well as to imagine what possibilities for the future they portended. The rise of the old 'new' nationalism was a major form of collateral damage of the sovereign debt crisis. The recent past of 2012 was prologue to the events of 2015 and beyond. If analysts had been looking, the elections of 2016 and 2017 should not have been a surprise. Until analysts and policy makers recognize the *political facts* of the last five years, the nationalist right only needs to show up to be a salient political force – and that is today's challenge to democracy.

Notes

1 Using Triandafyllidou and Gropas (2007) and Zincone, Penninx, and Borkert (2011) as sources, I completed a survey of European immigration law in 14 European national states from 1945 to the present that supports this claim.
2 I track the electoral salience of right parties from 1970 to the present in 181 parliamentary elections using Mackie and Rose (1991) and the NSD (2017) for all statistical references in this chapter.
3 On the longstanding relation between the French right and the working classes see Viard (1997); on Marine Le Pen's strategy see (Berezin, 2013, pp. 250–254).
4 See Berezin, 2013, pp. 240–241 for a summary of these opinions.
5 The raw numbers for years and chapters (years/articles) are: 2009/2363; 2010/2009; 2011/2103; 2012/2259; 2013/2713.
6 Fella and Ruzza, 2013 provide an early assessment of this election.
7 See Lacroix and Nicolaidis (2010); Mudge and Vauchez (2012) following Pierre Bourdieu describe this phenomenon as a 'weak field'.
8 On the class differentiation among European citizens and support for Europe, see Diéz-Medrano, 2003; Favell, 2008; Fligstein, 2008.
9 *National experience* in contrast to the over-worked *national identity* is a more dynamic concept and accounts for variability and stability over time.

References

Art, D. (2011). *Inside the radical right: The development of anti-immigrant parties in Western Europe*. New York: Cambridge University Press.

Bale, T. (2012). Supplying the insatiable demand: Europe's populist radical right. *Government and Opposition*, *47*(2), 256–274.

Berezin, M. (2009). *Illiberal politics in neoliberal times: Culture, security, and populism in the New Europe*. Cambridge: Cambridge University Press.

Berezin, M. (2011). Europe was yesterday. *Harvard International Review*, Web Symposium January 7. Retrieved from http://hir.harvard.edu/europe-was-yesterday?page=0%(2C(2.

Berezin, M. (2012). Events as templates of possibility: An analytic typology of political facts. In J. C. Alexander, R. Jacobs, & P. Smith (Eds.), *The Oxford handbook of cultural sociology* (pp. 613–635). New York: Oxford University Press.

Berezin, M. (2013). The normalization of the right in post-security Europe. In A. Schäfer & W. Streeck (Eds.), *Politics in the age of austerity* (pp. 239–261). Cambridge: Polity Press.

Betz, H.-G. (1994). *Radical right-wing populism in Western Europe*. New York: St. Martin's Press.

Blyth, M. (2013). *Austerity: The history of a dangerous idea*. New York: Oxford.

Brubaker, R. (1992). *Citizenship and nationhood in France and Germany*. Cambridge: Harvard University Press.

Capital Economics. (2014). NExit: Assessing the economic impact of the Netherlands leaving the European Union, London. Retrieved from www.capitaleconomics.com.

Cohn-Bendit, D., & Marquardt, F. (2013). The fix for Europe: People power. *New York Times*, 3 September. Retrieved from www.nytimes.com/2013/09/03/opinion/the-fix-for-europe-people-power.html.

CSA (2013). *Les Français et François Hollande*. Sondage CSA pour BFMTV. Etude N. 1300628A April.

Díez-Medrano, J. (2003). *Framing Europe: Attitudes to European integration in Germany, Spain, and the United Kingdom*. Princeton, NJ: Princeton University Press.

Dinas, E., & Lamprini, R. (2013). The 2012 Greek parliamentary elections: Fear and loathing at the polls. *West European Politics*, *36*(1), 270–282.

Durkheim, E. ([1895] 1964). *The rules of sociological method*, translated by S. A. Solovay & J. H. Mueller. New York, Free Press of Glencoe.

Eichengreen, B. J. (2007). *The European economy since 1945: Coordinated capitalism and beyond*. Princeton, NJ: Princeton University Press.

Elysée. (2012). Présidence de la République. Discours de M. le Président de la République lors du cinquantenaire du discours du général de Gaulle à la jeunesse allemande. *Accueil*, Discours 2012.

European Council EUCO. (2012a). Conclusions, 28/29 June, EUCO 76/12. Retrieved from http://data.consilium.europa.eu/doc/document/ST-76-2012-INIT/en/pdf.

European Council EUCO. (2012b). Herman Van Rompuy, Speech to the Parliament of Romania, 25 April 2012. EUCO 68/12, europa.eu/rapid/press-release_PRES-12-170_en.pdf.

Eurostat. (2017). Retrieved from http://epp.eurostat.ec.europa.eu/statistics_explained/index.php/Unemployment_statistics.

Favell, A. (2008). *Eurostars and Eurocities: Free movement and mobility in an integrating Europe*. Oxford: Blackwell.

Fella, S., & Ruzza, C. (2013). Populism and the fall of the centre-right in Italy: The end of the Berlusconi model or a new beginning?. *Journal of Contemporary European Studies*, *21*(1), 38–52.

Fligstein, N. (2008). *Euroclash: The EU, European identity, and the future of Europe*. New York: Oxford University Press.

Fourcade, M., Steiner, P., Streeck, W., & Woll, C. (2013). Discussion forum: Moral categories in the financial crisis. *Socio-Economic Review*, *11*(3), 601–627.

Frijda, N. (1993). Moods, emotion episodes and emotion. In M. Lewis & J. M. Haviland (Eds.), *Handbook of emotions* (pp. 381–403). New York, Guilford.

Front de Gauche. (2011). *L'humain d'abord: Le programme du Front de Gauche et de son candidat commun Jean-Luc Mélenchon*. Paris: Flammarion.

Habermas, J. (2009). *Europe: The faltering project*. Cambridge: Polity.

Habermas, J. (2012). *The crisis of the European union: A response*. Cambridge: Polity.

Kaldor, M., & Selchow, S. (2012). The 'ubbling up' of subterranean politics in Europe. Working Paper Civil Society and Human Security Research Unit, London, School of Economics. Retrieved from www.gcsknowledgebase.org/europe/wp-content/themes/SubPol(2/SubterraneanPolitics_June(201(2.pdf.

Keynes, J. M. ([1919] 1920). *The economic consequences of the peace*. London: Macmillan.

Kitschelt, H. (1995). *The radical right in Western Europe: A comparative analysis*. Ann Arbor, MI: University of Michigan.

Klaus, V. (2013). Democrats of Europe, wake up!. Retrieved from https://www.klaus.cz/clanky/3435.

Kriesi, H. (2014). The political consequences of the economic crisis in Europe: Electoral punishment and popular protest. In N. Bermeo & L. M. Bartels (Eds.), *Mass politics in tough times: Opinions, votes and protest in the great recession* (pp. 297–333). Oxford: Oxford University Press.

Lacroix, J., & Nicolaidis, K. (2010). *European stories: Intellectual debates on Europe in national contexts*. Oxford: Oxford University Press.

Le Pen, M. (2013). Non, à l'injustice fiscale. Retrieved from https://twitter.com/mlp_officiel/status/394448584651067393.

Mackie, T. T., & Rose, R. (1991). *The international almanac of electoral history*. Washington, DC: Congressional Quarterly Inc.

Mair, P. (2013). *Ruling the void: The hollowing of Western democracy*. London: Verso.

Moravcsik, A. (1998). *The choice for Europe: Social purpose and state power from Messina to Maastricht*. Ithaca, NY: Cornell University Press.

Mudde, C. (2007). *Populist radical right parties in Europe*. Cambridge and New York: Cambridge University Press.

Mudge, S. L., & Vauchez, A. (2012). Building Europe on a weak field: Law, economics, and scholarly avatars in transnational politics. *American Journal of Sociology*, *118*(2), 449–492.

Müller, J.-W. (2007). *Constitutional patriotism*. Princeton, NJ: Princeton University Press.

New York Times. (2013). Editorial board, Europe's populist backlash, 10/15/2013. Retrieved from www.Nytimes.com (accessed 10/21/2013).

NSD. (2017). European election database. Retrieved from www.nsd.uib.no/european_election_database/index.html.

OECD. (2012). OECD employment outlook. OECD. doi: 10.1787/empl_outlook-(201(2-en.

Parsons, T. ([1942] 1954). Propaganda and social control. In T. Parsons (Ed.), *Essays in sociological theory* (2nd ed., pp. 142–176). Glencoe: The Free Press.

Pew Research Center. (2012). European unity on the rocks, global attitudes project. Retrieved from www.pewglobal.org/2012/05/29/european-unity-on-the-rocks/.

Pew Research Center. (2013). The new sick man of Europe: The European Union. Retrieved from www.pewglobal.org/2013/05/13/the-new-sick-man-of-europe-the-european-union/.

Poggi, G. (1979). *The development of the modern state*. Stanford, CA: Stanford University Press.

Renan, E. ([1882] 1992). What is a nation?. In E. Renan (Ed.), *Qu'est-ce qu'une nation?*, translated by E. Rundell. Paris: Presses-Pocket.

Sewell, W. H. (1996). Historical events as transformations of structures: Inventing revolution at the Bastille. *Theory and Society*, *25*(6), 841–481.

Soini, T. (2011). Why I don't support Europe's bailouts. *Wall Street Journal*, May 9. Retrieved from www.wsj.com/articles/SB10001424052748703864204576310851503980120 (accessed 8/4/2011).

Stuckler, D., & Basu, S. (2013). *The body economic*. Princeton, NJ: Princeton University Press.

The European House Ambrosetti. (2012). Intelligence on the world, Europe and Italy, September 7–9. Retrieved from www.ambrosetti.eu/en/summits-workshops-forums/forum-villa-deste/forum-villa-deste-edizione-2012/.

Triandafyllidou, A., & Gropas, R. (2007). *European immigration: A sourcebook*. Aldershot: Ashgate.

Wagner-Pacifici, R. (2010). Theorizing the restlessness of events. *American Journal of Sociology*, *115*(5), 345–390.

Weber, E. (1976). *Peasants into Frenchmen: The modernization of rural France, 1870–1914*. Stanford, CA: Stanford University Press.

Wilders, G. (2013a). The resurgence of national pride and the future of Europe. *Wall Street Journal*, June 9. Retrieved from www.geertwilders.nl/index.php/in-de-media-mainmenu-74/nieuws-mainmenu-114/1829-speech-geert-wilders-los-angeles-june-9–2013.

Wilders, G. (2013b). The resurgence of European patriotism. How to ruin the day of bureaucrats and politicians in Brussels. *Wall Street Journal*, November 21. Retrieved from www.wsj.com/articles/the-resurgence-of-european-patriotism-1385066982.

Zincone, G., Penninx, R., & Borkert, M. (2011). *Migration policymaking in Europe*. Amsterdam: Amsterdam University Press.

8 The coterminous rise of right-wing populism and superfluous populations

David A. Snow and Colin Bernatzky

Introduction

Our objective in this chapter is to consider and theorise the interactive relationship between populism and superfluous populations.[1] We will focus on a variant of populism characterised by virulent anti-pluralism and argue that it is, by its very nature, a seedbed for the germination of one or more superfluous populations. In doing so, we argue that superfluous populations are not just structurally or demographically determined, but are also socially constructed and, thus, can be 'talked into existence' via strategic framing and identity work. However, we also contend that the degree of population superfluity and how 'that problem' is dealt with are contingent on three intervening conditions: the existence or development of abeyance systems, the presence or absence of structural or status vacancies, and the expansion or contraction of cultural spans of sympathy. Finally, we will briefly consider the alternative ways in which superfluous populations might be, or have been, dealt with, referencing some historical examples, and then raise the question of whether there is a kind of elective affinity between populism and the emergence of superfluous populations and the manner in which they are dealt with strategically. Throughout, we draw on the political discourse of the United States' populist President Donald Trump for illustrative purposes. Given our focal interest in exploring and amplifying the relationship between right-wing populism and superfluous populations, we begin with the discussion of the two concepts and their intersection.

Right-wing populism

As with many concepts in the social sciences, there is no consensus on how best to conceptualise populism. Questions have been raised as to whether populism is a variant of fascism, whether it is a distinctive type of social movement or a political or movement strategy, and whether it is a political ideology or logic (Berman, 2016; Judis, 2016; Mudde, 2016). Given these questions, it is not surprising that there is some debate as to its core defining features. This definitional contestation notwithstanding, there are two core features of populism that are central to most conceptualisations: anti-elitism and anti-pluralism. These two defining characteristics are accented, for instance, in Müller's (2016) *What is Populism?* and Mudde's (2004, 2016) definition, which posits the division between two homogenous and antagonistic groups – the pure people and the corrupt elite – as the hallmark of populism. Somewhat similarly, Kazin, in his book on American populism, views it as:

> a language whose speakers conceive of ordinary people as a noble assemblage not bounded narrowly by class; view their elite opponents as self-serving and undemocratic; and seek to mobilize the former against the latter.
> (Kazin, 1995, p. 1)

These overlapping conceptualisations are useful as a point of departure in considering populism, but they are not particularly helpful in distinguishing variants of populism, such as the left/right distinction as embodied in the 2016 US presidential campaigns of Bernie Sanders and Donald Trump.

Since we are interested in right-wing populism is this chapter, we consider briefly the distinctions between left-wing and right-wing populism. It is worth noting that this dichotomisation is not universally embraced among scholars, and that 'left-wing populism' as it is conventionally understood may be a mischaracterisation. For example, Müller states that:

> [it] is a failure of political judgment to think that simply because political actors appeal to 'Main Street' or defend the downtrodden they must be populist, [and as such] it is crucial to understand that populists are not simply anti-elitist: they are also necessarily anti-pluralist
> (Müller, 2015, p. 88, f.)

The major difference between left and right populism, we contend, is that right-wing populism is much more exclusionary. The exclusionary nature of right-wing populism is rooted in what Judis (2016, p. 15) identifies as its triadic character, in contrast to the dyadic character of left-wing populism. In the case of the latter, it is the 'people writ large' against the elite or those on the top, as illustrated by the Occupy Wall Street Movement's frequently voiced slogan, 'We are the 99 percent'. In contrast, 'rightwing populists champion the people against an elite they accuse of coddling a third group' (15). This presumably elite 'favoured' and/or 'protected' group functions as a 'negative other' for the right-wing populist, a 'negative other' that is used as a comparative referent for framing the obstacles to the 'pure' or 'true' people's interests and rightful standing. Just as reference to 'the People' is 'an empty signifier' (Laclau, 2005) in that it is a socially constructed identity that can encompass almost any category of people variously clustered within the sociocultural context, there is no single social category automatically constitutive of the comparative 'negative other'. Rather, the list of social categories that might comprise this third triadic leg of right-wing populism is an open slate; in today's world it might consist of welfare recipients, various racial/ethnic or religious groups and nationalities, immigrants, feminists, LGBT individuals, college and university professors, climate scientists, evolutionary biologists, and so on.

Thus, the anti-pluralism of right-wing populism takes the form of a Manichean project – that is, a dualistic worldview that provides clear contrast conceptions between 'the People' and 'the negative others', and some configuration of enabling elites. It is in this demagogic construction of a scapegoat – which the elites are seen as coddling and favouring – that accounts in part for the potency of right-wing populism.

But there is another factor at work as well. We refer to the almost 'messianic' tenor of right-wing populism, which provides a sense of expectancy not only of better days to come but of a kind of collective transposition, somewhat akin to what the historical Jesus told his disciples when they asked about the prospects of a wealthy young man getting into heaven: 'So the last will be first, and the first will be last' (Matthew 20: 16). Similarly, the right-wing populist argues that if it were not for the elite's coddling of its favoured groups, the life situation of the neglected or forgotten people – that is, the metaphoric pure people – would be dramatically reversed. We are not claiming that populists firmly believe such claims, but they do make such claims. For example, Pat Buchanan, who ran in the US presidential primaries of 1992 and 1996, claimed that he would 'make this country what it used to be – God's country'. And Trump, of course, has made numerous messianic, transpositional claims, as when he said, in one of his unrelenting flow of 'tweets' while campaigning in Wisconsin in April 2016: 'If I win, all bad things in the US will be rapidly reversed.' As one observer noted about Trump's voters, or at least some of them, they 'are motivated by a kind of faith: They believe in the man, and his promise that all their losing will come to end' (Manseau, 2016).

This belief or faith also suggests the operation of a personality cult of the kind Arendt noted in reference to the 'Führer-principle' with respect to Hitler in Germany and Stalin in the Soviet Union (Arendt, 1968, pp. xxxii-xxiii and elsewhere), suggesting that both 'exercised a fascination to which allegedly no one was immune' (305). Focusing on the fascination associated with Hitler, Arendt writes:

> The 'magic spell' that Hitler cast over his listeners has been acknowledged many times. . . . This fascination – 'the strange magnetism that radiated from Hitler in such a compelling manner' – rested indeed 'on the fanatical belief of this man in himself' . . . , on his pseudo-authoritative judgments about everything under the sun, and on the fact that his opinions . . . could always be fitted into an all-encompassing ideology
>
> (Arendt, 1968, p. 305, footnote 1).

With but a slight change or two in this assessment of the fascination associated with Hitler, this statement readily captures a portion of the character of, and fascination engendered by, many right-wing populists today and, arguably, their associated personality cults. In the case of Trump, for example, how else does one explain the Teflon-like shield that deflects his many outrageous comments, as

Populism and superfluous populations 133

when he boasted, while campaigning in Iowa in January 2016, that 'I could stand in the middle of 5th Avenue and shoot somebody and I wouldn't lose voters?'

The point here is that the quasi-religious, transpositional claims frequently associated with right-wing populists are bolstered and rendered more believable to their adherents by their sometimes 'fanatical belief' in themselves as the saviour or 'fixer' of whatever claimed ills and injustices they presumably suffered, as illustrated by Trump's claim during his 2016 Republican Convention address that 'I am your voice', and 'I alone can fix it'. As one journalist observed, unlike recent former Republican candidates and presidents, Trump

> did not appeal to prayer, or to God. He did not ask Americans to measure him against their values, or to hold him responsible for living up to them. He did not ask for their help. He asked them to place their faith in him . . . The most striking aspect of his speech wasn't his delivery. . . . It wasn't the specific policies he outlined, long fixtures of his stump speech. It was the extraordinary spectacle of a man standing on a podium, elevated above the surrounding crowd, telling the millions of Americans who were watching that he, alone, could solve their problems.
>
> (Applebaum, 2016)

It is this combination of religious-like prophetic claims and promises of better days to come for the populist's adherents, with his/her charismatic, messianic claims about being the only one who can solve the issues or ensure the promises, which give credence to the idea of some kind of transpositional order. Taken together, these intersecting elements of right-wing populism – the Manichean dualism juxtaposing the worthy, forgotten people and the elite-coddled others, the promise of a transpositional ordering of existing or constructed status groups or classes, and the spewing of prophetic, charismatic claims about one's unique and special powers – suggest that an exclusionary form of identity politics is at the core of right-wing populism. We thus turn to consideration of two underlying mechanisms of this exclusionary identity politics: identity work and collective action framing.[2]

Identity work and framing

The concept of identity work, initially conceptualised by Snow and Anderson (1987), refers to the range of activities individuals and/or collective entities engage in to signify and express who they are and what they stand for, in relation or contrast to some set of others. At its core, identity work is the generation, invocation, and maintenance of symbolic resources used to bound and distinguish the collectivity, both internally and externally, by accenting commonalities and differences. It manifests itself in at least four ways or modalities: (1) through procurement or arrangement of physical settings and props, as illustrated by interior and exterior decoration, the cars we purchase and stickers we slap on their bumpers, and the political signs and banners and protest placards we construct

134 *David A. Snow and Colin Bernatzky*

and display to signal our political identity; (2) through cosmetic face work or the arrangement of personal appearance via the use of makeup, body ornamentation such as tattoos, hair styles, and dress; (3) through selective association with other individuals and groups such as cliques, gangs, friends, or networks; and (4) through identity talk/discourse involving the verbal or written construction and avowal and attribution of personal or collective identities via framing.[3]

Of the four types of identity work, we contend that identity talk via framing is most relevant to populism for two reasons: first, because its tell-tale sign is the verbal or discursive construction and differentiation of at least two antagonistic groupings; and second, because it fertilises the soil for the other types of identity work. To illustrate this exclusionary identity work via framing, we turn to Trump and his divisive, Manichean language, which not only divides America into antagonistic segments, but also drives a wedge between the US and the rest of the world. His 2017 inaugural address alone provides ample illustration, as indicated by the following statements:

- We are transferring power from Washington, D.C. and giving it back to you, the American People.
- January 20th 2017, will be remembered as the day the people became the rulers of this nation again.
- The forgotten men and women of our country will be forgotten no longer.
- You will never be ignored again.
- We must protect our borders from the ravages of other countries.
- This American carnage stops right here and stops right now.
- From this moment on, it's going to be America First.

To get another handle on Trump's exclusionary populist talk, we turn to a more fine-tuned, nuanced assessment of his inaugural address by assessing the frequency of selected word usage in comparison to Obama's first inaugural address.

Table 8.1 Selected word usage in Obama's and Trump's inaugural addresses

	Obama	*Trump*
We	60	46
Our	69	48
Us	23	2
Your	3	11
You	10	10
I	3	3
My	2	1
America/American	15	34
Some variant of 'people'	8	9

Table 8.2 Usage of 'people' in Obama's and Trump's inaugural addresses

	Obama	*Trump*
America-centred	3	8
	The people (2)	The people (4)
	The American people (1)	The American people (1)
		God's people (1)
		Our people (2)
Other-centred	5	1
	A people (1)	People of the world (1)
	Other peoples (1)	
	Its people (referring to Iraq) (1)	
	Your people (other countries) (1)	
	The people of poor nations (1)	

The comparisons in Tables 8.1 and 8.2 point to several interesting differences that underscore Trump's exclusionary orientation both domestically and internationally. In Table 8.1, for example, Obama's inaugural address was more inclusionary, with many more references to 'We', 'Our', and 'Us' (151 to 96). In Table 8.2, we see that Obama's inclusionary tone extends beyond the US, and is thus more other-centred, whereas Trump's tone is America-centred. The exclusionary character of Trump's America-centric rhetoric is even more evident in his endless tweets regarding immigration, refugees, the border, and the border wall. Consider the following:

- Everybody is arguing whether or not it's a BAN. Call it what you want, it is about keeping bad people (with bad intentions) out of the country! (2/1/2017)
- Can you believe it? The Obama Administration agreed to take thousands of illegal immigrants from Australia. Why? I will study this dumb deal! (2/1/2017)
- People say my wall idea is crazy. China built a wall and guess how many Mexicans they have. (1/2/2016)
- We MUST have strong borders and stop illegal immigration. Without that we do not have a country. Also, Mexico is killing US on trade WIN! (6/20/2015)
- The border is wide open for cartels & terrorists. Secure our border now. Build a massive wall & deduct the costs from Mexico foreign aid! (3/30/2015)

Such tweet-based populist identity work functions to either provide or concretise for a segment of the population the idea that they have been neglected, overlooked, short-changed, forgotten by some cluster of decision makers and privileged folk – the elite – in part because of the elite's privileging of other clusters of the population, thus giving rise to a new identity group and collective identity.

Although not recognised as a populist, Nixon engaged in populist identity work in solidifying and mobilising the so-called 'Silent Majority' (Lassiter, 2006) and 'hard hats'. Trump, who borrowed from Nixon's playbook, did likewise by tapping into the collective identity of what might be deemed the 'neglected white American'. These strategic efforts to mobilise and speak directly to this identity group seemingly paid off, as nearly 60 per cent of white voters supported Trump over all, including fully two thirds of white voters without college degrees as well as over 80 per cent of white evangelicals (Cillizza, 2016; Tyson & Maniam, 2016). Recall who he was speaking to in his inaugural address with such phrases as: 'The forgotten men and women of the country will be forgotten no longer', and 'You will never be ignored again'. These characterisations are all illustrative of populist identity work and framing.

So what is the connection between such populist framing and identity work and superfluous populations? Our argument is that such framing and identity work, which is hardly peculiar to Trump, appropriates, exploits, and ratchets up whatever empirical basis there is for the populist Manichean project, which, consistent with the triadic conceptualisation of right-wing populism, is generative of 'superfluous populations'. In other words, populist framing serves to make superfluous populations more noticeable and problematic to the rank-and-file adherents of populism. We now turn to consideration of superfluous populations themselves.

Superfluous populations

Dictionary definitions of the adjective 'superfluous' include: exceeding what is sufficient or required; not necessary or relevant; uncalled-for; serving no useful purpose. Any of one of these overlapping definitions implies *surplus, redundancy, and expendability*. The initial use of the term *superfluous people* occurred in Arendt's (1968) monumental tome, *The Origins of Totalitarianism*. Arendt emphasised throughout the book that human populations sometimes come to be defined as superfluous and may thus be conceived as expendable, and thereby as candidates for various forms of social exclusion, social death, and liquidation. As she wrote toward the end of her masterful book:

> [Today], with populations and homeless everywhere on the increase, masses of people are continuously rendered superfluous. . . . Political, social, and economic events everywhere are in silent conspiracy with totalitarian instruments devised for making men superfluous.
>
> (Arendt, 1968 p. 439)

But what exactly did she mean by superfluousness? Here she is only marginally helpful by conflating 'uprootedness' and 'superfluousness'. To be uprooted, she wrote, is 'having no place in the world that is recognized and guaranteed by others; to be superfluous is not to belong to the world at all' (475). Uprootedness can lead to superfluousness, and may often be a step in that direction, but uprootedness is not a necessary or automatic condition for superfluousness. As

Arendt writes: 'Uprootedness can be a preliminary condition for superfluousness, just as isolation . . . can be a preliminary condition for loneliness' (475).

Implied in this juxtaposition of uprootedness to superfluousness is the existence of one or more conditions that give rise to a social category's superfluity. No doubt that is true, but what it gives short shrift to is the constructionist dimension of groups becoming superfluous. In other words, superfluous groups or social categories do not emerge only in the wake of a number of material conditions, but they can and are also 'talked into existence' via identity work and strategic framing, as Trump has done with his repeated framing of himself as the saviour of the country's 'forgotten' and 'ignored' white, working-class Americans. That the majority of this social category were passed by or over by the confluence of automation, the associated decline of the manufacturing sector, plant and job relocation, and the increasing financialisation of capital has certainly contributed to their plight, but whether they have been forgotten or ignored is open to debate. After all, many of the so-called 'forgotten' benefit from federal programs, such as Medicare and even the Affordable Care Act. The more important point, however, is that many of these folks appear to believe – according to Arlie Hochschild's (2016) ethnographic interviews with a handful of them in Louisiana, and Vance's (2016) autoethnographic memoir of a segment of the Appalachian experience – that they have been forgotten or passed over by the federal government. It is folks like this that both left-wing and right-wing populists appeal to, but right-wing populism, in keeping with its triadic structure, goes another step further by engaging in exclusionary identity work entailing the identification of a collective, antagonistic other that is framed as the beneficiary of governmental programs and resources, and thus as the coddled other. Who are these coddled others? According to Hochschild (2016, p. 137), they are the metaphoric 'line cutters'. As she writes in her composite summary sketch of the diagnostic view of her informants:

> Look! You see people *cutting in line ahead of you*! You're following the rules. They aren't. As they cut in, it feels like you are being moved back. How can they just do that? Who are they? Some are black. Through affirmative action plans, pushed by the federal government, they are being given preference for places in colleges and universities, apprenticeships, jobs, welfare payments, and free lunches, and they hold a certain secret in people's minds. . . . Women, immigrants, refugees, public sector workers – where will it end? Your money is running through a liberal sympathy sieve you don't control or agree with. These are the opportunities you'd have loved to have had in your day – and either you should have had them when you were young or the young shouldn't be getting them now. It's not fair.
> (Hochschild, 2016, p. 137)

We have, then, *two strikingly different superfluous categories in the case of right-wing populism*: one that has been framed as forgotten and superfluous but is now framed as a worthy candidate for populist rescue and resurrection, and another that is framed as superfluous and unworthy, and thus out of place or in a place they do not deserve. These differing categories of superfluousness – which might be termed the 'worthy People' and the 'negative other' – are often invoked in tandem with one another, with populists serving as the vanguards who will salvage the former and prevent further encroachment by the latter.

Another way to grasp this flip side of the superfluousness coin is by drawing on the work of the cultural anthropologist Mary Douglas, her most recognised books, *Purity and Danger* (1966) and *Natural Symbols* (1970), and her classification thesis in the vein of Durkheim. The crux of that thesis is that, for all cultures, everything has a place and that things out of place are constitutive of pollution and defilement. She postulated an almost universal cognitive block regarding things out of place, arguing that '[unclassifiables] provoke cognitive discomfort and reactions of disgust, hence negative attitudes to slime, insects, and dirt in general' (Douglas, 2017). The relevance of Douglas's scheme to understanding superfluousness is that it suggests that populations for whom there is not a place or niche comprise excess baggage that draws on and dilutes existing resources, thus rendering them redundant and expendable.

A third line of theorising is also helpful in conceptualising superfluousness. Here we refer to an essay on 'the visibility of evil' in which Lewis Coser (1969) coined the concept of 'spans of sympathy' to focus attention on the degree to which the propensity to sympathise with victims of injustice and misfortune fluctuates within and across societies. Describing a sense of moral invisibility that can envelop a society, Coser argued that 'we share at all times the capacity for not seeing what we do not wish to see', in part because we have only so much emotional energy and yet we live in a world filled with inhumanity and suffering (Coser, 1969, p. 104). In order to protect ourselves both emotionally and morally, it is argued that we are thus inclined toward denial or what Myrdal (1944) referred to as 'the convenience of ignorance'. There are factors other than emotional overload or compassion fatigue that contribute to variability in our spans of sympathy, of course (see Bunis, Yancik & Snow, 1996). But the implication of such observations is that there is no necessary or direct correspondence between the empirical visibility of those who suffer in a society or the world and the extent to which it enters the perceptual and emotional field of others. Accordingly, national and community expressions of sympathy are not simply an automatic response to some set of empirical conditions. Rather, sympathy/compassion is a sentiment or emotional response that is culturally embedded and temporally variable, and therefore subject to the intersection of varying conditions, including manipulation, for which populists like Trump, Le Pen, and Erdogan, among others, have demonstrated a robust aptitude. The implication for understanding the emergence and construction of superfluous people is that a fundamental accoutrement of being out of place is the contraction or retraction of any semblance of sympathy and compassion.

Current and ongoing examples of potentially superfluous people include today's hundreds of thousands of uprooted people that are all known from a distance: the refugees and asylum seekers from various parts of Africa and the Middle East,

Populism and superfluous populations 139

and in the Americas the people fleeing conflict-torn zones in Central and South America. Other examples include the homeless and border-crossing migrants in search of a greener pasture.[4] It is arguable that the rise in populist sentiments, candidates, and elected officials is due in no small part to the surge in out-of-place, unclassifiable people – that is, the ground swell of refugees and immigrants – across much of the world. Yet it is also arguable that there is not a linear relationship between the magnitude of increase in uprooted/displaced persons into a county and the rise and magnitude of populism. The US and the rise of Trumpism provides an illustrative case of this disjunction. As reported in a summary of the findings of an ongoing visualisation study of refugee flows throughout the world since 2000:

> By 2015, the greatest number of refugees were coming from Syria ... and *because most of those refugees went to neighboring countries rather than Europe, the migration received less media attention.* In 2015, the US resettled 69,933 refugees; Uganda, with a population roughly eight times smaller, took in more than 100,000 people. *Developing countries host nearly 90% of the world's refugees.*
>
> (Peters, 2017, italics added)

Based on such findings, the study report concludes that 'the story we tell ourselves about the refugee crisis is very different from the reality' (Peters, 2017). And this is especially so when, as suggested in the above quote, we consider the population size and GDP of the hosting countries. Looking at which countries host the most refugees by overall population, for example, the UN reports for mid-year 2016 that the top hosting countries were, in order: Lebanon, Jordon, Nauru, Turkey, Chad, South Sudan, Sweden, Djibouti, Malta, and Mauritania (Gharib, 2017). Overall, studies of refugee flows over the past 15 years or so reveal that the US is 'almost a non-player on the global stage' (Weller, 2017). Clearly, then, there is no necessary strong relationship between the inflow of refugees and other migrants and the rise of populism.

Yet, in the case of the US and Trump's populist discourse, we are continuously told that the US not only is besieged by refugees and other unwelcomed migrants, but that it carries more than its fair burden. But are these displaced persons or refugees superfluous? Clearly they are uprooted, but Arendt neither specifies the conditions that connect uprootedness and superfluousness, nor identifies clearly other factors that might generate superfluousness in the absence of uprootedness, as in the case of voluntary migrants. In order to gain some clarity on this disconnection and associated question, we turn to consideration of abeyance processes.

Abeyance processes

Dictionary definitions of abeyance commonly refer to a pattern of temporary activity or suspension, as in 'Let's hold that problem in abeyance for a while'.

Common synonyms include: cold storage, deep freeze, doldrums, dormancy, cessation, holding pattern, moratorium, and suspended animation. Sociologically considered, abeyance has been conceptualised and examined historically most thoroughly in Ephraim Mizruchi's (1987) *Regulating Society: Beguines, Bohemians and Other Marginals*. For Mizruchi, abeyance is a process of holding people, which occurs within and between organisations or institutions, typically when there is a surplus or redundant population. Formulaically, abeyance systems or structures arise when there is a mismatch between available positions or statuses or places in a society (too few) and the supply of potential claimants to those positions or statuses or places (too many).

As such, abeyance systems or structures can be thought of as forms of social control that involve two phases that are often interactive: expulsion and absorption. Expulsion generally involves the involuntary movement of people to create spaces or positions for a more select population or program. Examples include the use of the Western frontier in the US as a 'safety valve' for urban surplus populations; the British distribution of surplus populations during its colonial era as with population movements to Northern Ireland and Australia; and current urban gentrification processes involving the dislocation of low income residents in favour of the influx of higher income residents and business supportive of their lifestyle.

Absorption generally involves attempts to control surplus populations, particularly when seen as troublesome or potentially so. Examples include state initiatives, such as in the case of the President Roosevelt's Works Progress Administration (WPA) in the 1930s in the US; public compulsory education as a means of controlling the youth and immigrants; evolving religious orders and their monasteries, abbeys and convents such as the Beguines that emerged in the thirteenth century as a means to absorb the surplus population of women who were unattached because of religious wars, the Crusades, and men being pulled into new religious orders, and the somewhat longer life expectancy of women (Mizruchi, 1987); countercultural movements, such as bohemian/hippie communes (Berger, 1981); and perhaps other systems of enclosure and/or confinement as with 'ghettos' (Duneier, 2016) and prisons (Wacquant, 2002), including the more recent refugee camps such as the former Calais Jungle in France with more than 5,000 residents in 2015, and shelters and other forms of housing for the homeless (Hopper & Baumohl, 1994).

Returning to the question of the link between the uprooted and superfluous populations, the foregoing provides a partial answer: the uprooted or displaced – refugees and involuntary migrants – become superfluous when the abeyance process is not operative with respect to them, thus making them difficult to classify in the sense suggested by Mary Douglas's scheme. This could be because the societal abeyance system is non-existent, overloaded because of resource deficits due to an imbalance between available slots or places and the demand for such, or because of a suspension of the process in respect to the uprooted in question. Right-wing populist appeal may come into play in relation to any of these factors, stoking fears about the threats and dangers of absorbing the uprooted in general or the uprooted from specific places. Trump has employed such fear-stoking appeals with his deportation efforts and promise to build a wall along the US-Mexico border, and his ongoing travel bans and restrictions for people from selected predominantly Muslim countries. Such populist efforts not only suggest publicly that these 'negative others' are out of place and/or unwelcome, but they also contract or suspend the cultural span of sympathy with respect to them, thus making them candidates for some of the more inhumane and unseemly strategies for dealing with superfluous populations. We thus turn to a consideration of these strategies.

Populist strategies for dealing with 'negative other' superfluous populations

Once a population has been rendered superfluous – whether in material/structural actuality, 'talked into existence' through populist discourse, or through a combination of both – there emerges a continuum of potential action that can be taken to resolve the central dilemma of superfluousness. Scholars examining the creation and destruction of the European Jews and the Holocaust have noted that there have been three basic policies for dealing with their constructed superfluity: conversion, expulsion, and annihilation (Hilberg, 1967; Rubenstein, 1975). However, we think the options are somewhat broader, at least for dealing with the superfluous targets of right-wing populism. Here, we identify six such strategies that may be pursued under the banner of populism.

Inaction: Just as superfluous populations can be talked into existence, the strategic action undertaken by populists can be little more than empty rhetoric as well. In some cases, the negative 'othering' levied against potentially superfluous populations may be a hyperbolic scapegoating tactic that serves political ends but offers little in the way of concretely achievable policy aims. Perhaps there is a limit to how much 'red meat' populists can throw at their angry base before their constituency demands more tangible action, but in the meantime, exclusionary populist talk in and of itself appears to be a viable strategy for gaining and maintaining political power. Moreover, if and when action fails to materialize, the triadic structure of right-wing populism enables populists such as Trump to shift blame towards the elites (e.g. the 'swamp' or 'deep state' in Washington, D.C.) for obstructing action.

Incorporation: Populations at risk of superfluousness can be brought into the fold of the dominant social fabric in at least two ways. The first is through the expansion of structural vacancies such as the previously mentioned WPA or other policy measures that significantly expand opportunities to rescue populations from potential superfluousness. The second method of incorporation occurs by placing potentially superfluous populations within abeyance structures, as was the case with the Western frontier in the US and the advent of monastic life in the thirteenth century (Mizruchi, 1987). Such strategies of incorporation are more likely to be embraced by populists when the group in danger of superfluousness is perceived to be on the worthy or deserving in-group side of the coin, as previously discussed. For example, the footprint of the US coal mining industry has dwindled to the point where it is now comparable to niche industries such as nail salons and bowling alleys (Ingraham, 2017), yet some populists are relentless in their efforts to preserve and expand jobs in the coal industry.

Conversion and/or assimilation: Superfluous groups that assimilate into the dominant social order may be perceived by populists as sufficiently transforming their social position. In this way, efforts of conversion or assimilation serve as an act of transmogrification that can reduce the distance between in-group and out-group and tone down the severity of 'negative othering'. German, Irish and Italian immigrants to the United States were all subjected to 'negative othering' and have since successfully been assimilated under the category of 'White-American'. This assimilationist approach is a staple of contemporary populism, including the emphasis placed on speaking English in the US, as evidenced by then-candidate Trump's comments during a presidential debate: 'Well, I think that when you get right down to it, we're a nation that speaks English. I think that, while we're in this nation, we should be speaking English', he stated, adding, '[whether] people like it or not, that's how we assimilate' (Gibson, 2015).

Structural confinement and isolation: When the spatial visibility of out-of-place populations cannot be resolved through the aforementioned strategies and can no longer be ignored, populists may embrace and undertake efforts to physically separate superfluous populations from society writ large. This process of making groups invisible via structural confinement and isolation can range from 'soft' efforts, such as the creation of out-of-sight homeless shelters, to 'hard' approaches, such as ghettoisation and imprisonment.

Population transfer/expulsion: Efforts to transfer or expel a superfluous population constitute a more extreme version of the structural confinement and isolation described above. This strategy of forced relocation is reflected in American history by the Trail of Tears, in which thousands of Cherokee were forcibly uprooted from their lands as a result of President Andrew Jackson's authorisation of the Indian Removal Act in 1830. In doing so, Jackson – the most frequently referenced populist US president until recently – sanctioned an attitude that had persisted for many years among many white immigrants. Even Thomas Jefferson, who often cited the Great Law of Peace of the Iroquois Confederacy as the model for the US Constitution, supported the forced removal of Native Americans as early as 1802. In the contemporary American landscape, the deportation of undocumented citizens is perhaps the most immediate and far-reaching example of population transfer/expulsion.

Liquidation/annihilation: The most severe and brutal strategy for dealing with superfluous populations is annihilation, as in the case of genocides. Clearly it is not a strategy that right-wing populists recommend outright, but as such populism turns to fascism, it may become part of an evolving repertoire of strategies for dealing with constructed superfluous populations, as occurred with the rise of Hitler and Nazism and the drift toward the Holocaust. Regarding this point, Arendt provides the following warning toward the end of *The Origins of Totalitarianism*:

> The Nazis and Bolsheviks can be sure that their factories of annihilation which demonstrate the swiftest solution to the problem of overpopulation, of economically superfluous and socially rootless human masses, are as much an attraction as a warning. Totalitarian solutions may well survive the fall of totalitarian regimes in the form of strong temptations which will come whenever it seems impossible to alleviate political, social, and economic misery in a manner worthy of man.
>
> (Arendt, 1968, p. 459)

To the extent that these six strategies arise sequentially in a stepwise fashion, we would be wise to heed Arendt's warning by paying close attention to the emergence and elaboration of superfluous claims made by populists in order to detect and prevent further escalation towards such final solutions.

Conclusion

We have argued in this chapter that there is a kind of elective affinity between right-wing populism and superfluous populations. Our view of right-wing populism builds on the triadic conceptualisation offered by Judis (2016), in which the populist message pits the rightful but neglected 'people' against some set of underserving 'negative others', and some configuration of enabling elites. It is this demagogic construction of a scapegoat – which is perceived to be favoured and coddled by elites – that accounts in part for the potency of right-wing populism. We also argue that its potency is heightened by a 'messianic' sense of expectancy, provided by some populists such as Trump, not only of better days to come but of a kind of collective transposition in which the structural and cultural position of the rightful but neglected people – the pure or true people – and the resented 'negative others' are reversed. An additional source or potency is the populist's charismatic-like claims about their uniqueness and solitary powers to effect the changes, including the transpositional order which they have promised. It is these intersecting elements of right-wing populism that makes it a likely progenitor of superfluous people. By superfluous people we mean – based on our integration of the work of political philosopher Hannah Arendt (1968), anthropologist Mary Douglas (1966), and sociologist Lewis Coser (1969) – social categories for whom there is no niche or place, whether for social structural or constructionist reasons, and who are therefore seen as redundant and expendable populations who fall outside of the cultural span of sympathy.

Linking these constructions of right-wing populism and superfluous people, we have argued, with illustrative material drawn principally from the Trump presidential campaign, that right-wing populism is likely to be associated with two strikingly different and oppositional superfluous social categories: the 'worthy people', who have been framed as forgotten and superfluous to the existing elite but now as deserving candidates for populist rescue and resurrection, and the 'negative other', who are framed as superfluous and unworthy, and thus out of place or in a place that makes them candidates for various forms of social exclusion or worse. As argued earlier, this is not to say that right-wing populists necessarily generate or construct superfluous populations, but they often nurture the soil for that possibility by engaging in their Manichean exclusionary identity work and politics, often by exploiting certain existing trends, such as the flow of uprooted peoples and immigrants. However, caution also needs to be exercised so as not to assume a direct, linear relationship between escalating trends, such as the refugee flow, and the rise of populism. To do so would be to ignore the fact that 'populists have often distorted or even invented fact in order to make their case' (Zakaria, 2016, p. 15), as Trump, among others, has been given to do. However, we have also cautioned that whether populations targeted by right-wing populist rhetoric become fully superfluous is likely to be contingent on at least two other factors: the collapse or contraction of the abeyance process and the associated cultural span of sympathy. Finally, we have called attention to a continuum of ways in which populists may strategically deal with superfluous populations of 'the negative other' variety, with both abeyance processes and fluctuations in the cultural span of sympathy also functioning as important intervening factors in this dynamic.

Notes

1. We wish to acknowledge the helpful comments of John McCarthy of Pennsylvania State University and Eddie Hartmann of the University of Potsdam, Germany, for their helpful suggestions regarding the talk that formed the basis for the paper, and Roberta Lessor for her thorough reading of the chapter and her useful comments.
2. For discussion of the intersection of these two mechanisms, see Hunt, Benford and Snow (1994); Snow and McAdam (2000), and particularly Aslanidis (2016), in relation to populism.
3. See Snow, Vliegenhart & Ketelaars (2018) for an updated review of the framing literature on social movements.
4. For discussion of the scope and magnitude of this problem worldwide, and its relation to modernity and globalisation, see Fritz (2000) and Bauman (2004).

References

Applebaum, Y. (2016). I alone can fix it. *The Atlantic*, July 21. Retrieved from www.theatlantic.com/politics/archive/2016/07/trump-rnc-speech-alone-fix-it/492557/.

Arendt, H. (1968). *The origins of totalitarianism*. Orlando, FL: Harcourt.

Aslanidis, P. (2016). Populists social movements of the great recession. *Mobilization*, *21*(3), 301–332.

Bauman, Z. (2004). *Wasted lives: Modernity and its outcasts*. Cambridge: Polity Press.

Berger, B. M. (1981). *The survival of a counterculture: Ideological work and everyday life among rural communards*. Berkeley, CA: University of California Press.

Berman, S. (2016). Populism is not fascism, but it could be a Harbinger. *Foreign Affairs*, *95*(November/December), 39–44.

Bunis, W. K., Yancik, A., & Snow, D. A. (1996). The cultural patterning of sympathy toward the homeless and other victims of misfortune. *Social Problems*, *43*(4), 387–402.

Cillizza, C. (2016). The 13 most amazing findings in the 2016 exit poll. *The Washington Post*, November 10. Retrieved from www.washingtonpost.com/news/the-fix/wp/2016/11/10/the-13-most-amazing-things-in-the-2016-exit-poll/?utm_term=.e8aedf3d8a21.

Coser, L. A. (1969). The visibility of evil. *Journal of Social Issues*, *25*(1), 101–109.
Douglas, M. (1966). *Purity and danger: An analysis of concepts of pollution and taboo*. London: Routledge & Keagan Paul.
Douglas, M. (1970). *Natural symbols: Explorations in cosmology*. London: Barrie & Rockliff.
Douglas, M. (2017). A history of grid and group cultural theory. Retrieve from http://projects.chass.utoronto.ca/semiotics/cyber/douglas1.
Duneier, M. (2016). *Ghetto: The invention of a place, the history of an idea*. New York: Farrat, Straus and Giroux.
Fritz, M. (2000). *Lost on earth: Nomads of the new world*. New York and London: Routledge.
Gharib, M. (2017). Which countries host the most refugees relative to size and wealth?. *Goats and Soda*, March 27. Retrieved from www.npr.org/sections/goatsandsoda/2017/03/27/518217052/chart-where-the-worlds-refugees-are.
Gibson, G. (2015). Trump to bilingual Bush: 'We should be speaking English'. *Reuters*, September 4. Retrieved from http://blogs.reuters.com/talesfromthetrail/2015/09/04/trump-to-bilingual-bush-we-should-be-speaking-english/.
Hilberg, R. (1967). *The destruction of European Jews*. Chicago, NJ: Quadrangle Books.
Hochschild, A. R. (2016). *Strangers in their own land*. New York and London: The New Press.
Hopper, K., & Baumohl, J. (1994). Held in abeyance: Rethinking homelessness and advocacy. *American Behavioral Scientist*, *37*(4), 522–552.
Hunt, S., Benford, R. D., & Snow, D. A. (1994). Identity fields: Framing processes and the social construction of movement identities. In E. Larana, H. Johnson, & J. Gusfield (Eds.), *New social movements: From ideology to identity* (pp. 185–208). Philadelphia, PA: Temple University Press.
Ingraham, C. (2017). The entire coal industry employs fewer people than Arby's. *Washington Post*, March 31. Retrieved from www.washingtonpost.com/news/wonk/wp/2017/03/31/8-surprisingly-small-industries-that-employ-more-people-than-coal/?utm_term=.d2730b20c7b4.
Judis, J. B. (2016). *The populist explosion: How the great recession transformed American politics*. New York: Columbia Global Reports.
Kazin, M. (1995). *The populist persuasion: An American history*. New York: Basic Books.
Laclau, E. (2005). *On populist reason*. London: Verso.
Lassiter, R. D. (2006). *The silent majority: Suburban politics in the Sunbelt South*. Princeton, NJ: Princeton University Press.
Manseau, P. (2016). Is Trumpism its own religion?. *Los Angeles Times*, June 21. Retrieved from www.latimes.com/opinion/op-ed/la-oe-manseau-trump-religious-movement-20160621-snap-story.html.
Mizruchi, E. H. (1987). *Regulating society: Beguines, bohemians, and other marginals*. Chicago, IL: University of Chicago Press.
Mudde, C. (2004). The populist Zeitgeist. *Government and Opposition*, *39*(4), 541–563.
Mudde, C. (2016). Europe's populist surge: A long time in making. *Foreign Affairs*, *95*(6), 25–30.
Müller, J.-W. (2015). Parsing populism: Who is and who is not a populist these days?. *Juncture*, *22*(2), 80–89.
Müller, J.-W. (2016). *What is populism?*. Philadelphia, PA: University of Pennsylvania Press.

Myrdal, G. (1944). *An American dilemma: The Negro problem and modern democracy*. New York: Harper and Row.
Peters, A. (2017). Watch the movements of every refugee on earth since the year 2000. Retrieved from www.fastcompany.com/40423720/watch-the-movements-of-every-refugee-on-earth-since-the-year-2000.
Rubenstein, R. L. (1975). *The cunning of history: The Holocaust and the American future*. New York: Harper Colophon Books.
Snow, D. A., & Anderson, L. (1987). Identity work among the homeless: The verbal construction and avowal of personal identities. *American Journal of Sociology, 92*(6), 1336–1371.
Snow, D. A., & McAdam, D. (2000). Identity work processes in the context of social movements: Clarifying the identity/movement Nexus. In S. Stryker, T. Owens & R. White (Eds.), *Self, identity, and social movements* (pp. 41–67). Minneapolis, MN: University of Minnesota Press.
Snow, D. A., Vliegenhart, R., & Ketelaars, P. (2018). The framing perspective on social movements: Its conceptual roots and architecture. In D. A. Snow, S. A. Soule, H. Kriesi & H. McCammon (Eds.), *The Wiley-Blackwell companion to social movements*. Oxford: Wiley. (2nd ed.), new and expanded.
Tyson, A., & Maniam, S. (2016). Behind Trump's victory: Divisions by race, education and gender. *Factank: News in the Numbers*, Pew Research Center, November 9. Retrieved from www.pewresearch.org/fact-tank/2016/11/09/behind-trumps-victory-divisions-by-race-gender-education/.
Vance, J. D. (2016). *Hillbilly elegy: A memoir of a family and culture in crisis*. New York: Harper.
Wacquant, L. J. D. (2002). From slavery to mass incarceration: Rethinking the 'race question' in the US. *New Left Review, 13*(January/February), 41–60.
Weller, C. (2017). Mesmerizing maps show the global flow of refugees over the last 15 Years, *Tech Insider*. Retrieved from www.businessinsider.de/maps-flow-refugees-last-15-years-2017–5?r=US&IR=T.
Zakaria, F. (2006). Populism on the March: Why the West is in trouble. *Foreign Affairs, 95*(6), 9–15.

9 Toward a strategy for integrating the study of social movement and populist party mobilisation

John D. McCarthy

'May You Live in Interesting Times'

Introduction

In this chapter I bring to a consideration of populist movements a general approach to understanding forms of insurgent social movement mobilisation that has evolved during the last three decades within a robust community of North American and European scholars (McAdam, McCarthy & Zald, 1996; Snow, Soule & Kriesi, 2004). I believe that paradigm offers a relatively well curated theoretical kitbag useful for exploring which social, economic and cultural factors are important in accounting for variation in insurgent mobilisation across movements of all kinds, across time, and across national contexts, including, I will argue, populist political party mobilisations.

Theoretical tools in this kitbag have been employed recently by a number of scholars writing about populist radical right parties in Europe (Hutter, 2014; Klandermans & Mayer, 2006; Koopmans et al., 2005; Kriesi, 2014; Mudde, 2007), but they have rarely taken the methodological turn of pursuing comparative analyses of populist mobilisation by decomposing its discrete issues (or claims) to allow comparison with the full range of collective action into equivalent units of empirical analysis. It is that turn, I will argue, that led to the flourishing of empirical scholarship on the full range of collective action in its diverse forms (protest, social movement organisations (SMOs) and party formation and mobilisation). By neglecting to take that turn seriously most populist scholarship has focused primarily upon party voting and, therefore, remains un-integrated with the bulk of empirical scholarship on insurgent collective action, even in nations with flourishing populist parties.

In the following, I first recount what I argue was the decisive methodological shift in the study of social movements that allowed the comparative study of the full range of insurgent collective action claims by moving away from the use of the concept of social movement as the key theoretical unit of analysis. Second, I offer a critique of the research scholarship on populism from the methodological perspective I have described, suggesting how populist party mobilisation, as well as populist protest and SMOs, can be decomposed into clusters of issue claims facilitating analyses that allow comparison of them with the full spectrum of issue claim mobilisation. Third, I describe the three primary forms of insurgent collective action mobilisation, protest, SMO mobilisation and party mobilisation, and discuss how they vary in comparative frequency across national contexts. Finally, after reviewing the key theoretical factors now typically deployed by analysts of comparative collective action, I illustrate the use of a few of them in a glimpse at how they can be used to explain instances of the surge of populist issue collective action in the recent period in North America and Western Europe, widely described as a populist moment.

From social movements and SMOs to collective action claims and advocacy organisations

The now dominant approach to the study of social movements was heavily influenced by the conceptualisation and research of Charles Tilly (1978, 2005). Arguing that 'the prototype' social movement was the emergent socialist movement in Western Europe, Tilly focused his empirical approach upon collective action claims by collective actors, both movement and non-movements. Research in the US, previously dominated by collective behaviour frameworks, had regularly focused upon spelling out the key dimensions of what we now call campaigns of collective action that were deemed to constitute social movements, many of them very different in goals and structure from socialist movements. This regularly led to disputes about whether particular empirical instances were or were not social movements. (e.g. right-wing movements, religious movements, feminist movements) Social movement textbooks invariably began with such a definitional exercise, and still do (della Porta and Diani, 2006; Snow and Soule, 2010). For example, Snow and Soule define that

> social movements are collectivities acting with some degree of organisation and continuity, partly outside institutional or organisational channels, for the purpose of challenging extant systems of authority, or resisting change in such systems, in organisation, society, culture, or world system in which they are embedded.
>
> (Snow & Soule, 2010, pp. 6–7)

Before what I will call the theoretical/methodological turn, such definitions led researchers to narrow their focus to a subcategory of collective action, impeding wide comparative analysis. A key dimension of disagreement among analysts, as the above definition demonstrates, has been the centrality of unconventional (or disruptive) tactics to the definition of a social movement, even though most analysts accepted Michels' claim of the ultimate triumph of the 'iron law of oligarchy' (Michels [1911] 1962), organisational processes that resulted in the mainstreaming of tactics for any successful social movement over time.[1] A similar dispute came to dominate the study of social movement organisations (SMOs), as analysts began to recognise their pervasiveness and directly study more formally organised collective actors. Was the National Association for the Advancement of Colored People (NACCP) an SMO or an interest group? Interest groups were on the turf of political scientists, and constituted a part of the informal conventional system of governmental influence. SMOs were unconventional, and outsiders, employing unconventional tactics. Tilly's early depiction of polity insiders and outsiders contributed to hardening this barrier, in my opinion, theoretically marginalising the analysis of the full range of what have since come to be termed 'advocacy organisations' (AOs) (Andrews & Edwards, 2004) in contrast to his path-breaking leadership toward analysing collective action claims (or issues) of insurgents.

These two related theoretical/methodological turns were, then, in my opinion, the shift from using social movement as the central units of analysis toward using collective action claims (issues) as the unit of analysis across all forms of insurgent collective action; and, the shift from focusing only upon SMOs toward comparative study of the full range of advocacy organisations. The turns allowed analysts to study the full range of protest events and AOs comparatively across time and across place. I briefly review the emergence and flourishing of research following the turns.

Insurgent claims analysis spread rapidly, following Tilly's lead, and became known among its practitioners as 'protest event analysis' (PEA). Heavily relying upon print sources, most frequently newspapers, PEA analysts expanded their focus to speech acts (see Koopmans et al., 2005), public gatherings of all types, as well as press releases and law suits. The basic unit of analysis in the approach is events where a collective actor makes a claim in the name of more than a single individual. An early example of the approach is that of Kriesi and his colleagues (Kriesi et al., 1995), who gathered events from national newspapers in four European nations (France, Germany, Switzerland and the Netherlands) between 1975 and 1989, analysing their comparative features through time and across the four nations.[2] Typically, such datasets employ a claims category scheme, attempting to differentiate all the specific claims (issues) that are advanced from one another. Events may focus upon a single claim or on multiple claims, which is common.

A more recent example of a PEA dataset is that of the 'dynamics of collective action' (DOC). The extensive research that it has facilitated demonstrates the potential of PEA for the comparative study of insurgent collective action. Collected by Sarah Soule, Susan Olzak, Doug McAdam and John D. McCarthy, it consists of all of the protest events mentioned in the *New York Times* from 1960 through 1995, and is available online for downloading and analysis.[3] The codebook, provided online, includes a two-page description of a collective action event. The data has been used as the basis of scores of published papers analysing protests events, a small subset of which are listed on the web-site. The list of possible claims advanced by protesters is seven pages long, dominated by 'rights' claims, a distinctive US focus. Several good examples of what can be done with the data are seen in Soule and Earl's (2005) examination of the full range of protest issues across more than two decades in the US; the paper by Walker, Martin and McCarthy (2008) which shows how the tactics employed by collective actors vary by the targets they choose. Another paper by King, Bentele and Soule (2007) examines the variation over time in protest on rights issues and similarly US congressional attention to rights issues.

The equivalent theoretical/methodological move toward a focus upon the full range of AOs is clearly displayed in the early work of Debra Minkoff, a pioneer of this approach. Using the *Encyclopedia of Associations* (a source devoted to including all national associations in the US, published and updated annually, she tracked all women's and African-American advocacy associations over an extended period of time. She showed that the majority of them were not primarily devoted to protest, but instead most were devoted to providing services. Analysing all of the AOs exhibiting claims about women's and African-American issues allowed Minkoff (1994) to show how rare protest was as the primary tactic for these AOs, and, also how they evolved over time away from protest as a primary tactic as a result of environmental forces. Making the issues AOs emphasised and examining the entire range of AOs, then, put the protest mobilisation around women's and African-American issues into broader theoretical and empirical collective action context.

Following Minkoff's lead, many other researchers have drawn on the same data source to investigate a variety of issues about the shape, size and trajectory of the full spectrum of AOs in the US over extended periods (Bevan et al., 2013). For instance, Walker, McCarthy and Baumgartner (2011), coding AOs by their primary issues, show how important issue categories of AOs grew over the late twentieth century, and that the growth was similar for both membership and non-membership organisations, in contrast to arguments of observers that newly formed AOs had been less likely to recruit members than more traditional ones. Finally, Wang and Soule (2012) use the DOC PEA dataset to create an issue cross-walk to link organisational information from the EA to SMOs present at protest events to investigate diffusion of protest tactics across AOs. Increasingly, issue cross-walks between systematic datasets will facilitate combining various forms of evidence on insurgent collective action and AOs, as well as many other types of organisations and evidence, and, importantly, the issues political parties mobilise around.

I have claimed that these theoretical/methodological turns led to a flourishing of research, and the evidence supports my claim, as the dominance of publications in top US peer-reviewed journals as they occurred shows an astonishing trend. As shown in Figure 9.1, by 2005, more than 25 per cent of the publications in these journals focused primarily upon collective action and social movements. The calculations displayed there are based upon summing the total number of articles in seven sociology disciplinary journals (*American Sociological Review*, *American Journal of Sociology*, *Social Forces*, *Social Problems*, *Sociological Forum*, *Sociological Perspectives*, and *Sociological Quarterly*), and then, based upon a key word search strategy, identifying those articles that focused upon social movement/collective action topics. As issue-based empirical analyses of collective action began to take hold among social movement researchers, the rate of publications about it in disciplinary journals skyrocketed.

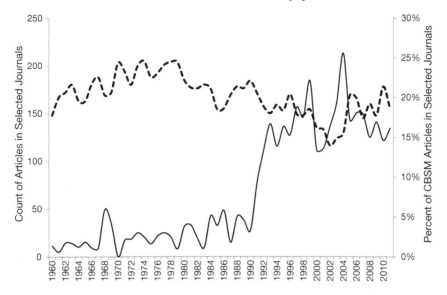

Figure 9.1 Time-series of total and collective behaviour/social movement publications appeared in top four US sociology journals, 1960–2012

Note: Solid line represents the raw count of social movement articles (left Y-axis). Dashed line represents the proportion of social movement articles over the all of the articles published in selected journals (right Y-axis).

Studying populist protest and party mobilisation

Reading widely across the scholarly literatures on populism published during the last several decades, I have been struck by three central features: 1) a predominance of case studies or small N studies; 2) the agonising lengths to which many analysts go in attempting to delimit the phenomenon they label populism; and 3) the extensive focus upon populist political parties, and especially voting, as an index of popular support for populism, thereby conflating the specific mix of issues (claims) each party espouses, claims which they often times share with other parties (e.g. immigration), and the reality that the centrality of a party's focus upon an issue can change dramatically over time. (e.g. law and order). My impressions regarding the first two features are affirmed in an observation by Jansen, in his recent extensive review and critique of that literature, when he says:

> Over the past 50 years, scholars from various disciplines have disagreed not only about how to best explain populism's historical emergence, but more fundamentally about what it *is*. Most of what has been written has come not in the form of theoretical statements or comparative analyses, but as historical studies of individual populist cases.
>
> (Jansen, 2011, p. 78)

These impressions are also clearly illustrated in two widely noted recently published, more popular, analyses of populism by North American analysts (Judis, 2016; Müller, 2016), interest in them being spurred by the Donald Trump Presidential run. In selecting notorious cases and putting great effort into arriving at a definition of the thing to be explained, both authors struggle to integrate instances of what they term populism in the US with Western European populism, mostly party emergence and voting.

Cas Mudde, perhaps the most theoretically astute empirical researcher of right-wing European populist parties, begins his analyses of those parties with a typical, but incisive, effort to specify the most important common features of populist right-wing parties, what he terms a party family.[4] Although each differs from one another in what he terms less central characteristics, they together share, he claims, an enthusiasm for nationalism (encompassing anti-globalisation), xenophobia, strong states and welfare chauvinism (Mudde, 2007, p. 21). I would add to Mudde's list a pretty consistently expressed hostility toward ruling elites. He terms these ideological features of parties rather than claims. He also lists eight other features, subsumed under the primary features, not always present in the cases he examines. Those features look closer to being what PEA analysts' term claims. The direction I suggest for integrating analyses such as Mudde's with the broader research community employing discrete claims for analysis, would be to turn these major and minor features into discrete claims that can be coded independently as present or absent from party platforms, press releases, speeches and campaign materials, and the like. The presence or absence of each can be tracked over time, and, especially for the concerns of analysts such as Mudde, their co-presence can be analysed. Then, the presence of these claims can be analysed along with similar analyses of other parties' claims, as well as the claims of protesters and advocacy organisations. I will return to further discussion of this strategy below but let me say that with such comprehensive data in hand that allows the analysis of the full range of insurgent collective actor claims across the full range of actors, it would become rather straightforward identifying actors with multiple claims thought to be populist from other actors, thus identifying trends in more or less right-wing populist mobilisation. Let me stress that Mudde is definitely not guilty of Jansen's charge, offering systematic and convincing comparative analyses of populist parties in Europe. And, while he discusses their variable strength in terms of demand and supply side causal factors that has become common among comparative analysts of populist parties (Goulder, 2016; Rydgren, 2007), tellingly, however, neither the word protest nor the term social movements appear, for instance, in the index to Mudde's (2007) *Populist Radical Right Parties in Europe*, or in his analyses therein of populist party mobilisation. What I have come to discover in my dive into these literatures is that a systematic dynamic approach to Populist Party mobilisation is only just emerging.

Three primary forms of insurgent mobilisation

I want to distinguish between three forms of insurgent mobilisation: 1) organising and fielding protest events, 2) the formation and growth of AOs, and 3) political party formation and mobilisation. Activists aiming to advance grievance issues can choose to put their efforts into one or another of these action forms, or some combination of them. I will argue that right-wing populist groups in European parliamentary systems have tended to favour political party electoral mobilisation, but the situation has been quite different in the US In doing so, I follow Jansen when he says, 'I propose a shift away from the problematic notion of "populism" and toward the concept of *populist mobilization*' (Jansen, 2011, p. 81). The thing to be explained, then, is temporal and spatial patterns in different forms of populist mobilisation, not in isolation from one another, but in contrast to the full range of protest, AO and party mobilisation. Once the several forms have been delineated, I will turn to a selective consideration of some important theoretical factors that have been implicated in the rate and timing of movement mobilisation in general, and their relevance to recent populist issue mobilisation in particular.

Protest events

A massive research literature has emerged aimed at explaining variation in public protest over time and across nations. Depending primarily upon newspaper and media reports of protest, as well as, sometimes, drawing on police reports, scholars have explored a wide variety of factors thought to explain variation in protest mobilisation. Protest has become widespread and normative in Western democracies, leading some observers to speak of the 'Social Movement Society' (Meyer & Tarrow, 1997). And, the standard research template that came to be known as Protest Event Analysis (PEA) has been deployed by researchers both in Western democracies and around the world, with the aim of systematically exploring variation in protest mobilisation. The extent and average size of protest events varies across nations and through time, being quite a bit more common in Western European democracies than the US in recent decades (Norris, 2002). Some protests occur spontaneously, but they tend to be relatively small. Large protests are typically organised by activists involved in SMOs but more recently researchers have shown the increasing importance of social media in assembling large protest demonstrations (Bennett & Segerberg, 2014; Tufekci, 2017). But, in general large-scale protests depend upon the agency of activists and groups, and the best predictor of who participates is who is asked to do so (Schussman & Soule, 2005). Right-wing populist protest has been generally rarer in Western European nations and the US in recent decades than protest by other issue groups, especially those espousing left and new social movement issues. This is seen clearly in Hutter's data (2014, p. 118) that shows protest around left issues substantially more extensive across several Western European democracies than protest around right-wing issues.

Advocacy organisations' density

Advocacy organisations are more or less organised vehicles created to facilitate collective action aimed at creating social change on behalf of a social issue. They are a common form of social movement collective action, and have proliferated very extensively in the US (e.g. Walker, McCarthy & Baumgartner, 2011), while not so widely in Western European democracies. While right-wing populist AOs have emerged in Europe, for instance, 'Activists Against Islamisation' (Benveniste & Pingaud, 2016) in France, and PEGIDA in Dresden (Kocyba, 2017) and beyond Germany (Berntzen & Weisskircher, 2016), my strong impression is that AOs in general are far more prevalent in the US across the spectrum. Blee and Creasap (2017) describe in great detail the panoply of right-wing conservative advocacy organisations and campaigns that have flourished in the U.S in recent decades. They attribute this surge importantly to 1) alliances that were forged between social conservatives and free market conservatives, and 2) to the entry of large numbers of conservative Evangelical Protestant conservatives into politics, discussed in more detail below.

Research on protest and organisational mobilisation in the US has been criticised for being 'movement centric', and, especially for ignoring interactions between protest, movement spawned groups and political parties (McAdam & Tarrow, 2013) or any serious consideration of party mobilisation around issues. European populism research reflects the flip-side of that problem – it pays little attention to the extra-party mobilisation of direct action protest and the founding and activities of advocacy organisational vehicles, nor does it pay more than scant attention to party mobilisation mechanisms.

Party formation and mobilisation

Preceding Jansen's recent call for a focus upon the mobilisation as an approach to understanding populist political parties, some scholars had already been working within a movement mobilisation framework in trying to understand the recent rise of populist parties in Western Europe (e.g. Veuglers, 1997, 1999). Veuglers (1999) makes a cogent case that the study of parties by sociologists was moribund by the turn of the century, pretty much ignoring the dynamics of party formation and mobilisation. I want to call particular attention, however, to a recent book that develops a robust theoretical framework for understanding such mobilisation.

Building blocs: how parties organise societies

The editors' 'Introduction' to *Building Blocs: How Parties Organize Societies* (de Leon, Desai & Tuğal, 2015) sketches a thorough critique aimed at understanding parties as far more than simply a reflection of the pre-existing structures and sentiment cleavages in a society (what had been the dominant framework for understanding them). Parties are seen, rather, as active agents that cobble together elements of the social structure, cultural elements and civil society organisations into emergent and evolving mechanisms for electoral mobilisation, a process they call political articulation. They say:

> We define political articulation as the process by which parties 'suture' together cohesive blocs and cleavages from a disparate set of constituencies

and individuals, who, even by virtue of sharing circumstances many not necessarily share the same political identity

(de Leon, Desai & Tuğal, 2015, p. 2)

This approach views political parties as important in creating societal cleavages and shaping what my colleagues and I have called sentiment pools (Kim & McCarthy, 2016; McCarthy & Zald, 2002). I suggest, then, that a full understanding of populist issue mobilisation requires including all forms of mobilisation across the full range of issue claims, allowing the analyst to put party populist claims into comparative context. This has become the standard approach for studies of protest and AO mobilisation, and by combining all political party issue mobilisation in similar analyses and integrating them with the flourishing protest and AO movement mobilisation literature, I contend, studies of populist party mobilisation can be integrated into direct dialogue with the flourishing movement research.

Understanding populist issue mobilisation: the movement mobilisation paradigm

Many social movement analysts in both North America and Western Europe during the last decades of the twentieth century worked within a broad consensus in regularly invoking three key theoretical factors in explaining variation in insurgent mobilisation: 1) resources/material and organisational; 2) political opportunities, and 3) framing and media processes (see McAdam, McCarthy & Zald, 1996). In the following section I will touch upon each of these in emphasising a particular instance of populist issue mobilisation. I begin with discussion of the role of grievances which had been back grounded by those working within this paradigm. However, the role of grievances has begun to be reemphasised among movement researchers in recent years, and particularly with respect to populist mobilisation.

Grievances

Classical social movement analysts relied heavily upon grievances in accounting for insurgent movement mobilisation, which, nevertheless, was shown in many cases to be an inadequate, or at least a wholly incomplete, explanation of such mobilisation. For North American analysts, the emergent 'civil rights' movement called out for explanations beyond grievances since it occurred at a time when, by many indicators, life circumstances for African-American citizens had been steadily improving. The important books by Doug McAdam (1982) and Aldon Morris (1984) offered complementary, and highly convincing, accounts of the mobilisation of the US civil rights movement by invoking a variety of other factors beyond grievances. In an effort to change the subject from grievances, John McCarthy and Mayer Zald made a claim that many scholars later found outrageous when they said:

We are willing to assume that there is always enough discontent in any society to supply grass-roots support for a movement if the movement is effectively organised and has at its disposal the power and resources of some established elite group.

(McCarthy & Zald, 1977, p. 1215)

A burst of research in the 1980s and 1990s subsequently elaborated many important factors beyond grievances in attempting to best account for insurgent movement mobilisation. In fact, however, subsequent scholarship has clearly shown the importance of grievances in explaining mobilisation, especially economic grievances, and those scholars have brought grievances back into the discussion of how to explain variation in mobilisation. I will briefly discuss some of that work here, and how it pertains to populist mobilisation. I finally then turn my attention to the other theoretical factors I believe are important for making sense of movement mobilisation, and in doing so, highlight some specific examples drawing upon evidence of recent populist mobilisation in the US and Western Europe.

It is untenable to focus upon recent populist mobilisation without considering the role of the economic crisis of 2008 and its consequences. The crisis was followed in short order by anti-austerity protests and invigorated populist party activity across Western Europe. And, in the US it was quickly followed by the rapid formation of local Tea Party groups and their extensive protests and the proliferating Occupy Wall Street contentious occupations of public spaces across the country. Research showing the impact of economic deprivation (sometimes both objective and subjective) had already begun to accumulate before the crisis, and has expanded since, such impact seen in spurring public protests, right-wing social movement organisations and populist party activity.[5]

In a study of homeless protests across seventeen US cities, Snow, Soule and Cress (2005) showed that one of the strongest set of predictors of the number of annual protests by homeless groups was measures of economic deprivation. Snow and Soule (2010) went on, in their concise summary of social movement research, to develop a vigorous defence of the importance of grievances to understanding insurgent mobilisation. Caren, Gaby and Herrold (2017) have just published a systematic effort to assess the role of economic breakdown (indicated by an annual decline in per capita gross domestic product) on collective action (in their case, protests and riots) for 145 countries for the period 1960–2006. They conclude their extensive analyses by saying,

we find that economic adversity and collective action are linked so strongly as to suggest that economic conditions cannot be overlooked as an important precursor to social movement mobilization.

(Caren, Gaby & Herrold, 2017, p. 151)

The time series they employ ends in 2006, just prior to the 2008 financial crisis, but another study by Mario Quaranta carried out a similar analysis for the

2000–2014 time period, with similar results. Assessing evidence from 25 European nations, using the Global Dataset on Events, Locations and Tone (GDELT) he investigated the impact of variation in an economic performance index (including the factors of inflation, unemployment and deficit growth) and a consumer confidence indicator on 'anti-government protests'. He concludes by saying:

> the analyses have demonstrated that a relationship exists between objective economic conditions and subjective economic evaluations, and the number of anti-government protests, and that this association is robust.
> (Quaranta, 2016, p. 749)

There exists a bit of evidence that economic grievances also are related to the rate of right-wing patriot/militia organisations mobilised within a state in the US during the mid-1990s. Van Dyke and Soule (2002), for instance, show that the number of such groups organised in a state in the US is strongly related to the loss of manufacturing jobs and the loss of farms in a state. These groups are primarily grass-roots ones with little outside support. The fact that SMOs of any scope and size require extensive resources means that, in general, we would not expect economic grievances to automatically translate into the founding and flourishing of such movement groups. So economic jolts like that of the 2008 financial crisis can be expected to generate increased numbers of potential supporters for such groups if they manage to secure enough resources to get organised. Hanspeter Kriesi makes a convincing argument about the more general impact of the major financial shock of 2008. He says:

> Grievances constitute the starting point: an exogenous shock like the Great Recession creates a tremendous amoung of popular discontent. People with grievances seek to express them, and they do so by raising their voice by exiting ... one of the first signs of popular discontent are sharp shifts in voting patterns.
> (Kriesi, 2016, p. 68)

Of course, a number of grievances are obviously the focus of recent right-wing populist mobilisations beyond economic ones, especially issues of immigrants and immigration, as indicated clearly by the agendas (and platforms) of populist parties, and the issues raised by populist protests and advocacy organisations.[6]

Resources

My own work on mobilisation has laid heavy emphasis upon the availability of resources to activists who seek to mobilise protest, organise and recruit members to social movement organisations and organise and mobilise members of political parties to challenge mainstream institutions of the state, corporations and powerful non-profit organisations such as universities, and mainstream political parties

(McCarthy & Zald, 1978; Walker et al., 2011). Since most insurgent groups lack extensive resources of their own, the availability of outside resources, especially financial and social organisational ones (Edwards & McCarthy, 2004), are many times key to understanding both mobilisation potential and mobilisation success. So it is not surprising to find the existence of important flows of such resources from outside sources to successful right-wing populist mobilisation efforts. Both the Bolsheviks and the Symbionese Army activists robbed banks to provide resources for their movements, but modern activists seek resources in a variety of more or less legitimate places, especially in state sources and groups of wealthy elite supporters in the US. I illustrate this with evidence for the French National Front Party and the US Tea Party.

Key Resource Flows to French National Front: Even without much in the way of national parliamentary success, several European right-wing populist parties have been able to draw extensively on European Parliamentary resources to fund their extensive mobilisation efforts, particularly Marine Le Pen's National Front and the UK Independence Party (UKIP). In an analysis of this pattern Birnbaum says:

> Many of the strongest bids to tear apart the E.U. are being underwritten by E.U. cash. . . . As many as a third of the European Parliaments' 751 members are Euro-sceptics, including 23 members of Le Pen's National Front Party.
> (Birnbaum, 2017)

UKIP has had a similar level of success recently with 22 members of the European Parliament (MEPs). Recall that these two parties then held almost no seats in their respective national parliaments. This is significant, why? Because EU Parliamentary membership is accompanied by lavish salaries and extensive expense allowances and allowances for Parliamentary assistants. With over twenty MEPs, then, the National Front, through its MEPs, has access to extensive resources for mobilisation of support.

Key Resource Flows to the Initial Tea Party Mobilization. I relate a series of observations from Jane Mayer's brilliant reporting on the flow of outside resources, both infrastructural and financial, to the US Tea Party during its initial burst of mobilisation.

'In 1991, Citizens for a Sound Economy (a Koch brother's funded organisation) promoted what was advertised as a massive "reenactment of the Boston Tea Party" in Raleigh, North Carolina, to protest tax increases' (Mayer, 2016, p. 168). In 2007, '[the] Koch's new organization, Americans for Prosperity, tried to stage another Tea Party protest against taxes, this time in Texas. It too was a dud' (169). Within hours of the Santaelli rant, (thought by many to be the rallying cry for the initial Tea party mobilisation) 'another Web site called *TaxDayTeaParty.com* appeared on the internet, organised by a long time associate of the Koch's (Eric Odom) (176). 'Odom also formed what he called the nationwide Tea Party Coalition with other activists, including operatives from Dick Armey's group, FreedomWorks and the Koch's group, Americans for Prosperity. APF quickly registered a Web site called *TayPayerTeaParty.com* and used its network of fifty-some staffers to plan rallies across the country' (180).

No organization played a bigger early role than FreedomWorks, the estranged sibling of Americans for Prosperity, which was funded by donations from companies such as Phillip Morris and from billionaires such as Richard Mellow Scaife. 'I'd argue that when the Tea Party took off, FreedomWorks had as much to do with making it an effective movement as anyone', said Armey (Mayer, 2016, p. 182).

Elite framing and media processes in consensus mobilisation

Bert Klandermans, several decades ago, made a strong distinction between what he dubbed the theoretically distinct processes of consensus mobilisation and action mobilisation. In his words: 'Consensus mobilization implies a struggle for the minds of the people, action mobilization means the struggle for their resources – their money, time, skills, or expertise' (Klandermans, 1997, p. 7). Many of us who pursued resource mobilisation lines of analysis concentrated very heavily upon action mobilisation and pretty well neglected consensus mobilisation processes because we assumed pre-existing pools of potential adherents already existed for most mobilisation efforts around some of the most salient issues, such as civil rights and the plight of the working class. I was certainly guilty of ignoring the central importance of consensus mobilisation. In recent years, however, there has been extensive work on major consensus mobilisation campaigns, showing how crucial they can be in creating large pools of adherents, and shaping the possibilities of subsequent action mobilisation campaigns. Consensus mobilisation campaigns can, over longer periods, change the shape of national sentiment pools, preparing the way for action mobilisation campaigns. In practice, it can sometimes be difficult to untangle consensus from action mobilisation, of course, because the process of mobilising people and their resources may also have important consequences for how those targeted think about how their concerns articulate with whatever issue is the focus of action mobilisation. Elite collective actors, including large foundations and think tanks, as well as well financed advocacy groups, have in recent decades waged very effective consensus mobilisation campaigns. One of the best known and highly successful has widely sown the seeds of climate denial among US citizens (McCright & Dunlap, 2011), convincing a large proportion of US adults that 'climate change' is a hoax. I want to very briefly describe another one that has been responsible for shaping the sentiment pool available to Tea Party organisers when they began their efforts, one which cultivated the widespread belief in 'burdensome taxation' among US citizens.

I describe what I call the 'burdensome taxation' consensus mobilisation campaign. By campaign I mean a concerted effort that lasted for an extended period of time and included extensive collective action by a variety of interlinked collective actors. The most useful unit of analysis for bounding campaigns of all kinds is, as I have argued for mobilisation in general, the central issue(s) upon which a campaign focuses. Such campaigns are typically waged over a number of years, sometimes even decades. When successful, they shift the taken-for-granted understandings of large segments of a citizenry, making action mobilisation potentially more likely on one side of the issue at stake or the other as a result. That was the consequence of this campaign in providing fertile ground for the anti-tax message that was central to the Tea Party mobilisation, becoming one of its signature issues.

Ever since the passage of the Sixteenth Amendment to the US Constitution, wealthy collective actors organised to either abolish the federal income tax it authorised, or to make sure that rates were as low as possible (Martin, 2013). There have been recurrent bursts of collective mobilisation aimed at reducing federal taxes since, one of which began with the help of President Ronald Reagan and focused upon balancing Federal Budgets through tax limitation. By the late 1980s, two thirds of US citizens thought the federal income tax they paid was too high compared to one third who though it was 'about right' (Gallup, 2007). Tom Edsall describes the early phases of this campaign:

> During the 1970s, the political wing of the nation's corporate sector staged one of the most remarkable campaigns in the pursuit of political power in recent history. By the late1970s and early 1980s, business, and Washington's corporate lobbying community in particular, had gained a level of influence and leverage approaching that of the boom days of the 1920s.
>
> (Edsall, 1984, p. 107)

He goes on to say:

> Over the past decade, the community of corporate interests has achieved an unprecedented political mobilization, its members joining forces – in grass-root lobbing efforts, in the funding of conservative intellectual institutions, in the financing of a broad spectrum of political campaigns, in the formation of ad hoc legislative lobbying coalitions, in the political organizations of stockholders and management-level personal, and in de facto alliances with conservative ideological groups – to convert what had been in 1974 an anti-business Democratic Congress into, by 1978, a pro-business Democratic Congress; and to change in general terms of the *national tax and spending* debate, preparing the way for the election of Ronald Reagan and the sharp shift to the right in 1981.
>
> (Edsall, 1984, p. 21)

These developments led to recurrent efforts to require federally balanced budgets between 1978 and 1989. Some key collective actors in subsequent phases of the campaign included Americans for Prosperity (the central node of the Koch brother's political organisation), already mentioned as a key backer of early Tea Party groups, the US Chamber of Commerce, which had a massive presence by the turn of the century, including 1,200 Staff, and a $70.000.000 annual budget by 2015. The Chamber informs, trains, equips, and encourages

Do you consider the amount of federal income tax you have to pay as too high, about right, or too low?

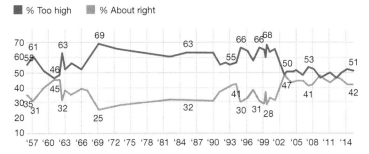

Figure 9.2 Estimation of income tax burden
Source: Gallup, 2017.

members to participate in policy-making at federal, state, and local levels and in legislative and political action at the national level, and lobbies consistently for tax reductions. The chamber is a 501(C)6 organisation, with no restrictions on the amount of lobbying it can do or the amount of money it can spend on lobbying. Quite central to these efforts, too, was the AO organised by Grover Norquist in 1985, the Americans for Tax Reform. This AO began a campaign to pressure federal legislators sign a Taxpayer Protection Pledge, and by 2012, 238 of the 242 Republican House Members and 41 of the 47 Republican Senators had signed the pledge. The net effect of this ongoing campaign was the reduction of Federal taxes on all brackets, especially the super-rich, now seen as one of the important factors contributing to the rapidly increasing wealth inequality in the US

The results of the early phases of the campaign can be seen in the above figure (Gallup, 2017), where in 1969, 69 per cent of US adults thought they paid too much in taxes, and, even in spite of the many subsequent tax reductions, a majority still thought so as the 2008 recession set the stage for the emergence of the Tea party and its mobilisation around the issue of burdensome taxation when the economic crisis of 2008 struck.

Political opportunity (PO)

The extent and variety of political opportunities available to challenging groups has been one of the most widely invoked factors in explaining the mobilisation of social movements, especially the extent and size of protest events and the founding and trajectory of social movement organisations. Doug McAdam's (1996) summary of the central dimensions of PO still remains a useful one, where he explicates four widely recognised dimensions: 1) the relative openness or closure of the institutionalised political system, 2) the stability or instability of the broad set of elite alignments that typically undergird a polity, 3) the presence or absence of elite allies, and 4) and the state's capacity and propensity for repression.

Regardless of this long-standing attention to political structures, social movement analysts have, for the most part, until recently, ignored political parties and how variation in their national structure and processes affect social movement mobilisation. Recent theoretical efforts by movement analysts to bring political parties in to the mobilisation equation for the US have, in general not gone very far in illuminating the role of parties (see McAdam & Tarrow, 2013). I will argue that taking a comparative and historical perspective toward the role of parties can provide important context for understanding the trajectory of the Tea Party in US party politics since its formation in 2009. My argument will proceed in three steps. First, I will briefly describe important trends in party identification and voter turnout in recent decades, common in both Western European democracies and in the US, that have provided activists on both sides of the Atlantic new opportunities for the penetration of national party systems, as dissatisfaction with mainstream parties has increased. These opportunities, however, are quite different in the US two-party system than they are typically in European multi-party parliamentary systems. Second, I will draw upon some new scholarship that aims to directly describe and account for how social movements and movement activists participate in modern US political parties by sometimes organisationally penetrating one or another party, and/or moving between movement activism and party activism, depending upon whether a movement is in opposition. Finally, I will describe the trajectory of the Tea Party movement as a participant in Republican Party politics and subsequent elections.

Trends in party identification and electoral turnout in Western Democracies. The level of support for traditional mainstream parties in the US and Western Europe has declined dramatically in recent decades. These trends are well known but worth remembering. The figure below quite dramatically shows a long-term trend in declining party identification for the UK, France, Germany and the US. This evidence was systematically assembled by Russell Dalton (2016): trends that have been well and widely documented earlier for European Democracies (see van Beizen, Mair & Poguntke, 2012) and trends in the US where '[currently], 39% Americans identify as independents, 32% as Democrats and 23% as Republicans' (PEW Research Center, 2017). These trends in declining party identification have been interpreted as indicating both de-alignment of traditional left/right cleavages and growing disenchantment with the ideas and policies of mainstream elite parties (Blais & Rubenson, 2013; Brooks, Nieuwbeerta & Manza, 2006) and also as reflecting the growing participation in protest as a substitute for electoral politics.[7]

Similar trends have marked voter turnout in elections, although those trends are more erratic, varying from election to election. These several trends reflect, as Hanspeter Kriesi (2008) has convincingly argued, a dramatic decline in party control over voters. It also reflects, on the other hand, wide opportunity for political party insurgencies, either in the form of new parties and/or in penetration by insurgents of existing party structures. The form that such mobilisation takes is importantly a function of the party system in which it occurs, where in Western European parliamentary systems opportunities for the creation of new parties are

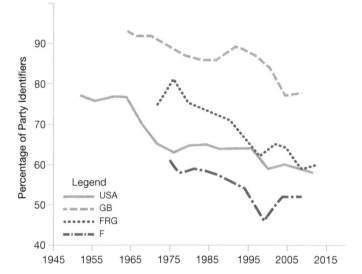

Figure 9.3 Party identification and elector turnout in Western democracies

extensive, as seen in the emergence of many populist parties and dramatically shown in new insurgent parties such as Emmanuel Macron's 'En Marche!', which soon after its formation took control of the French parliament.

System differences in electoral party mobilisation. European Parliamentary party systems are multi-party with generally quite low entry requirements and available state subsidies after modest electoral successes. This has led to the formation of many political parties in France, for instance, where there exist scores of parties, some only regional and many having achieved no elected representation. Forming a political party and attempting to mobilise supporters for it, ultimately becoming partisan voters, then, offers an attractive alternative for insurgent collective actors. France has two traditional parties of left (Socialists) and right (Republicans), and approximately 20 additional parties contending to some extent at broader than the local level, including, importantly for our focus, the National Front.

In the US, in contrast, a weak two-party system with high barriers to new party ballot access, that must be achieved in every state separately, has meant that few recent new party efforts have been fielded in the last several decades, and those that were mounted showed little broad electoral success, at best playing the role of spoiler in a few states in Presidential elections. The two US national parties are quite weak organisationally, and as a result electoral mobilisation tends to be heavily candidate based, as seen in the electoral mobilisation of the Obama campaigns (McKenna & Han, 2014). Theda Skocpol and Alexander Hertel-Fenandez (2016) provide evidence that in 2016 the Koch brothers' Americans for Prosperity commanded a larger national structure of operatives and activists than did the Republican National Committee, the primary vehicle of the national

Republican Party. Nevertheless, insurgent collective actors in the US do regularly attempt to penetrate those weak party structures.

A growing body of scholarship has begun to examine the relationship between social movements and political parties. An important historical pattern for US parties, analysed by Schlozman is that 'the alliances between labor and the Democrats and the Christian Right and Republicans have defined parties' basic priorities, and exerted long-term influence away from the median voter' (Schlozman, 2015: 3). While some contemporary observers suspected that the Tea Party movement might represent another such "movement anchor" for the Republican Party, I argue below that this has not come to pass.

Another useful direction for understanding insurgent penetration of US weak national parties in seen in the work of Heaney and Rojas (2011, 2015), who trace the ebb and flow of activism once institutionalised political parties affiliated with a movement gain political power. Analysing the movement against the Iraq War, Heaney and Rojas (2015) emphasise the dual identifications of many activists, simultaneously tying their political identities to the movement and the Democratic Party. As the latter gained political power through electoral victories, the movement demobilised as a result of identity shifts. Over time, activist identification with the Democratic Party trumped feelings of connectedness with the anti-war movement. The decline of street-level activism in that case, therefore, was a result of a movement's activists securing some measure of institutionalised political power within the Democratic Party rather than only a decision by leaders to abandon protest efforts.

The trajectory of the Tea Party in electoral mobilisation. Two surveys of local Tea Party (TP) leaders were completed the year after the groups had staged more than 1,000 Tax Day rallies on April 15, 2009 (Gardner, 2010; Skocpol & Williams, 2012). Results of Gardner's survey showed that during their first year, TP local leaders indicated that they were not typically campaigning for specific electoral candidates and were concentrating primarily on "get out the vote" efforts. So they began being electorally engaged, and even though they leaned toward supporting Republican candidates, they were far less partisan than public opinion surveys showed non-activists TP supporters to be. And, they were almost universally unwilling to support Republicans they did not agree with. What happened subsequently? Relying upon interviews with TP activists in 2013 and responses to web-based surveys in 2015 McCarthy et al. (2017) generated a pretty clear picture of the electoral mobilisation/participation trajectory of the Tea Party. That picture suggests that only about half of the remaining local chapters (substantially less than half of those that existed in 2010) continued to be electorally active in later years, very few of them staged protests, less than a dozen in 2015, and they remained generally critical of the Republican party. Rafail and McCarthy (2018) analysed blog posts of TP groups from 2009 to 2016 and found that the TP leaders consistently defined themselves as conservatives, and only secondarily as Republicans. In contrast, FOX News defined them primarily as Republican and only secondarily as generally conservative. This evidence, in sum, suggests that

TP activists did not, for the most part, penetrate the Republican Party. In fact, as both early surveys showed, local TP groups were very modest affairs with few members and few resources. So their electoral trajectory is not consistent with either of the historical precedents I have discussed above. They did not abandon Republican Party politics entirely, but they did not become party activists on the other hand.

This analysis shows a complex relationship between the Tea Party and the Republican Party. While, of course, there was extensive overlap between the two, we find little evidence that the disappearance of the Tax Day rallies or the decline in the number of local groups was a product of electoral gains or conservatives securing positions of political power, even from movement-affiliated politicians. Instead, as the Tea Party evolved from top-down to grassroots mobilisation, disenchantment with the Republican Party grew too, as the politicians were viewed as self-interested and misaligned with movement goals. This trajectory is quite distinct from demobilisation as a product of channels of access to institutional politics opening as a result of movement successes. In short, we find that for the Tea Party, in many cases movement identity transcended party identity.

Conclusion

My central argument urges analysts of populist party mobilisation to link their analyses to those of the wider research communities studying insurgent collective action in general, regardless of the claims advanced by insurgents. The suggested steps are quite straightforward: decompose populist party issue claims into discrete issues that can be related to all insurgent protest claims, including populist ones, and all AO claims, including populist ones, through issue (claim) cross-walks. Such cross-walks are issue catalogues constructed to facilitate comparison of insurgent mobilisation across collective action forms. The great potential of such a strategy is illustrated in Swen Hutter's (2014, p. 118) analyses, which provide a model of my suggested methodological turn by incorporating both the claims of protesters and the claim contents of party platforms across a number of European democracies. He uses an updated and extended version of an existing PEA dataset gathered by Kriesi and his colleagues, discussed above, from newspaper reports (Kriesi et al., 1995), and one that captures protest claims over extended time periods. He then creates an issue cross-walk to an existing dataset assembled by the Comparative Manifestos Project (Budge, et al., 2001), which provides the electoral manifestos of parliamentary parties in the same European nations continuously from 1945 through 2003. With this painstakingly assembled dataset, he is able to show that when parties espousing left issues are in power, protest groups espousing left issues are more energetic, but that when parties that espouse right-wing issues are in power, protest espousing those issues becomes even less common. This conclusion constitutes a finding that I judge to be quite important theoretically, since it allows a systematic examination at the dynamics of insurgent claims-making across collective action forms, particularly linking party claims mobilisation with protest claims mobilisation.

Notes

1 For a critique see Zald and Ash (1966).
2 The original authors each produced extensive further analyses of this data as did other scholars after the authors made the data set publicly available.
3 See https://web.stanford.edu/group/collectiveaction/cgi-bin/drupal/.
4 I am going to ignore 'left-wing' populist parties in my discussion, but by adopting the issue/claim approach, they are easily integrated into empirical study of insurgent mobilisation.
5 I ignore for the most part here the Occupy Wall Street mobilisations in the US.
6 Echoing the theoretical assumption of most scholars working within the paradigm I lay out here, Bert Klandermans and Nona Mayer say: 'Xenophobic and anti-system sentiments alone are not enough to establish an enduring political movement' (Klandermans & Mayer, 2006, p. 274).
7 For a summary of such claims, see Immerzeel, Rijken and Klandermans (n.d.).

References

Andrews, K., & Edwards, B. (2004). Advocacy organizations in the US policy process. *Annual Review of Sociology*, *30*, 479–506.

Bennett, W. L., & Segerberg, A. (2014). *The logic of connective action: Digital media and the personalization of contentious politics*. New York: Cambridge University Press.

Benveniste, A., Campani, G., & Lazaridis, G. (2016). Introduction. Populism: The concept and its definitions. In G. Lazaridis, G. Campani & A. Benveniste (Eds.), *The rise of the far right in Europe: Populist shifts and 'othering'* (pp. 1–23). London: Palgrave Macmillan.

Berntzen, L. E., & Weisskircher, M. (2016). Anti-Islamic PEGIDA beyond Germany: Explaining differences in mobilization. *Journal of Intercultural Studies*, *37*(6), 556–573.

Bevan, S., Baumgartner, F. R., Johnson, E. W., & McCarthy, J. D. (2013). Understanding time-lags and measurement validity in secondary data: The encyclopedia of associations database. *Social Science Research*, *42*, 1750–1764.

Birnbaum, M. (2017). Marine Le Pen wants to kill the European union: But it actually helps pay her bills. *The Independent*, April, 15. Retrieved from www.independent.co.uk/news/world/europe/le-pen-kill-european-union-pay-her-bills-eu-brexit-ukip-bnp-a7684796.html.

Blais, A., & Rubenson, D. (2013). The source of turnout decline new values or new contexts? *Comparative Political Studies*, *46*, 95–117.

Blee, K., & Creasap, K. A. (2017). Conservative and right-wing movements. In C. Mudde (Ed.), *The populist radical right: A reader* (pp. 200–217). New York: Routledge.

Brooks, C., Nieuwbeerta, P., & Manza, J. (2006). Cleavage-based voting behaviour in cross-national perspective: Evidence from six post-war democracies. *Social Science Research*, *35*(1), 88–128.

Budge, I., Klingemann, H.-D., Volkens, A., Bara, J., & Tanenbaum, E. (2001). *Mapping policy preferences: Estimates for parties, elections, and governments 1945–1998*. Oxford: Oxford University Press.

Caren, N., Gaby, S., & Herrold, C. (2017). Economic breakdown and collective action. *Social Problems*, *64*(1), 133–155.

Dalton, R. J. (2016). *Groups and identities, political behavior, political values, beliefs, and ideologies*. Retrieved from http://politics.oxfordre.com/view/10.1093/acrefore/9780190228637.001.0001/acrefore-9780190228637-e-72.

de Leon, C., Desai, M., & Tuğal, C. (2015). *Building blocs: How parties organize societies.* Stanford, CA: Stanford University Press.

Della Porta, D., & Diani, M. (2006). *Social movements: An introduction* (2nd ed.). Oxford: Blackwell.

Edsall, T. B. (1984). *The new politics of inequality.* New York: W.W. Norton.

Edwards, B., & McCarthy, J. D. (2004). Resource mobilization and social movements. In D. A. Snow, S. A. Soule & H. Kriesi (Eds.), *The Blackwell companion to social movements* (pp. 116–152). Oxford: Blackwell.

Gallup. (2017). Tax trends. Retrieved from http://news.gallup.com/poll/1714/taxes.aspx (accessed 12/17/17).

Gardner, A. (2010). Gauging the scope of the tea party movement in America. *Washington Post*, October 24. Retrieved from www.washingtonpost.com/wp-dyn/content/article/2010/10/23/AR2010102304000.html.

Goulder, M. (2016). Far right parties in Europe. *Annual Review of Political Science, 19*, 477–497.

Heaney, M. T., & Rojas, F. (2011). The Partisan dynamics of contention: Demobilization of the antiwar movement in the United States, 2007–2009. *Mobilization, 16*(1), 45–64.

Heaney, M. T., & Rojas, F. (2015). *Party in the street: The antiwar movement and the democratic party after 9/11.* New York: Cambridge University Press.

Hutter, S. (2014). *Protesting culture and economics in Western Europe.* Minneapolis, MN: University of Minnesota Press.

Immerzeel, T., Rijken, A., & Klandermans, B. (n.d.). Complimentary or substitute pathways to politics: Explaining the relationship between party politics and movement politics, department of sociology. *Discussion Paper*, Vrije Uniersiteit Amsterdam.

Jansen, R. S. (2011). Populist mobilization: A new theoretical approach to populism. *Sociological Theory, 29*(2), 75–96.

Judis, J. B. (2016). *The populist explosion: How the great recession transformed American and European politics.* New York: Cambridge Global Reports.

Kim, H. W., & McCarthy, J. D. (2016). Socially organized sentiments: Exploring the link between religious density and protest mobilization, 1960–1995. Social Science Research, *60*, 199–211.

King, B. G., Bentele, K. G., & Soule, S. A. (2007). Protest and policymaking: Explaining fluctuation in congressional attention to rights issues, 1960–1986. *Social Forces, 86*(1), 137–164.

Klandermans, B. (1997). *The psychology of social protest.* New York: Blackwell.

Klandermans, B., & Mayer, N. (2006). Through the magnifying glass: The world of extreme right wing activists. In B. Klandermans & N. Mayer (Eds.), *Extreme right activists in Europe: Through the magnifying glass* (pp. 269–276). New York: Routledge.

Kocyba, P. (2017). An overview of current research on right-wing protests in Germany (Pegida). Unpublished Paper, TU Chemnitz (Germany).

Koopmans, R., Stathaam, P., Giugni, M., & Passy, F. (2005). *Contested citizenship: Immigration and cultural diversity in Europe.* Minneapolis, MN: University of Minnesota Press.

Kriesi, H., Koopmans, R., Dyvendak, J. W., & Giugni, M. G. (1995). *New social movements in Western Europe: A comparative analysis.* Minneapolis, MN: University of Minnesota Press.

Kriesi, H. (2008). Political mobilization, political participation and the power of the vote. *West European Politics, 31*(1–2), 147–168.

Kriesi, H. (2014). The populist challenge. *West European Politics, 37*(2), 361–378.

Kriesi, H. (2016). Mobilization of protest in the age of austerity. In M. Ancelovici, P. Dufour & H. Nez (Eds.), *Street politics in the age of austerity: From indignados to occupy* (pp. 67–90). Amsterdam: Amsterdam University Press.

Martin, I. (2013). *Rich people's movements: Grassroots campaigns to untax the one percent.* New York: Oxford University Press.

Mayer, J. (2016). *Dark money: The hidden history of the billionaires behind the rise of the radical right.* New York: Doubleday.

McAdam, D., & Tarrow, S. (2013). Social movements and elections: Toward a broader understanding of the political context of contention and contentious politics: Building conceptual bridges. In J. van Stekelenburg, C. M. Roggeband, & B. Klandermans (Eds.), *The future of social movement research* (pp. 325–346). Minneapolis, MN: University of Minnesota Press.

McAdam, D. (1982). *Political process and the development of black insurgency, 1930–1970.* Chicago, IL: The University of Chicago Press.

McAdam, D. (1996). Political opportunities: Conceptual origins, current problems, future directions. In D. McAdam, J. D. McCarthy & M. N. Zald (Eds.), *Comparative perspectives on social movements* (pp. 23–40). New York: Cambridge University Press.

McAdam, D., McCarthy, J. D., & Zald, M. N. (Eds.). (1996). *Comparative perspectives on social movements.* New York: Cambridge University Press.

McCarthy, J. D., Rafail, P., Reuning, K., & Kim, H. W. (2017). Movement success and demobilization: The tea party's short romance with protest demonstrations. Unpublished Manuscript, Department of Sociology, Pennsylvania State University.

McCarthy, J. D., & Zald, M. N. (1977). Resource mobilization and social movements: A partial theory. *American Journal of Sociology*, *82*(6), 1212–1241.

McCarthy, J. D., & Zald, M. N. (2002). The enduring vitality of the resource mobilization theory of social movements. In J. H. Turner (Ed.), *Handbook of sociological theory* (pp. 533–565). New York: Kluwer Academic/Plenum Publishers.

McCright, A. M., & Dunlap, R. E. (2011). The politicization of climate change: Political polarization in the American public's views of global warming. *Sociological Quarterly*, *52*(2), 155–194.

McKenna, E., & Han, H. (2014). *Groundbreakers: How Obama's 2.2 million volunteers transformed campaigning in America.* New York: Oxford University Press.

Meyer, D. S., & Tarrow, S. (1997). The social movement society. Lanham, NY: Rowman and Littlefield.

Michels, R. ([1911] 1962). *Political parties: A sociological study of the oligarchical tendencies of modern democracy.* New York: The Free Press.

Minkoff, D. C. (1994). From service provision to institutional advocacy: The shifting legitimacy of organizational forms. *Social Forces*, *72*(4), 943–969.

Morris, A. (1984). *The origins of the civil rights movement: Black communities organizing for change.* New York: Free Press.

Mudde, C. (2007). *Populist radical right parties in Europe.* Cambridge: Cambridge University Press.

Müller, J.-W. (2016). *What is populism?* Philadelphia, PA: University of Pennsylvania Press.

Norris, P. (2002). *Democratic phoenix: Reinvesting political activism.* New York: Cambridge University Press.

PEW Research Center. (2017). Trends in party identification, 1939–2014. Retrieved from www.people-press.org/interactives/party-id-trend/.

Quaranta, M. (2016). Protesting in 'hard times': Evidence from a comparative analysis of Europe, 2000–2014. *Current Sociology*, *64*(5), 736–756.

Rafail, P., & McCarthy, J. D. (2018). Making the tea party republican: Media bias and framing in newspapers and cable news. *Social Currents*, March 2018, 1–17. Retrieved from https://doi.org/10.1177/2329496518759129.

Rydgren, J. (2007). The sociology of the radical right. *Annual Review of Sociology, 33*, 241–266.

Schlozman, D. (2015). *When movements anchor parties: Electoral alignments in American history.* Princeton, NJ: Princeton University Press.

Schussman, A., & Soule, S. A. (2005). Process and protest: Accounting for individual protest participation. *Social Forces, 84*(2), 1083–1108.

Skocpol, T., & Williams, V. (2012). *The tea party and the remaking of republican conservatism.* New York: Oxford University Press.

Skocpol, T., & Hertel-Fernandez, A. (2016). The Koch effect: The impact of a cadre-led network on American politics. Paper prepared for presentation at the Inequality Mini-Conference, Southern Political Science Association San Juan, Puerto Rico, January 8, 2016.

Snow, D. A., & Soule, S. A. (2010). *A primer on social movements.* New York: W.W. Norton.

Snow, D. A., Soule, S. A., & Cress, D. M. (2005). Identifying the precipitants of homeless protest across 17 US cities, 1980 to 1990. *Social Forces, 83*(3), 1183–1210.

Snow, D. A., Soule, S. A., & Kriesi, H. (2004). *The Blackwell companion to social movements.* Malden, MA: Blackwell.

Soule, S. A., & Earl, J. (2005). A movement society evaluated: Collective protest in the United States, 1960–1986. *Mobilization, 10*(3), 345–364.

Tilly, C. (1978). *From mobilization to revolution.* New York: Addison-Wesley.

Tilly, C. (2005). *Popular contention in Great Britain, 1758–1834.* New York: Routledge.

Tufekci, Z. (2017). *Twitter and tear gas: The power and fragility of networked protest.* New Haven, CT: Yale University Press.

van Beizen, I., Mair, P., & Poguntke, T. (2012). Going, going, . . . gone? The decline of party membership in contemporary Europe. *European Journal of Political Research, 51*(1), 24–56.

van Dyke, N., & Soule, S. A. (2002). Structural change and the mobilizing effect of threat: Explaining levels of patriot and militia organizing in the United States. *Social Problems, 49*(4), 497–520.

Veugelers, J. W. P. (1997). Social cleavage and the revival of far right parties: The case of France's national front. *Acta Sociologica, 40*(1), 31–49.

Veugelers, J. W. P. (1999). A challenge for political sociology: The rise of far-right parties in contemporary Europe. *Current Sociology, 47*(4), 78–100.

Walker, E. T., Martin, A. W., & McCarthy, J. D. (2008). Confronting the state, the corporation, and the academy: The influence of institutional targets on social movement repertoires. *American Journal of Sociology, 114*(1), 35–76.

Walker, E. T., McCarthy, J. D., & Baumgartner, F. (2011). Replacing members with managers? Mutualism among membership and non-membership advocacy organizations in the United States. *American Journal of Sociology, 116*(4), 1284–1337.

Wang, D. J., & Soule, S. A. (2012). Social movement organizational collaboration: Networks of learning and the diffusion of protest tactics, 1960–1995. *American Journal of Sociology, 117*(6), 1674–1722.

Zald, M. N., & Ash, R. (1966). Social movement organizations: Growth, decay and change. *Social Forces, 44*(3), 327–340.

Index

Note: Page numbers in *italics* refer to figures; numbers in **bold** indicate a table.

5SM *see* Five Star Movement (FSM; M5S)

abeyance processes 139–41, 144
advocacy organisations (AOs) 148, 149, 152, 153–4, 157, 165
AfD *see* Alternative für Deutschland (AfD)
Alfonsín, Raul 69
Alleanza Nationale (Italy) 7
alternative facts 39
Alternative für Deutschland (AfD): as anti-immigration party 37, 52; as populist movement 7, 27, 52; radicalization of 1; and the *Volk* 23–4
American Revolution 93, 94, , 96
Americans for Prosperity 158–9, 160, 163
Americans for Tax Reform 161
anti-elitism 131; *see also* elite, corrupt
anti-Europeanism 58
anti-institutionalism 32
anti-intellectualism 33
anti-Islam 58, 109
anti-liberalism 25
anti-pluralism 130, 131–2
anti-politics 81
anti-Semitism 23, 54, 58, 113
Arendt, Hannah 132, 142–3
Argentina 6–7, 52, 63, 69, 71, 72
aristocracy 93
Armey, Dick 158–9
asylum-seekers 37, 41 113, 138–9
austerity policies 1, 11, 37, 57, 109, 110, 113, 115, 116, 119, 120, 122, 124, 156
Austria: centre-right government in 1; democracy in 95; elections in 27, 34; nationalist parties in 112; *see also* Austrian Freedom Party (FPÖ)
Austrian Freedom Party (FPÖ) 1, 7, 71, 112
authoritarianism 1, 8, 20, 27, 70, 72

banking crisis *see* crises, banking
behaviour/social movement publications *151*
Berlusconi, Silvio 42n8, 52, 83, 119
Blair, Tony 104
Bolivia 69, 71
borders and bordering: defending 25; defining 25; fenced 37; national 99, 105, 141; open 39; out of control 37–8; sovereign 99; tightening 113, 134–5; *see also* boundaries
boundaries: community 59, 98; cultural 48, 54; ethnic 99; interpersonal 98; moral 48; national 31, 35; political 23, 58; social 91, 98, 99, 102, 105; spatial 99, 102; symbolic 98, 99, 102, 105; temporal 125; *see also* borders and bordering
Brexit referendum 1, 19, 20, 27, 34, 37, 38, 39, 52, 66
Buchanan, Pat 36
Bush, George W. 69

capitalism 2, 11, 115; and populism 7–9
Central Europe 95; *see also* Europe; European Union (EU); *specific Central European countries by name*
Chad 139
charisma 68–9, 83
Chávez, Hugo 69, 72, 83
Christian Democrats 56

Index   171

Christian Right 164
Citizens for a Sound Economy 158
citizens' rights 48, 82, 95, 99, 113; civil 103, 155, 159; claims of 149–50; deprivation of 56, 100; of groups 94, 101; human 113; individual 97; legal 58, 59, 80; migrant 57; minority 32, 57; rights of man 96; social 6, 7, 55; women's 105
class movements 21
cleavages 9, 91, 154, 155, 162
clientelism 63, 68, 73
climate change 159
climate denial 159
Clinton, Hillary 31, 33
closure, social 54, 58, 59, 91, 92, 98–102, 104–106
closure theory 91, 99, 106, 107n4–5
Cohn-Bendit, Daniel 122–3
collective action 11, 133, 147; dynamics of 149; insurgent 147–8
collective behaviour 148
collective mobilization; action 148, 159, 160; consensus 159; insurgent 147, 152, 155, 156, 165
communism 62
community building 99–100
Comparative Manifestos Project 165
competition, as core value 8–9
concepts, contested 2, 3, 6; framework for 3–4
conceptual history 2, 5, 6
conspiracy theory 84
consumer confidence 157
context; of populism 102–6; for populism debate 6–7
Correa, Rafael 69
Coser, Lewis 138, 143
crises: banking 1, 9, 56; financial 1, 9, 36–7, 56, 72, 110, 119, 124, 125, 156, 157; legitimation 53; sovereign debt 11, 36, 110, 114, 115, 116–17, 118, 119, 120, 122, 124, 125
Cyprus 1
Czech Republic 122

Dalton, Russell 162
Danish Progress Party (FP) 113
debt crisis *see* crises, sovereign debt
Declaration of Human Rights (UN) 113
deficit growth 157
democracy: challenges to 26, 125; changing nature of 5; definitions of 6; ideology of 28; illiberal 20; liberal 9, 11, 24, 55, 91, 94–5; modern 25; organic 95; political 11; and populism 18, 73–4, 92, 93; radical 25; representative 17, 18, 33, 74, 79, 94; social 103, 112; in the United States 95–7
democratic regimes 18, 22, 71, 73, 92, 93; *see also* democracy
demography 35, 39, 130
demos 18, 24, 28, 66, 94
Djibouti 139
Dornbusch, Rüdiger 69
Douglas, Mary 138, 140, 143
Durkheim, Emile 55, 111, 138
dynamics of collective action (DOC) 149–50

economic performance index 157
economic policies: neo-liberal 9, 97; and populism 69
Ecuador 69
Edwards, Sebastian 69
elections: in Europe (2010-2012) 111–12, 125; in Finland 114; in France 109, 113, 114, 117–19; in Greece 109, 114, 115; as historical events 111–12; in Italy 119; national 19, 23, 110; in the Netherlands 109, 113, 114, 115, 116–17; presidential 1, 163; right-wing salience in *114;* in Sweden 114; voter turnout 162–3, *163*
electoral parties; mobilisation of 163–4; and social movements 164; *see also* populism, parties and movements
electoral turnout 162–3, *163*
elite, corrupt 30, 53, 54, 58, 64, 65, 66, 70, 71, 72, 80, 91, 131
entrepreneurs, political 53–5, 57–8
Erdoan, Recep Tayyip 27, 38, 138
Erréjon, Iñigo 23, 25
ethnocentrism 112
ethnos 24, 28, 94
Europe: defined 120–1; idealistic vision of 121; institutional vision of 121; neo-liberal vision of 121; populist parties in 72; *see also* European Union (EU); Western Europe
European Central Bank 118
Europeanisation 124
European Monetary Union (EMU) 113, 114, 122
European Union (EU) 17, 20, 25, 32, 67, 74, 106, 117, 120, 123, 124, 158; austerity politics in 1, 109, 110, 116;

Index

Compact for Jobs and Growth 110; debt crisis in 110, 115; elections in (2010-2012) 111–12; expansion of 114; fears of dissolution 118–19; globalisation in 31; immigration policies 38; institutional crisis of 36–7; nationalism in 112–15; political normality in 18–19; populism in 35, 74; weak support for 121–2; *see also* Europe
Europhobia 117
Euroscepticism 67, 109, 113, 123
Eurozone 34, 36, 37, 109, 110, 117, 118, 125
events 2, 5, 6, 34, 53, 66; electoral 109, 110, 112; templates of possibility 112, 115, 125; *see also* elections
exclusion 7, 11, 24, 52, 53, 54, 58, 91, 92, 99, 101, 102, 105, 106, 124, 136, 143; norms of 100

fake news 39
fascism 8, *104*, 109, 118, 130, 142; neo- 7; and populism 9–10, 11
Fidesz (Hungarian Civic Alliance) 33
financial crisis *see* crises, financial
Finland 114, 115
Five Star Movement (FSM; M5S) 27, 119
FN *see* Front National (FN)
frames 55, 65, 72, 81, 84, 106, 137, 138, 143
framing 71, 82, 130, 131, 133–6, 137, 155, 159; elite 159–61; strategic 130
France 6, 7, 17, 20, 21, 25, 34, 37, 97, 120, 123, 140, 149, 154; elections in 27, 34, 102, 109, 117–19; electoral parties in 163; nationalism in 113; party identification in 162; populism in 52; terrorist attacks in 41; *see also* National Front (FN)
Francoists 23
Freedom Party (Austria) *see* Austrian Freedom Party (FPÖ)
Freedom Party (Netherlands) 109
FreedomWorks 158–9
free market 7, 8, 9
Freiheitliche Partei Österreichs (FPÖ) *see* Austrian Freedom Party (FPÖ)
French Revolution 93, 95–6, 111
French Socialist Party 120
Frijda, Nico 119
Front National (FN) 1, 7, 25, 63, 109, 113, 114, 117–18, 163; key resource flows 158
Fujimori, Alberto 72

genocide 142
geo-politics 106
Germany: elections in 27; on European unity 123; Green Party 122; Hollande's speech in 121; party identification in 162; populism in 1, 118, 154; refugee crisis in 37, 39, 41, 53, 56, 97; terrorist attacks in 122; *see also* Alternative für Deutschland (AfD); Hitler, Adolf
Global Attitudes Project (Pew Research Center) 123
Global Dataset on Events, Locations and Tone (GDELT) 157
global financial crisis *see* crises, financial
globalisation 7, 31, 37, 124; economic 19–20, 25; neo-liberal 18; opposition to 152
Golden Dawn 109, 115
Great Depression 55
Great Law of Peace (Iroquois Confederacy) 142
Great Recession 36, 57, 67; *see also* crises
Great Society 8
Greece 7, 20, 70, 114, 119, 123; austerity politics in 1, 56; elections in 109, 114, 115; refugee crisis in 37; Syriza party 7, 27, 34, 70, 115; unemployment in 37
Green Party (Germany) 122
Grillo, Beppe 33, 119
Grounded Theory 49

Habermas, Jürgen 121
Hertel-Fernandez, Alexander 163
historical events 5, 111–12
history; conceptual 5–6; factual 5–6
Hitler, Adolf 132, 142
Hochschild, Arlie 137
Hofer, Norbert Gerwald 34
Hollande, François 109, 117, 120, 121
Holocaust 141, 142
homogeneity 102, **104**
humanism 18
Hungary 1, 18, 52, 114; autocratic regime in 1; Fidesz 33; refugee crisis in 37–8
Hutter, Swen 165

ideal types 10, 42, 49–50, 51, 71; assessment 47, 54, 58; ideal-typical 47, 50, 52, 54, 58, 59; methodology 50, 52
identity/ies; collective 135; creation of 99; European 121–2; movement 165; national 116, 124, 126n9; party 165; political 134, 155; populism of 20–2; socially constructed 131

Index 173

identity politics 133
identity work 130, 133–6, 137; exclusionary 11, 144
ideology 3, 28, 33, 62, 64, 65, 68, 69, 71, 79, 80, 85, 106, 123, 130, 152; thin 10, 64, 65
Iglesias, Pablo 22
immigrants; as outsiders 31; as superfluous population 11; *see also* immigration
immigration; large-scale 35; opposition to 36, 37, 69, 102; policies addressing 23; and populism 20; and the refugee crisis 37; restrictions on 1, 113; *see also* immigrants
imperialism 31
implicit consent 99
India 27
Indian Removal Act 142
Indignados 21
individual rights 97
inflation 157
insurgent claims analysis 149, 165
insurgent mobilization, understanding 155–9
interest groups 149
Ireland 1
Iroquois Confederacy 142
Islam 38, 39, 105, 115; and anti-Muslim politics 1; Muslim asylum-seekers 37; radical 39
Islamisation 37, 117, 154
Islamophobia 54
issue cross-walks 165
Italian Social Movement Party (MSI) 112, 113
Italy 52; elections in 119; nationalist parties in 112; Northern League (LN) 38, 63; *see also* Five Star Movement (FSM; M5S)

Jackson, Andrew 142
Jefferson, Thomas 142
Jordan 139
Judis, John B. 25

Kaczyski, Jarosław 52
Katsambekis, Giorgos 32
Kazin, Michael 68, 131
Keynes, John Maynard 124–5
Kirchner, Christina 6–7
Kirchner, Néstor Carlos 6–7
Kitschelt, Herbert 68, 69
Klandermans, Bert 159

Klaus, Vaclav 122–3
Koch brothers 158, 163
Kriesi, Hanspeter 157, 162, 165

labour, immigrant 35
Laclau, Ernesto 22, 23, 24, 32, 58, 63
Latin America: imperialism in 31; populism in 3, 6–7, 31, 63, 64, 67, 68, 69, 70, 72, 79, 83, 105
Law and Justice Party (Poland) 27
leadership, charismatic 62, 68–9, 82, 83
Lebanon 139
Left Front (France) 117, 118
Lega Nord (LN) *see* Northern League (LN)
legitimation 52, 53, 92, 95
Le Pen, Jean-Marie 7, 113, 117
Le Pen, Marine 7, 25, 34, 39, 52, 102, 109, 116, 117–18, 138, 158
Levitsky, Steven 71
liberalism 5, 8, 18, 35, 38, 85, 92, 97, 103; *see also* democracy, liberal; neo-liberalism
Libya 38
line cutters 137
Lipset, Seymour Martin 92–3
London School of Economics 47
Lucke, Bernd 23

Maastricht Treaty 110, 123, 124
Macron, Emmanuel 40–1, 118, 163
Maduro, Nicolás 72
Mair, Peter 119
majoritarianism 32
male suffrage 93
Malta 139
Mandela, Nelson 68
Manichean dualism 11, 65–8, 70, 82, 132, 133, 134, 136, 144
Mann, Michael 24, 94
marginalisation 97, 105, 149
Marquardt, Felix 122–3
Marshall, Thomas H. 93
Marxism 24, 101; opposition to 113
Mauritania 139
Mayer, Jane 158
McAdam, Doug 149, 155, 161
McCarthy, John D. 149, 155
media, and politics 34–5
media processes, in consensus mobilisation 159–61
Mélenchon, Jean-Luc 22, 25, 27, 34, 37, 117, 118, 120
Meléndez, Carlos 66

174 Index

Merkel, Angela 23, 38, 40, 41, 56, 119, 121
migrants *see* immigrants; immigration
migration *see* immigrants; immigration
militarization 8
Minkoff, Debra 150
minorities: protection of 1; racialised 31
misogyny 93
Mizruchi, Ephraim 140
mobilization: consensus 159–61; of electoral parties 163–4; insurgent 147–8, 152–4, 156; party 147–8, 151–4, 165; populist 147–8, 153, 156, 165; potential for 158; protest claims 165; SMO 147–8; success rate 158
Monti, Mario 119
Morales, Evo 69, 71
Morocco 38
Morris, Aldon 155
Mouffe, Chantal 22, 23, 24, 32
movement of squares 21, 120
movements, social *see* social movements
Movimento Sociale Italiano (MSI) 7
Mudde, Cas 29, 64–5, 66, 79–80, 131, 152
Müller, Jan-Werner 28, 131
multiculturalism 39, 69
Murphy, Raymond 102

narodniki 21
National Alliance (AN) 112
National Front (FN) *see* Front National (FN)
nationalism 25, 28, 48, 69, 109, 118, 152; European 123; in France 113; in Netherlands 113; old 'new' 125; radical 58; right-wing 112–15, 120–4
National Socialism 23; *see also* Nazism
nation-states 56, 57, 69, 94, 101, 111, 113, 120, 122–4
Native Americans 96–7, 142
nativism 69
Nauru 139
Nazism 8, 23, 24, 142–3; neo- 109, 115
neo-fascism 7; *see also* fascism
neo-liberalism 7, 8, 9, 18–19, 25, 55, 106, 113, 114, 124; economic 97; economic policies 19, 22, 32; policies 49, 56; and populism 8–9; *see also* liberalism
neo-Nazism 109, 115; *see also* Nazism
Netherlands 1, 123, 149; elections in 27, 40, 109, 114, 115, 116–17; nationalism in 113

New Deal 8, 55, 56, 57
Nixon, Richard 136
normality, political 18–19
Norquist, Grover 161
Northern League (LN) 38, 63
Nuit debout 21

Obama, Barack 68, 105, 163; inaugural address **134–5**
Occupy Wall Street (OWS) movement 21, 36, 71, 72, 120, 131, 156
Offe, Claus 93
oligarchy 148
Olzak, Susan 149
Orbán, Viktor 27, 37–8, 52
Organisation of American States 74
Ostiguy, Pierre 71, 85
other; conceptualization of 22; internal 97; negative 11, 131, 141–3

Parkin, Frank 101
party identification 162–3, *163*
party mobilisation 147–8, 151–4, 165
patriotism 25, 110, 117
patriot/militia organisations 157
People's Party (North America) 21, 25
Perón, Juan Domingo 72
Péronism 6, 52, 63, 71
Perot, Ross 36, 83
personality cults 132
Peru 72
Philippines 27
pluralism 66, 97, 105
Podemos (Spain) 1, 7, 22, 23, 27, 70
Poland 52, 114; autocratic regime in 1; Law and Justice Party 27
political articulation 154–5
political facts 112, 125, 126
political opportunity (PO) 35, 161–5
politicisation 21, 25, 32; re-politicisation 32
politics: anti-Muslim 1; anti-politics 81; austerity 1; as conspiracy theory 84; and culture 111; democratic 92, 93, 95, 106; exclusionary 102; geo- 106; inclusivist 103; mediatisation of 34–5; populist 80, 91–2, 104, *104;* as religion 82–4; unsettling 85; as war 82; *see also* unpolitics
populations, superfluous 2, 11, 130, 136–9, 140, 144; conversion/assimilation of 142; inaction toward 141; incorporation of 141–2; liquidation/annihilation of 142–3; as

negative other 11, 131, 141–3; strategies for dealing with 141–3; transfer/expulsion of 142
populism: and anti-elitism 131; bottom-up 71, 83; and capitalism 7–9; causes and effects of 48; and charismatic leadership 68–9, 83; cleansing **104**; and clientelism 68; combining strategies for 104–5; conceptual history of 5–6; conceptualisation of 10; conflation with other ideologies 67–70; considerations for future work on 9–11; as contested concept 2–4, 17–20, 27–8; context-sensitivity of 6–7, 10–11, 102–6; cultural liberal 97, 102, 103, *103*, 105; dealing with 73–4, 93; and democracy 73–4, 93; as discursive and stylistic repertoire 29–30; diverse describability of 3, 19, 47–8, 62; economic liberal 97, 102, 103, *103*, 104; as economic phenomenon 19; and economic policies 69; epistemological 33; and exceptionality 41; and fascism 9–10, 11; field of 21, 92; and framing 134–6; ideational approach to 70; of identity 20–2; and identity work 133–6; as ideology 79–81; and immigration 20' in Latin America 3, 6–7, 31, 63, 64, 67, 68, 69, 70, 72, 79, 83, 105; left-wing 1, 7, 17, 20, 22–5, 26, 31, 32, 47, 58, 91, 107n4, 131; liberal 103, *103;* liberal economic 104; minimal definition of 64–7; national-populist 37; and the negative other 11, 131, 141–3; negative valuation of 3; as (neo-)fascism 7; nineteenth-century American 7, 25, 83–4; organic 91, 97, 102, 103, *103*, 104, 105; organisational dynamics of 71; pan-European 27, 34, 42n13; parties and movements 6–7, 11, 19, 21–2, 25, 26, 27, 37, 52, 56, 58, 59, 66, 70–2, 104, 115, 147, 152, 154–8, 163, 165; and 'the people' 30–1, 56–7, 65, 66–7, 71, 74, 80, 84, 91, 94, 97–8, 131, 143; plebeian 20–2; as political phenomenon 1, 52–5; as political strategy 98–100, 102; populist conjecture 31, 32, 34, 36; populist moment 10, 27, 34, 36, 40, 148; and public knowledge 39–40; research on 153–5; right-wing 1, 3, 9, 11, 31, 47, 58, 130–6, 143–4; in Russia 83; as social phenomenon 1, 11, 55–9, 72, 91, 94; sociological research on 48–9, 54; stigmatisation of 17–18, 27, 53–4, 63; and strategies of social closure 100–2; strategy 98, 99, 100, 101, 102, 141; subtypes of 70–2; thin ideology 10, 64, 65; top-down 71; trans-Atlantic 27, 34, 42n13; tropes of 81–4; typology of 51–2, 59; and 'unpolitics' 79, 80–1, 85–6; in the US 3, 6, 7, 21, 35, 52, 57, 68, 71, 79, 83–4, 130–2, 152; in Western societies 92; and xenophobia 21, 69–70
Portugal 1
post-security polity 124
post-truth era 39
power: balance of 55; and conspiracy theory 84; separation of 1
precariousness 11, 21, 38
protectionism 33, 35
protest event analysis (PEA) 149–50, 152–3
protests: anti-austerity 156; anti-government 157; homeless 156; against the Iraq War 164; left-wing 153; populist 147–8, 151–4; right-wing 153; youth 120
Pure People 30, 64, 65, 66, 67, 70, 71, 72, 80, 91, 131, 132
PVV (Party for Freedom) 115

Quaranta, Mario 156

racism 1, 54, 58, 93
Reagan, Ronald 160
Reaganomics 9, 56
refugee crisis 37–8, 67, 138; *see also* immigrants; immigration
religion, and politics 82–4
Renan, Ernest 123
repertoires 29, 30, 32, 33, 36, 40, 142
re-politicisation 32; *see also* politicisation
revolution, Democratic 91, 92, 93, 95, 96, 99, 106
rhetoric: America-centric 135; anti-immigration 37, 113; anti-party 33; economic 116–17; moderate 92; populist 41, 48, 58, 67, 141, 144; style 3, 29, 33, 48
rights of man 96
Roberts, Kenneth 67
Roosevelt, Franklin Delano 140
Rovira Kaltwasser, C. 66
rule of law 1
Russia 83, 95
Rutte, Mark 40

Sanders, Bernie 34, 72, 131
Sarkozy, Nicolas 117, 120
Schengen system 34, 38
Schröder, Gerhard 104
security 9, 11, 20, 26, 35, 38, 39, 109–11, 120, 123; practical 124
security policies 20, 124
Sen, Amartya 118
sentiment pools 155
Sewell, William H. 111
Shils, Edward 83
Silent Majority 40, 81, 136
Skocpol, Theda 163
social boundaries 91, 99, 102, 105
social closure theory 91, 98, 100–1
social Darwinism 97
social democracy 103, 112
Social Democrats 37
social disenfranchisement 120
social exclusion 101–2, 143–4; *see also* exclusion
social facts 111, 112
social inclusion 106
social inequalities 19, 22, 35, 95–7, 99
socialism (socialist movement) 11, 148: democratic 62; in France 109; in Greece 115
social movement organisations (SMOs) 147–9; grievances of 155; and political opportunity 161–5; resources of 157–9
social movements 70, 71, 72, 147, 150, 152, 161; analysis of 162; collective action by 153–4; defined 148; mobilization of 11; and political parties 164
Social Movement Society 153
social pluralisation 98
social pluralism *see* pluralism
social research 49–52
social stratification 96, 98, 102, 104
society, liberal-democratic 9, 11, 24, 55, 91, 94–5
Soini, Timo 116
Soule, Sarah 149
South Sudan 139
sovereign debt crisis *see* crises, sovereign debt
sovereignists 25
sovereignty: national 25, 32, 117; of the people 28, 53, 54, 92; popular 20, 25, 41, 66, 68, 70, 80
Spain 1, 37
spatial boundaries 99
Stalin, Joseph 132

Stanley, Ben 80
Stavrakakis, Y. 32
storytelling 99
Sweden: elections in 27, 114, 115; refugee crisis in 37, 139
Swedish Democrats 115
Swiss People's Party (SVP) 112
Switzerland, nationalist parties in 112
Syriza party 7, 27, 34, 70, 115

Taguieff, Pierre-André 62
Tarragoni, Federico 21
taxation, burdensome 159–61, *161*
Tea Party 36, 68, 71, 72, 156, 159–60, 161, 162; and electoral mobilisation 164–5; key resource flows 158–9; and the Republican Party 164–5
terrorist attacks 38–9, 41, 100
Thatcherism 9, 56
theory building: sociological 51; typological 49–50
Tilly, Charles 148, 149
Trail of Tears 142
True Finns 115, 116
Trump, Donald J.: America-centric rhetoric 20, 72, 135–6, 144; anti-immigration rhetoric 105, 141, 142; election of 1, 19, 27, 34, 37, 52, 63, 66, 131, 152; inaugural address **134–5;** messianic claims of 132–3, 143; personality cult of 132–3; populism of 67, 83, 104, 130, 137, 138; and the refugee crisis 38–9; Twitter communications 33, 39
Trumpism 63, 138–9
Tunisia 38
Turkey; authoritarianism in 1; democracy in 95; refugee crisis in 38, 139

UK Independence Party (UKIP) 158
unemployment 21, 37, 110, 111, 119, 124, 157
United Kingdom (UK): as democracy 6; immigration issues 97; party identification in 162; populism in 1, 52; Tory party 68; UK Independence Party (UKIP)158; *See also* Brexit referendum
United States (US): advocacy organisations in 154; democracy in 95–7; economic policies 69; electoral parties in 163–4; Great Society 8; and immigration 141; imperialism 31; and Native Americans 142; New Deal 8, 55, 56, 57; party identification in 162;

Index 177

patriot/militia organisations in 157; political situation in 17, 22, 37; populism in 3, 6, 7, 21, 35, 52, 57, 68, 71, 79, 83–4, 130–2, 152; protest events in 153; refugees in 38, 139; social movements in 72, 148–9, 150, 155, 156, 158–61, 162; sociology in 49; Works Progress Administration (WPA) 140; *see also* Trump, Donald J.
unpolitics 79, 80, 81, 83, 84, 85–6; defined 81
usurpation 101

van Hauwaert, Steven M. 66
van Kessel, Stjin 66
Van Rompuy, Herman 118–19
Venezuela 69, 72
Volk 23–4
Volksgemeinschaft 24
voter turnout *163*

Wallace, George 36
Wall Street Crash (1929) 55
war, and politics 82
Weber, Max 49–50, 51, 100–1
welfare system 56, 57, 58, 95–7; neo-liberal remodeling of 55; opposition to 152

Western Europe: advocacy organisations in 154; immigrants in 31; populism in 35, 152; protest events in 153, 156; right electoral salience in 114; social movements in 155, 156, 162; socialist movement in 148; and the welfare state 96; *see also* Europe; European Union (EU); *specific Western European countries by name*
We the people 74, 91, 92, 94–8
Weyland, Kurt 64–5
Wilders, Geert 33, 40, 109, 115, 116–17
Wildt, Michael 23–4
Wilkinson, Steven 68
Wittgenstein, Ludwig 29
Works Progress Administration (WPA) 140
world trade 106

xenophobia 19, 20, 21, 52, 58, 63, 68–70, 73, 112, 113, 152; rejection of 24–5

youth protest 120

Zald, Mayer 155
Zolberg, Aristide 38

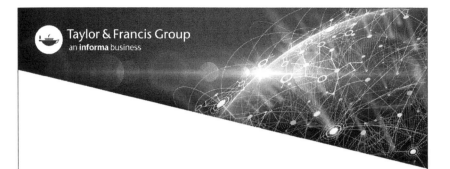